AN OPEN DOOR

The Story of Zvi Eyal

Petra van der Zande

ISBN 978-965-7542-50-7

Photos: Zvi Eyal, Petra van der Zande and the internet.

Order information:

E-mail: tsurtsinapublications@gmail.com

Website: www.lulu.com

www.tsurtsinapublications.com

A *Tsur Tsina* Production

Layout: Petra van der Zande

**This book is dedicated to my parents
Isaac and Esther Klafter-Mok z"l
And to my brother Freddy, z"l**

My father was murdered in Auschwitz, my mother survived
Theresienstadt and Freddy too survived the Second World war.
I am so grateful that my parents, from an early age, taught me to be
proud of my Jewish tradition. Like described in *Hatikva*, 'The Hope':

*"As long as the Jewish spirit is yearning deep in the heart,
With eyes turned toward the East, looking toward Zion,
Then our hope - the two-thousand-year-old hope -
will not be lost: To be a free people in our land,
The land of Zion and Jerusalem."*

This was and continues to be the driving force that led me to the
experiences shared in this biography.

I had the privilege to take part in that wonderful, continuing process
of Israel's rebirth – a dream that came true!

Zvi Eyal
Spring 2017
Jerusalem, Israel

Table of Contents

> *"While it becomes further in years,*
> *the experience draws nearer."*
>
> *Amos Gomes de Mesquita*

Table of Contents

Zvi and the writer on his roof top terrace

It was such a surprise when Zvi recognized himself on a picture of 1946

PREFACE

It was such a privilege to be able to write Zvi's life story.

The first interview, about his escape from Westerbork, took place in the summer of 2013. This was followed by at least ten more interviews that lasted about three hours. Then came the weekly visits to edit the written story during which time even more treasures were unearthed. Those were gold-plated days!

Being almost ninety and then having to go back in time, it is almost impossible to remember certain details. In those cases I have taken the liberty to fill in the lacking historical information.
To make Zvi's story more personal, it is written in first person and in order to enhance the historical value of the story, I sometimes added background information which Zvi, of course did not know at the time. It will draw the reader deeper into the story and help him understand better on how it was to be living during that time.
Some information has been supplemented by written material from Zvi's brother, Freddy, a report from an Amcha worker and books about the specific time periods.

Zvi will appreciate your reaction to his life story. You can write to email: tsurtsinapublications@gmail.com and I will make sure that he receives it.

Petra van der Zande,
2017, Jerusalem, Israel

> *"When you listen to a witness,*
> *you become a witness."*
> **Elie Wiesel**

My parents, Esther and Izaäk
Klafter-Mok

Perfumary Apollo Oudegracht 111, ca. 1930

CHAPTER 1
1925-1939

Harry Klafter, that was my name when I was born on the first of November in the Lange Viestraat in Utrecht, Netherlands. Manfred, my six-year older brother was called Freddy. My father, born in 1917 in Galicia, didn't want to serve in the German army, so he went to the Netherlands. In Amsterdam, he rented a room in the house of the Mok family in the Lepelstraat. Isaac fell in love and married the daughter, Esther. When the opportunity came to become manager of an Apollo perfumery affiliate, they moved to Utrecht. He later bought the perfumery shop on Oudegracht number 111. The family lived in the house above the shop.

I still remember what the house looked like: a stairway leading to the front and the back of the house where the living room, kitchen and master bedroom was. Freddy's room was in the back of the house. Through the courtyard, you reached the warehouse and enter the garden. My room overlooked the courtyard. It had a fold-away bed, a table and a violin standard (I took many violin lessons). I loved music and would often lay awake at night listening to the choir practicing in the building next door.

Even though my parents strictly adhered to Jewish tradition, they did not consider themselves as orthodox Jews. Mother kept a kosher household and on Shabbat and on holidays we went to the *Shul* (synagogue). Because most of the staff employed by my father were non-Jews, the shop remained open on Saturdays and Jewish holidays.

Two of my friends lived on the nearby Steenweg: Bobbie from bakery Strauss and Loeki, from widow Pines' deli. Flip Vorst lived on the Mariaplaats. For us, the centre of Utrecht was one big playground where we could roller-skate, cycle and play football. On Vreeburg and Neude's wide square we often played hockey by using old walking sticks.

The Saturday market, including the puppet show, was always held on Neude. Considering their original way of selling merchandise, the Amsterdam market vendors were always very popular. Astonished I watched a vendor wrapping a stocking around the neck of his wife. "Murder and manslaughter!" she screamed. The moment they had a crowd of curious spectators, the selling began.

Gazelle was the first company that sold bikes with drum brakes. In 1930 a 6-minute-long video was made in which Piet Pelle on his Gazelle flew to the North pole by zeppelin to install a radio device. I lost count of the times when I stood before the shop window where the video was shown. To me, it didn't matter that it was always the same video.

There weren't a lot of cars on Oudegracht— our neighbour drove a Chevrolet and Father had a Ford. Due to his small stature, he couldn't reach the accelerator pedal, but he solved this problem by increasing the height of the pedal.

On Saturdays, we always went out for a walk. "Loafers" the lanky youth were called who sat on the canal fences, whistling at the girls.

One day Mother allowed me to join my friend Hennie to have lunch at the Hema restaurant on Bakkerstraat.

"What have you eaten?" mother wanted to know when I came home.

"Shrimp roll."

"Shrimps? Oh, horrible!" mother cried out. "Brush your teeth immediately! And promise me not to tell your father!"

Thankfully, I could buy candy and liquorice laces without conscientious objection in a nearby alley.

A bag of peanuts from the Chinese 'Peanut men' promoting their wares with, "Peanut, peanut, *lekkah, lekkah* (tasty)!" During the Summer, I loved eating ice cream from the Italian ice vendor.

While my father played cards with Mister Groen, who owned a furniture store in the Schoutenstraat, I played with their dog Snoekie. The spacious store was also a wonderful place to chase their cat. And the small rope elevator was an amazing contraption. The Groen family had three children – Inge, Mary and sonles, who studied pharmacology. His friend, Tus Harvey studied medicine. Tus later became a beloved family doctor who had many Holocaust survivor patients, among them my mother.

Boldoot 4711 was a famous brand of eau de cologne that was also sold at my father's shop on 111th Oudegracht. Father decided to make his own brand in a washtub in the attic from distilled alcohol to which he added different scents and colors. The brand label, printed in the same colours as 4711, read '12467' – our telephone number. When a customer requested Boldoot's 4711 mother, let the woman smell a test vial of our 12467. Because our label was significantly cheaper than the Boldoot brand, it quickly became popular.

Just before Christmas, there was a big demand for luxurious soap, eau de cologne and perfume which were sold in pretty boxes. During extra busy times, I had to help out by showing the customers where they could find the products they were looking for.

Keeping up the display window was no easy task. My father had to crawl into the narrow area and with white chalk change the prices on the black cardboards.

Having to work in the busy shop all day my mother wasn't home much. In those years, it was normal to employ a German girl as a housekeeper and kind of nanny. Martha learned to speak Dutch and became part of the family until she married and left us. After the war, I met her again at the estate of Kaiser Wilhelm in Doorn, where her husband worked.

After Martha came to Fiene and later Hedy from Austria, which by that time already had been annexed by Germany.

Martha and I

Fiene

On the Oude Gracht, the residents and shop-keepers generally got on well with each other.
Near the Jansbrug, not far from us was the menswear shop from Ben Hendrinks. One of their sons studied for priesthood. One day, while my friends and I were playing football at Neude, the aspiring priest walked by. "Filthy Jew!" he shouted, aiming a heavy bolt at my head. Bleeding profusely, my friends rushed me to Hendriks' shop to show them what their son had done. The shocked parents punished their son and did their best to reconcile this unprovoked attack. During the war, my brother Freddy left our photo albums and valuables at the Ben Hendriks family for safe keeping.

I loved sports, whether it was canoeing in the Oudegracht, sailing on the Loosdrechtse Plassen, swimming at the Utrecht swimming club or in winter skating on the canals. I had lots of friends, Jewish and non-Jewish.

Since the Utrecht Jewish community was small, I went to the public Regentesseschool. On Sunday and Wednesday afternoons, I attended Jewish school where we studied Torah and Biblical Hebrew. After primary school, I went to the HBS-B at the 62nd Catharijnesingel in Utrecht. Considering the fact that I had to go to school on Shabbat, we made an agreement with the teacher that I didn't have to write that day. On my free Sunday morning, I attended the Jewish Youth Federation. It was busy but wonderful life.

One of my idols was Chaim Weizman – a Jewish chemist, Zionist and politician. Weizman later became the first president of Israel. Once, I even drew a picture of him during art class.

Our classroom chemistry experiments
ended up in the school book.

In the eyes of my friends, I was the 'chemistry expert.' My room had turned into a laboratory. At the drug store and other shops, I bought different chemicals so we could do our own experiments. According to my chemistry textbook, you could extract phosphorus from urine, so that's what we were going to do. After collecting my friends' urine, I mixed it with sand and transferred it to a large Erlenmeyer flask – a cone shaped bottle with a cylindrical neck. A gas flame brought the concoction to boiling point. The result was overwhelming: the stench spread throughout the whole house. I can't remember my mother's reaction to my antics.

I grew up with Zionism. Father was treasurer of the JNF (Jewish National Fund) and Freddy was *madriech* [guide/mentor] of the Zionist Youth Federation. At first, the meetings were held in the basement of the 111th Oudegracht, but later, Father used the warehouse and shed. It wasn't unusual that Father convened with JNF board members while Freddy at the same time met local leaders of the Zionist Youth Federation in his room upstairs. Mother dutifully went back and forth with coffee, tea and cake.

A few times a year the JNF organized special campaigns for which specific products from Palestine were sold. During the Almond- and Honey Campaign, I went door-to-door selling these products, making sure to take the Maliebaan. Most people did not give more than one guilder, except Lord Elzas, who always give me two and a half guilders!

The Utrecht Jewish Youth Federation "Bnei Amenu" organised weekly meetings, bike rides, and during the summer holidays went camping in the Vierhouten forest. It often happened that youth groups from other cities met halfway to have a picnic together. The Sunday youth meetings were not only to have fun. We were also supposed to learn and make notes of the various objects that were taught.

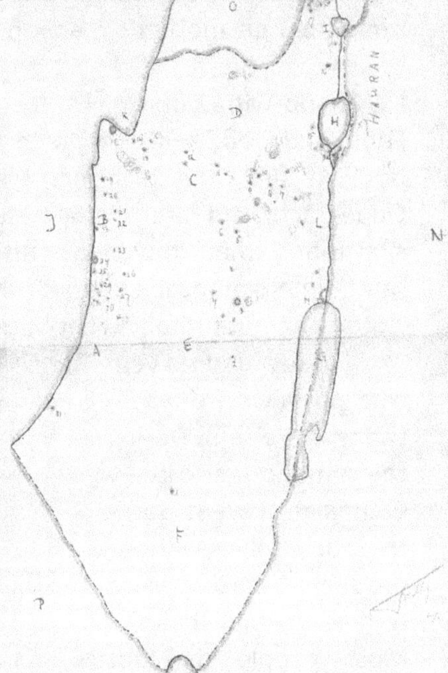

MAANDPROGRAMMA MEI

Sjabbath 3 Mei 3.00 uur.

Onze nieuwe secretaresse laat van zich horen.Zij doet haar intrede in B.A. met een boekbespreking."Opstandige Jeugd" van Schmarja Levin.

Zondag 4 Mei. Twee fietstochten.

1e.Een ontmoeting met Arnhem in Renswoude.Deze tocht is alleen voor oudere leden bestemd.
We vertrekken precies om 8 uur van het Beth.Am. en wachten niet op Langslapers.zelfs niet op de penningmeester van het C.B.
Het wordt een mooie tocht.Brood mee.Goede banden.Weer thuis om 6 uur.

2e.Een ontmoeting met Gouda in Woerden.Deze tocht is alleen voor de jongere leden bestemd.
Vertrek om precies 9 uur van het Beth.Am. Ook geldt hetzelfde als voor de 1e tocht. Alleen om 5 uur thuis.
Beide tochten gaan voor een gedeelte door de bloeiende boomgaarden, volgens de zomerprogramma-commissie.

It was great to receive special visitors from Palestine because they taught us the latest Hebrew songs. Some home owners didn't like loud singing youngsters in their attic, forcing us to relocate. In the warehouse on the St. Jansveld we organized a *shuk* [market] to raise money for the JNF. Official invitations were sent out to JYF members. Everybody called each other by their first name, but only in correspondence titles like *chaver* (friend) or *madrich* (coach, counsellor) were used.

The leadership encouraged initiatives or when someone gave a presentation about a specific Jewish object. It was a great opportunity to develop our talents. A lot of work had to be done for the Jewish Youth Federation: typing reports and newsletters, duplicating stencils, delegating tasks, and so on. Freddy later took over the Presidency of *Bnei Amenu* from Ab Horneman.

Due to the increasing demand for hairdressing articles, Father had to look for a larger factory. In 1938 he refurbished an old power plant in the Bilt. That same year, our parents travelled to Palestine to explore the possibilities of setting up a company there and maybe even emigrate.

Freddy decided that while our parents were in Palestine, we would host the *Bnei Amenoe* Seder meal at our house. He cleared the living room and turned the whole house upside down so we could accommodate the youth group.

Text on the Note card: about the lack of interest in the Shuk, and if people would come, they were not going to stay overnight in Utrecht.

A'dam, 6 Mei '40.

Chaw. H. Klafter, Utrecht.

Beste Harry,

Wij hebben op Zichron laten uitroepen of er liefhebbers voor de sjoek, die jullie organiseert, zijn, maar niemand meldde zich aan. Misschien dat er enkelen toch nog per fiets of trein de sjoek bezoeken, maar het is hun bedoeling dan niet in Utrecht te blijven overnachten. Veel succes en hartelijk Sjalom,

Namens het H.B. Zichron,

Secretaris.

In 1938, when I was a 15-year-old youth member, my older brother examined me and awarded me a seven plus for my knowledge of the Zionist movement and Jewish history.
Freddy was my idol. He studied at the Gymnasium and his textbooks appealed greatly to me. As Mother only finished primary school and Father went to a German elementary technical school, Freddy had a major influence on my intellectual development. Since discussion was central at our home, reading was of secondary importance.

As I was an average HBS-student and not very diligent, my parents insisted I receive private tutoring. Being too active and unmotivated to learn, I preferred to play outside and spend time at the Youth Association. During the weekend we always visited family. I had my friends and my hobbies.
What more could a boy 15-year-old wish for?

CHAPTER 2
1939-1941

At the Oudegracht we could hear the large bells of the Dom Church clearly. That trusted sound was so different from the hysterical screams coming from the radio my parents kept in the storehouse. The moment I entered the front door I heard Hitler's roars. The hatred of that man was almost palpable. Father had no illusions about Hitler's plans and took his threats to the Jews serious. The situation in Germany was on the forefront of our minds. Ever since Hitler had come to power in 1933, German Jews had become more and more isolated. A few decided not to wait and fled to the Netherlands. The *Kristallnacht*[1] unleashed a stream of refugees.

Between 1933-1939, many German-Jewish refugees settling in the Netherlands also found their way to our home. These people needed a job to provide for their families. Father knew many people who were willing to help and thanks to his private 'employment office' several found work. If possible, Father helped refugees to emigrate. Our whole family was involved in helping these refugees.

---

[1] *Kristallnacht*, also called *Reichspogromnacht*, was a by the Nazis organized action against the German Jews took place on the night of 9 and 10 November 1938. Jews were attacked all over Germany and between 1,000 and 2,000 synagogues were torched (firemen were not allowed to extinguish the fire.) About 7,500 Jewish shops and businesses were destroyed and Jewish houses, schools, cemeteries and hospitals were also attacked. 400 Jews were killed or committed suicide.

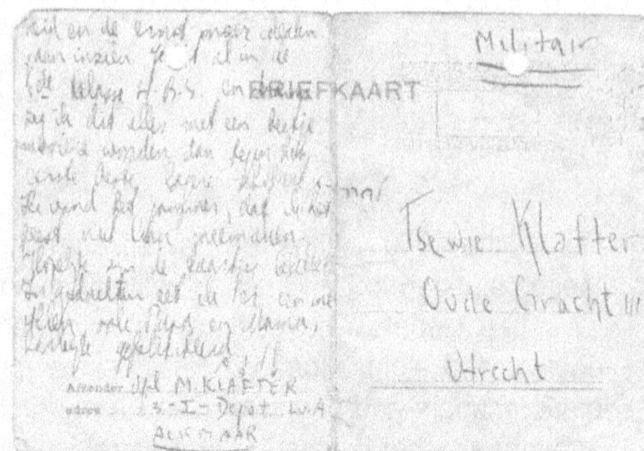

The Dutch army had been mobilized since September 1939. Freddy was stationed in Alkmaar.

Postcard dated "MILITAIR" d.d. 1-11-1939 Tsewie Klafter, Oude Gracht 111, Utrecht, From: M. Klafter 3-I-Depot Lv.A Alkmaar
Dear Zvi (in Hebrew) – Congratulations! I hope your 14th birthday will be the start of a period filled with knowledge, happiness and insight. Being one year older also brings responsibilities; the number of mistakes one makes, become less. It requires more gratefulness for the sacrifices of our parents. Do you understand? A good listener only needs a few words and I even give you a whole sentence. I presume you understand what I mean. For us, Zionists, becoming older means we stop our shallowness and seriously think about our ideals. Because you are already in the 3rd class of the HBS I use different words than I would say to a first grader. I'm sorry having to miss the party. I hope the cake is delicious. I imagine eating one as well. Congratulate Papa and Mama as well.

After fleeing Germany, my aunt, her husband and four children also came to Utrecht. Uncle became warehouse manager of the NV Negum factory and my cousin, David Reichman, worked as a carpenter.

Ergica Katscher fled Czechoslovakia and became my parent's foster daughter.

A few years previously, it had been normal for people to employ a German maid, but nobody wanted to have them anymore. My stepsister assisted my mother in running the household.

Mother and Ergica 1941

Refugee absorption was being paid for by Jewish individuals. Not liking the idea of those German-Jewish refugees living throughout the Netherlands the Dutch government suggested the creation of a central refugee camp. Queen Wilhelmina didn't want the camp to be on the Veluwe, that would be too close to her palace 'Het Loo' in Apeldoorn. The government found the 'perfect' place to build the camp: on the wild, barren moors of Westerbork, in the province of Drenthe. Unemployed laborers, forced to work if they were to receive an allowance, began building the barracks in 1939. In October that year, the Camp opened its doors to the first 22 residents. By the end of January 1940, 167 people lived at Camp Westerbork and in April, 749. The German-Jewish residents didn't feel safe being so close to the German border.

"I cannot remember a month of May so very beautiful. It is as if nature wants to bring comfort during so much suffering." Ina Boudier-Bakker

May 10, 1940. At 3.30 am, a dull humming noise and continuous shooting woke me up. From the window, I saw many airplanes against the clear sky – too many for the anti-aircraft guns to handle. Huddled around the radio in our pajamas to our astonishment we heard that the German army had invaded the Netherlands. This shocking news was followed by a flaming protest from Queen Wilhelmina. I dressed quickly and ran to my friends.

Rumors were rife and everyone was warned to look out for German spies. The streets became dangerous when nervous Dutch soldiers stationed on the Dom tower began shooting because they thought they were seeing traitors. Women ran to the stores to stock up supplies.

"We are only allowed to buy groceries for one day," Mother told me. "And Mayor Ter Pelkwijk told us we must use water, gas and electricity sparingly."

That evening I helped to darken the windows with black asphalt paper. Even when a little light was visible, someone from the air-defense would ring the bell and order it to be fixed. Cyclists and cars could only use a very small light.

Everywhere you went, the radio was turned on. Since we had to keep abreast with the war situation, also in the shop we kept it on. The chief rabbi even ordained that on Shabbat the radio was to be kept on always.

May 12, the shocking announcement came that the royal family had fled to England. The military command ordered citizens to keep all windows closed and people were discouraged to leave the house. A curfew was established: after 8 p.m. it was forbidden to be on the street.

The next morning, my friends and I watched the long line of vehicles deporting the imprisoned Dutch soldiers. In opposite direction came the evacuated people from eastern Netherlands.

May 14 the streets were full of little papers. The German leaflets warned that Utrecht would be bombarded if the Dutch army didn't surrender.

Utrecht occupied by the Germans

To let us know they meant business, the same afternoon the Germans bombarded Rotterdam.[2]

Realizing that with each passing day the chance to flee became smaller, Father said, "It's now or never!" he said. In great haste, we drove to IJmuiden, hoping to find a ship that could bring us to England. We were not the only ones: thousands of cars were lined up. One glance at the burning oil tankers (bombed by the British) and we knew our escape route had been cut off. Disillusioned we returned to Utrecht.

That evening at 7 p.m., general Winkelman announced over the radio that the Netherlands had capitulated. Safe in England, Queen Wilhelmina called on the Dutch people to hold their ground.

On the streets, shocked neighbors were talking softly to each other. Everyone was friendly and people even struck up conversations with complete strangers.

After their breakthrough at the Grebbeberg, on May 15 the German army entered Utrecht via the Viebrug. Schools were closed during those first days of the war; I witnessed the entry of German soldiers on BMW sidecar motors. The Dom square was full of Wehrmacht lorries.

---

[2] Ca. 1943, a German propaganda film showed a 'German' city that had been bombed by the 'British.' Nobody recognized the German footage of the bombing of Rotterdam, during the first day of the war in 1940.

During dinner, Father told us that many Jews had committed suicide.

"Premature. We don't believe Jews will be persecuted here. Those unfortunate people – many were intellectuals – have lived under pressure for so long that this continued stress became unbearable."

Ina Boudier-Bakker

In all aspects, Father had become a Dutch citizen and at home, we only spoke Dutch. Convinced of the approaching disaster he tried to warn the Dutch Jews about the dangers of the occupation. Most of them shrugged it off. "It won't be as bad as that." Even family and friends reacted lukewarm to his warnings. "Those atrocities you mention, it will never happen in the Netherlands." Mother's family, who for generations had lived in Holland, predicted that the war would soon be over.

The first thing the German occupier initiated was 'German time'[3], causing many people to be late for work.

An NSB provoked brawl on Vredenburg had been beaten off by the people of that district. On May 16, when we had to return to school, I found an anonymous note on my desk. Written on NSB letterhead paper, it read:
"You are a dirty Jew!"
When I showed it to the director, he responded, "Ah! Don't you worry!"
Mr. Brunner, a known NSB-man, and my teacher said, "Harry! If they want to hurt you, come to me. I will protect you."

3 Dutch summer (daylight saving) time was different from other European countries. NL 12 (noon) = Belgium: 12.40 p.m.– France: 12.40 p.m. – Germany 1.40 p.m. On May 15, Germany initiated German time in the Netherlands and later also in Belgium and France. In July 1940, all three occupied countries used the same German time and daylight saving time.

May 19, Dr. Arthur Seyss-Inquart was nominated by Hitler as *Reichskommissar* for the occupied Dutch area. His right-hand man told secretary-general of internal affairs, Mr. Frederiks, that in the eyes of the Germans there was no Jewish problem in the Netherlands. Utrecht was led by a civilian administration and the *Wehrmacht*. All over the city German signs appeared, showing the way to the many military bureaus. NSB members, its headquarters (National Socialist Movement) on Maliebaan, now openly wore their black uniforms. At first, the implications of the German occupation didn't seem too bad. Thanks to German orders, the steel factories suddenly had plenty of work. Visiting the municipality on June 21, Seyss-Inquart assured them that the occupiers had come with the best intentions.

    "You see?" the NIGU leadership responded.

Father didn't believe the Nazi's words.

From July 1, 1940, Jews were no longer allowed to man air-raid protection stations, Freddy was discharged. Father sent him to Rotterdam to find out if perhaps we could escape to Switzerland by riverboat. Getting on board without being spotted by the captain proved impossible. Without passports and travel documents we could neither travel to France via Belgium. Father, forever the optimist, grabbed each little straw. Unfortunately, in doing so he also lost view of reality, which eventually would become our downfall.

Within the *Bnei Amenu,* I carried a lot of responsibilities for a 15-year-old. This speech I held in July 1940.

"*Chavereem vechaverot,* the future is far but when you have an ideal, the most important is not that you reach it, but the striving itself is important. Same with the future – you can strive for it, even though it's far away. When everybody does his little share, each of us begins to understand the importance of deciding what his part will be. That can be working on this chapter of Jewish history as a chapter of renewing and building of the Jewish people. Ending the chapter of wandering. The tragic Jewish wandering of more than 2,000 years, through which we kept standing despite the hostilities, is similar to the 40 years of wandering through which the Jewish people were bettered. A new core had to be created to enter the country. I wonder if these 2,000 years have changed us enough to be able to go to *Eretz.* The answer is: determine your part. If each of us determines

Some of my notes

his share with the goal to build up *Eretz* than the Jewish, people won't have to wander around the third time and we can find a solution for this big question. The issue you now experience yourself. When you read in the papers that Haifa has been bombed[4], you feel it and are afraid. You feel the connection with the country you can be part of."

The new school year saw many changes. The portraits of the royal family no longer hung on the walls. Anti-German study books were banned from school and we received a list with forbidden study books. Pages had been ripped from history books and hymnals.

Parents received a letter containing the new behavioral school rules: they children could expect sudden bag-checks and books to see if students were carrying anti-German printed matter. Telling anti-German jokes was forbidden. Our history teacher, Mr. Brunner was nicknamed *"de boef"* – the scoundrel. Before the war, he taught more German propaganda than history, but had signed a declaration that he was not a member of the NSB. After May 15, he openly wore a NSB-pin on his lapel.

"Listen, Harry, you don't have to be afraid," he tried to put me at ease. "I will take good care of you."

4 In June 1940, the Italian Airforce bombed Haifa and other coastal cities in Mandate Palestine.

It was crowded in the Buurkerk where ration cards were distributed. Since the fall of 1939, the municipalities had been experimenting with ration cards, most women knew how the system worked. Besides personal informa-tion, the 'master' card also had a photo of the owner. Upon showing this card, Mother received the allotted ration cards for our family. Through the newspaper or radio messages, housewives learned which ration cards could be used during which period.

Distribution master card

That year's Yom Kippur services could not be held in the synagogue, therefore, prayer services were held in people's homes.
More food and other products became only available with coupons, and almost weekly something else became forbidden. These *Verordnungen* appeared like clockwork.
"Where is this leading to?" Father and Mother wondered.
For the non-Jewish Dutch citizen life continued as usual. Most people didn't realize the anti-Jewish measures became more and more severe.

OCTOBER: VERORDNUNG 189/1940:

Who is a Jew? Everyone who has more than two grandparents who belong to a Jewish ecclesiastical congregation.

According to *Verordnung* 6/1941, everyone with more than one Jewish grandparent had to register[5] at the Ministry of Interior. The NIGU, which followed the advice of the Jewish Council, called for the Jews in Utrecht to stay calm, to accept the German measures and to cooperate so things wouldn't get worse.

From October 1940, it had become illegal to hire Jewish civil servants or promote them. Non-Jews had to sign a so-called *Ariërverklaring* – a declaration the person was not Jewish.
In February, I came home with the news that all Jewish teachers at the HBS had been fired.
"All Jewish civil servants have been fired as well," Father said.
From March 12, Jews were banned from the trade and industry world and their companies taken over by a non-Jewish director. This Verwalter could either continue the business, liquidate it or give it to somebody else. Because Father had seen this coming, he had already taken steps so the

Brummer after the war

Negum factory and the two perfume shops could continue.

In May, I learned that 'the Scoundrel' denounced one of my teachers to the *Sicherheitsdienst* (SD) because of anti-German leaflets in the teacher's lounge. This NSB member also didn't like the fact that the director had promised the students that he would not check their school bags.

After the first razzias in Amsterdam, the illegal Communist Party called for a strike on February 25 and 26, 1941. Starting in Amsterdam, it soon spread to other areas in Holland, Hilversum and Utrecht. The surprised German occupiers forbade newspapers and radio to report these protests. On February 26, the Nazis managed to forcefully suppress the strike. During a speech on March 12 in the Amsterdam Concert Hall, Seyss-Inquart stated, "You are with or against us, there is no longer a third option."

5: This information was transferred to the *Zentralstelle fur Jüdische Auswanderung* in Amsterdam, supposedly to speed up emigration. In truth, this information was used to call up people for Westerbork. From there, many were deported to concentration camps.

NV Negum factory in De Bilt— father in the circle

On March 15, 1941, Jews had to hand in their radios and from April 1st, Jews were no longer allowed to enter a bar. The mayor of Utrecht was replaced by a NSB mayor, Cornelis van Ravenswaay. The aldermen in his council were convinced and fanatical NSB members.

"Baarn municipality - limited freedom of movement for Jews"

"Forbidden for Jews"

For practical reasons both youth organizations, Bnei Akiva and Bnei Amenu, joined forces. In our synagogue, we used the old, Mizrachi version of the Agudah, where we read, *"Adonoi."* I was happy with the new chazan in our synagogue who used the new Hebrew version. Now we had to say, *"Adonai."* For security reasons, the Shabbat services were now being held at different homes.

Loukie Danielsohn had a record player at home, so our friends and I often went there to dance. It was a pity we had to leave before curfew.
In the Summer of 1941, Bnei Amenu was forced to find another meeting place. During choir practice at the Jewish orphanage at the Nieuwe Gracht, I met a group of German and Austrian girls who were part of the so-called *Kindertransport.*[6] The Dutch Jewish community looked after these girls for a few weeks before they travelled to England.

August 8, Father was ordered to hand over his money, postal- and bank account and stocks to the Lippman-Rosenthal & Co bank whose Jewish leadership had been replaced by Germans. Real estate was also expropriated. The noose around the Jews was tightened even further.
During dinner, Father said, "I heard that British planes are landing on the Loosdrechtse Plassen to bring people to safety."

"Izaäk, you shouldn't believe all those fantastic tales that make the rounds!" Mother warned.

Just before the new school year was about to start, we were informed that Jewish students would no longer study at the municipal high school. I was not even allowed to say goodbye to my friends[7].

6. The *Kindertransport* (German for "children's transport") was an organized rescue effort that took place during the nine months prior to the outbreak of the Second World War. The United Kingdom took in nearly 10,000 predominantly Jewish children from Germany, Austria, Czecho-slovakia, Poland, and the Free City of Danzig. The children were placed in British foster homes, hostels, schools and farms. Often, they were the only members of their families who survived the Holocaust. Not many people know that almost 2,000 children stayed behind in the Netherlands. Before the war, one-third of them managed to escape to England or the USA; one-third survived in hiding or came out of the camps alive, and one-third died in the concen-tration camps.

Jewish Orphanage on the Nieuwegracht—my HBS per September 1,1941

From September 1st, I attended the Jewish high school (HBS) at the Jewish Orphanage. Suddenly I realized, "I, the Jew, Harry Klafter, am different. An outcast,"
In my new class, I noticed that the other students were much further in their studies than I was. That stung my pride and I decided to work harder at my grades.

From September 15, 1941, I was no longer allowed to enter OZEBI, the public swimming pool. Also, parks, libraries, zoos, theatres and musea had become off-limit for Jews. At the entrance of a village near Utrecht was even a sign that read, "Jews and dogs not allowed."

7 One of the students protested to the school management that I was no longer welcome. Guus Sluijter, my school friend, would never forget that my place in class suddenly was empty. Without obtaining permission, NSB teacher Brunner introduced Hitler's *Mein Kampf* and Goebbels' book to study. Because of a formal complaint against him, our director was fired in January 1942. In Brunner's class, more students were punished and told to leave the class because of disorderly behavior than in any other class.

My brother
Freddy

CHAPTER 3
Trapped! Autumn 1941

[I didn't remember much of these traumatic experiences. My mother told this story to an Amcha staff worker, many years later.]

Father fully trusted electrician Elsbach, a German-Jewish refugee whom he had given a job in his factory.

"Mister Klafter, sir, can I speak to you in private?" Elsbach asked one day. In the safety of Father's office, he said, "There is a possibility to obtain passage on a freighter to Sweden. Out of gratefulness for your help, I'm telling you this, nobody else." The soft-spoken man explained the escape plan. Besides travel costs, they also had to pay for a special German exit permit. Father decided to grab this unique chance. "Why don't you and your fiancé join our family?" he offered Elsbach.

Mother listened to Father's enthusiastic story about the captain he had met in Amsterdam. The man had shown him official-looking papers with German stamps. The transaction had been approved by the *Divisenschutzkommando* that was in charge of tracing and supervising the flow of foreign currency. This certificate permitted the captain to sail to Sweden as long as the ship stayed within the boundaries of German occupied territory.

"The offer is only valid for a short time," Father said. "And we must pay a certain sum up front, so they can buy food for the journey."
Mother didn't know what to think about this plan. A few weeks passed.
At the next meeting, the captain made more demands. Feeling trapped, Father was willing to make big concessions. Diamonds were easy to conceal, therefore a family member who worked as a diamond cutter helped Father to buy a lot of these precious stones. He also bought golden coins and American stocks and bonds. All their savings were used to escape the approaching calamity.

Wondering if this scheme was trustworthy, my pessimistic Mother suggested to Father, "Take Freddy to your next meeting with the captain."
Freddy studied at the Higher Textile school in Enschede, so he would have a profession in Palestine.

"I would like to see that ship," Freddy told the captain.

"It's presently being repaired in the dry dock," the greying man said. "But if you are willing to travel to Zwolle, I can show you a similar ship."
At the appointed time, the captain showed a moored freighter to Father and Freddy. Everything seemed all right.

"We'll let you know the day and time, then you'll travel by train to Enkhuizen. You'll have to board the ferry to Stavoren inconspicuously," the captain instructed. "From Stavoren you travel by train to Sneek from where the freighter to Sweden will depart." Sternly he added, "Neither suitcases nor hand luggage is permitted. The moment you diverge from the itinerary, we annul the trip. Travel expenses will not be returned. This plan must be kept secret."
The lips of the Klafter and Elsbach family were sealed.

Even though both Mother and Freddy felt uncertain about this escape plan, the families began to prepare for their day of salvation. From their last money, Elsbach bought a rucksack and a few warm sweaters.

The morning of their departure had arrived. Hidden under their warm, best clothes, the family wore their valuables in special fabricated pockets. Everybody was tense. The house was left as it was, and even the shop personnel didn't know about their escape plan.

Before leaving, Mother quickly dusted the living room and took a few snapshots with her. The hardest of all was having to leave her 78-year old mother without being allowed to say goodbye.

At Amsterdam Central station we transferred to the train to Enkhuizen. The ferry was already docked in the harbor. Since 1886 the timetable of the ferry Enkhuizen-Stavoren was connected to the train schedule. Even during the war the *SS C. Bosman* and the *SS R. van Hasselt* kept their ferry service between the two IJsselmeer cities. Father bought tickets and our little group went aboard the ferry boat.

In the smoking salon, we anxiously waited for the departure signal.
Bringing our coffee, the waiter whispered in Father's ear, "Are you Jews, on your way to another boat?"

3rd class train carriage, 1941

We acted as if we didn't know what he was talking about. When the waiter passed us again, Father wanted to know why he asked that strange question.

Enkhuizen train station and ferry

Promenade dek 3e kl. S.S.R. v. Hasselt.
Kajuit 2e klasse veerboot.
Veerdienst Enkhuizen-Stavoren.
Salon 1e kl. S.S.R. v. Hasselt.
Restauratiezaal veerbooten

"Yesterday, a drunken sailor came on board," the waiter said. "He told me that the Gestapo ordered him to look over this boat. He had to reserve a room for Jews planning to escape to England and the Gestapo would pay him richly for it."
Seeing the suddenly deadly frightened faces, the waiter asked, "Can I help you? Do you want to get rid of something?"

The Klafter and Elsbach family only wanted one thing: to get off the boat as quickly as possible. At that moment, the departure signal sounded.

The ferry departs

Paralyzed by fear we waited for the things that surely were going to befall us. The moment the ferry had passed the pier the so-called captain, who worked for the enemy, appeared. "There they are!" he told two men wearing civilian clothes.

"Come!" barked the Gestapo.
Like beaten dogs, we followed the agents to the reserved room. Everybody was frisked and everything of value was confiscated. Our world had collapsed. What was going to happen to us now? The short journey to Stavoren seemed never ending.

"You stay on board!" the Gestapo barked at us.
I felt the pitying and curious glances from passengers leaving the boat. Father was handcuffed and taken away. Nobody told us where to.

"You return to Utrecht," commanded the Gestapo to the rest of us. "Each day you report at the police station."

Nobody said a word during the seemingly endless journey back. It was as if Elsbach and his fiancé had turned to stone – they just sat there, staring straight ahead. All of us had fallen victim to a fellow Dutchman who betrayed his countrymen for 75 guilders plus a percentage of the booty.

Wolvenplein prison, Utrecht

Disillusioned we returned home. As Freddy was not registered in Utrecht, he decided to go into hiding in Amsterdam. With Father imprisoned in the Utrecht Wolvenplein goal and Freddy somewhere in Amsterdam, Mother and I had no other option than to report daily at the local police station. The Elsbach family, however, never showed up.

A few days later, Mother read a shocking news item in the newspaper. "In the Eems River near Eemnes, police found the bodies of a man and woman, bound together. Probably of foreign origin. From the note they left behind, we conclude they committed suicide. The capsized rowing boat they rented the day before was found nearby. Anyone who can give information is asked to report to the local police."
Mother never forgave herself that in her heart she had blamed the Elsbach family for what happened.

Years before the war, Frits Preuss a German rival of Father, had lost a court case against him. In the 1930's, Preuss became a leading Nazi in Duisburg. On December 17, 1941, he was installed as the *Verwalter* of the Negum factory.

In December 1941, when Mother and I reported again at the police post, the policeman told us we had to relocate to Westerbork.

"Why?" Mother demanded to know.

"All non-Dutch Jews have to relocate to Kamp Westerbork," the policeman replied.

"But we are Dutch!" Mother exclaimed.

The policeman looked at the paper in his hand. "The fact that your husband never became a Dutch citizen has rendered him stateless. Therefore, your son Harry is also stateless. That's why you are to relocate to Westerbork."

In January 1942, the Jewish citizens of Zaandam and Hilversum received a notice from the Jewish Council they were to relocate to Amsterdam. The Jews from Utrecht also had to move to Amsterdam. Mother and I didn't have to go there. Together with the other stateless Jews, we were 'allowed' to go straight to Westerbork. An NSB family moved into our apartment above Perfumery Apollo on the Oude Gracht.

CHAPTER 4
1942 Kamp Westerbork

Much we were not allowed to take with us to Westerbork. The list sent by the Jewish Council only allowed clothing, blankets and toiletries. All my science items were donated to my friend Johan Westdorp.

The winter of 1941-1942 was very cold. That January morning, I shivered

while waiting at the assembly point at Utrecht Central Station. Our little group travelled to Westerbork on a stamped travel permit and a ticket that was paid for by the Jewish Council. Mother and I boarded the train to the big unknown.

Bakkerbrug/ Oudegracht 1942

The Hooghalen train station in the Drenthe province was quite a distance from Camp Westerbork. Only people who had difficulty walking were given a ride in the lorry that was waiting at the station.

Mother and I had to walk three miles on foot, carrying our own luggage. On arrival, we were welcomed by an *Ordedienst* (O.D.) steward, dressed in green overalls, who showed us the way.

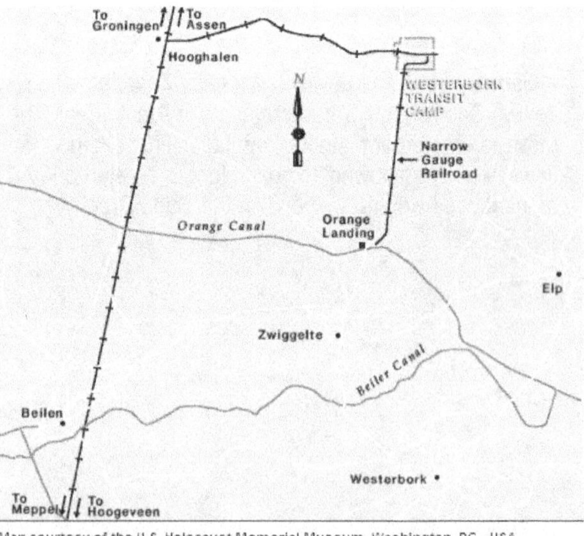

Map courtesy of the U.S. Holocaust Memorial Museum, Washington, DC - USA

After registration, I received a *Lagerkarte* and *Arbeitskarte* and was sent to barracks 21 – the youth barracks. The barracks leader assigned me one of the forty bunk beds.[1]

The guardhouse, entrance Kamp Westerbork

The bed didn't have springs but steel strips on which the mattress lay. "Roll call is twice a day. You must make your bed, for they keep strict control of the barracks. You will be told which work detail you'll be in."

I found Mother in another barrack that was divided in two; in the center was a small area with a heater, where she had her bed. Later this turned out to be a blessing because the big room was very crowded and noisy.
Every evening Mother was exhausted from the heavy work in the barrack kitchen. I joined the cleaning and maintenance detail but preferred to work in the hospital laboratory.

1 This was nothing compared with the later situation when hundreds of people had to sleep in three tier bunk beds, often without a mattress.

Kamp Westerbork was run by the so-called *Alte Kampinsassen* – the very first residents of the Camp. Among them were twenty-two people from the St. Louis ship[2].

In January, the Dutch anti-German lieutenant-colonel J. Schol was in charge of the Camp, that was guarded by fifteen Dutch military police. The German-Jewish refugees lived in small wooden barracks that were divided into living quarters. One of them was turned into 'post office.' Every two weeks I could send either two postcards or one letter. We were not allowed to seal the envelop because everything was being censored. It was forbidden to write about internal affairs, the work outside the camp and later about the transports that had left. Some of the letters I wrote to my friend Johan Westdorp survived the war.

2 On May 13, 1939, the St. Louis had sailed from Hamburg to Cuba with about 930 German Jews on board. Both the USA and Cuba refused them entry, thereby forcing the ship to return to Europe. Only a few European countries were willing to take in the refugees. The Netherlands took 181 (of whom 76 perished in German concentration camps). 22 people were sent to Camp Westerbork, amongst them MD Fritz Spanier, his wife and twin daughters. Doctor Spanier later became the chief physician of the camp, until it was liberated. After the war, he became chief physician of the DP camp Bergen-Belsen.

Dear Johan,

"I'm here already one week and have found my bearings. I probably can continue my studies, otherwise I'll have to work. How is your laboratory? I hope you didn't end up in hospital yet. They mailed my books and I expect to receive them soon. Yes, gone are the days we were hanging from your window, looking at the stars. Believe me, I often think back on those days with longing. Hopefully, this will help me to develop quicker to become an adult. Here, you learn the naked truth, even though we're still young. Still, next year I hope to be able to do my exams and fulfill my plans, which I often shared with you. For now, these are future expectations and dreams. Johan, you'll make me happy if you write regularly. A small effort on your part, and it will hopefully help me to get through these difficult times. Unfortunately, I cannot write often because I'm only allowed 2 sides per fourteen days. Can you please forward the bottom part of this letter?

Write me in detail about yourself, what you think, etc. Like we did when you visited me on Saturday afternoons. Until now I've been given a lot. While waiting at the Central Station in Utrecht, so many people came up to me, even those I didn't know, and gave me lots of sweets. Many of my friends were there as well. It's good to know you have real friends. Give my warm greetings to your parents and thank them for their hospitality when I visited you. Also, thank you for your help. Greet all my friends at school, also your sister. Dear Johan, best wishes and remember the Dutch saying: "everything will be all right". Warm greetings, and looking forward to your letters, your friend, Harry.

The German-Jewish Breslauer[3] family was also ordered to relocate to Westerbork. Breslauer, whose hobby was photography, was grouped with those that were 'needed' in the Camp. This privileged family was housed in one of the small barracks.

Because almost all the Camp residents spoke German, from February 1942 onwards, all rules and regulations were given in German. The mandatory school age was lowered to fourteen, thus I was grouped in a *Dienstzweig* (work detail) led by a *Dienstleiter* (work leader). Most of them had been living in Westerbork for a long time. Kurt Schlesinger, the new *Oberdienstleiter* was nicknamed the 'Mayor of Westerbork.'
Dr. Fritz Spanier became head of the medical staff and Arthur Piskhead of the *Ordnungsdienst* (OD) – previously the fire brigade.

Of course, there was no limit to sending uncensored or illegal letters. These we gave to trustworthy people that worked outside the Camp or to visitors.

6-3-1942

Dear Johan,

"First of all: thank you for your letter. In this letter, I can say more because this one will reach you via an illegal channel. Answer this letter as superficially as possible because all letters are being censored. So please don't write that you have received my letter, only, "thanks for the greetings."
That ends the technical part. Until now I had to work hard, which is difficult because of the snow and sand storms. Beginning on Monday I officially become a 'Selbstudent'. Not only is this camp an assembly point but also a 'work' camp. A pity I didn't receive my books, but that must be the transportation. Did you give my schoolbooks to Loekie? Work is hard and the food bad. That's not too bad, if one stays strong

3 Ursula Breslauer (now Chanita Moses, Israël) was a teenager when she arrived in the Camp. Because only a few people were living there at that time, everybody knew each other. Mrs. Breslauer worked in the registration barrack because she could type. Ursula helped the Birnbaum family take care of the orphans. Later she assisted her father with the developing of the many pictures that were needed for the *Lagerkarte*. When the big razzias began in June 1942, more than 3,000 pictures per day were taken.

spiritually and doesn't become dull. Which is what those who put us here are trying to achieve. For me it's not too bad because now I can study. I will try to develop myself so by the time I can leave here I'm not too far behind. How is your work? I'm glad your sister liked the books. At least somebody profited that I had to leave. You see: every bad thing has a good side. Here, I try to emphasize the good as much as possible. So much so, that perhaps I will forget the bad things. The barracks we sleep in are bad. There is no space you can call your own. Now you realize how much a person is attached to material things. It will be hard to imagine for you. Only gradually it begins to dawn on me that until now I have lived a reasonable easy life, like every boy should have in his youth. But that's why we are called the "chosen people". When the time comes and we have our own country, we won't be troubled any longer. Only then I can be the same as a Dutch boy, experiencing that feeling of having a homeland. Such a want you never had, no doubt about it; only in times like these you begin to understand a little what a homeland means. Johan, I must end. Warm greetings to your parents and sister and greet my school friends. And of course the girls in my former class, Annie, etc.
I don't have a poem like you sent me, and end with warm greetings and a strong 'paw' from your friend, Harry."

Early spring I noticed many SD-officers walking through the Camp. I learned they were looking at the infrastructure, the kitchen and the bathhouse. Rumors were strife until the announcement came that the moment the ground was defrosted, the camp was to be enlarged. It had to be finished by July. I had to assist building twenty-four huge, bad quality barracks. Each barrack could house between 250-300 people.[4]

From a distance, Camp Westerbork looked desolate and sad. Often, a mist created by the sand hung over the endless, barren and dry moors. On the horizon, a visitor spotted a chimney and three high white roofs.

4 At the time we build them, between 1,100-1,800 people lived in Westerbork; everybody wondered why this extension was needed. Would the Camp be able to cope with an influx of between 6,000 and 7,000 new people?

Besides the agricultural fields everything was brown and most of the time a sharp, icy wind blew over the lowland.

Whatever the weather, the inmates of Westerbork had to work.

"Why do we have to work in this rain?" someone protested.

"Rain?" the Dutch supervisor responded. "Nonsense! This is only wet wind! Keep on working!"

Wind on the Westerbork moor seemed like a sandstorm and a downpour like a deluge. Despite the rain, the sand kept flying about. I had to help dig, build barracks and work in agriculture. The physical work was difficult, especially for city people. Our spring menu consisted of kohlrabi, carrots, salted string beans (called barbed-wire we called them) and half rotten potatoes.

Thankfully, after a long workday, we could relax a little in the evening. Shalom Weiss, the son of one of the barrack leaders, already lived in Westerbork before the German invasion.

Drente, 1-4-1942

Dear Johan,

After not having been able to write you for some time I now have the opportunity to write you an illegal letter. Your letters are very uplifting. Your bird propaganda almost got me into trouble. One evening, about two hours before sunset, I walked to the moor, which is difficult for us to reach and most of it is swamp. How I enjoyed that sunset and the stunning view. Because someone had escaped and ended up in a concentration camp, my friend and I discussed all kinds of escape plans. There are not many animals on this wet flatland and I don't have enough knowledge to know which bird is which. So, when we returned to the Camp at 9.15 p.m we were accosted by the police who told us we were too late. We were not allowed to be outside after curfew and could end up in prison. The next morning, we had to appear before an officer and thankfully, because we were rather new here, they let us go after a stern warning. There is a lot of work going on here and I'm glad to be a self-student, which will free me from having to work. The moor is being cultivated and they are building new barracks that must be filled. So much is awaiting us.

Johan, you'll make me very happy by sending my books and notebooks. If possible, as soon as possible because I'm already getting behind with some subjects. Please, don't forget, it's very important to me. I just returned from roll-call where the guards scolded us. It looked like a concentration camp! Johan, I must mail this letter, otherwise you won't receive it. Greetings to your parents and sister, Thijs, Annie and Jo and finally yourself, warm greetings from your friend, Harry.

One evening, I breathlessly listened when his mother, a professional singer, sang music from Schubert.

I noticed they made haste to finish the camp and that German officers regularly inspected the progress.

The heavy-laden lorries, stacked high with iron bunk beds, had great difficulty not to get stuck in the mud. Inside the new empty barracks there was hardly room to move. *How can people live here?* I wondered.

And where can they store their belongings? There are no cupboards.

"It's as if the people won't have to stay here very long," somebody remarked.

The new toilets looked like a long egg-stand: two rows of holes in a large wooden slab over a cesspit. The men's urinals were on the outer wall above a sloping gutter. There was no privacy at all.

By the end of April, during morning roll call, lieutenant-colonel Schol read a notice from the Jewish Council:

"From Sunday, May 3, 1942 onwards, all Jews in the Netherlands must wear a yellow cotton sign on their clothes: the six-pointed "Jewish star," sown, not pinned. Adults and children older than 6 years are required to wear this star."

Dutch evening newspapers announced the introduction of the Jewish Star on Wednesday, April 29, 1942. To be on the safe side, this regulation was also enforced to the Westerbork residents.

I told Mother to make sure the squares of the rectangular piece of cotton were folded properly and sown at the right angle on my clothes.

Johan Westdorp (right). This picture was taken a few months before I was forced to leave high school. That's why I'm still smiling here.

3-5-1942

Dear Johan,

Thank you so very much for the books you sent me! I can use them very well. Are these all the books? Please, let me know. Thanks for sending me the curriculum, which is very helpful. I'm following the curriculum of the Jewish Lyceum and now can compare them. I've noticed that at school you still behave as badly as while I was studying there. Reading your stories about Pont [German teacher] and de Piel [math teacher] brought back nostalgic (for me at least) memories. What are your grades? Will you go to the next grade? I hope I can do my matriculation exam for the fifth grade but not sure if I will make it. Did you already see those yellow stains in Utrecht? How does the population respond to them? You see, they keep pestering us. But I hope that these difficult times will strengthen my Jewish People and that we'll come out stronger from this war than the people who want to oppress us and destroy us. I don't think that those living outside the camp, I mean the non-Jews, have any idea what we go through and how it feels being imprisoned. They are dealing with their own problems, because you no longer live in a free country, but there's a big difference. I hope you see this difference. Especially because we have so much perseverance and strong will to keep living and exist.... I'm sure that we, I mean the Jewish People, will survive this war. If we, as individuals will survive this war is something else. You see, these questions pain us youngsters besides the problems each boy our age struggles with. Perhaps this explains why the Jews seem so busy. But also, the other bad qualities people ascribe us we only embraced because of these suppressive measures. Thankfully, the new generation growing up in Palestine is different and better. In the future I want to be part of that. My ideal is to make Palestine in a model state. This is possible because she is still young, while other countries already have an established and set tradition. I hope my ideal will be realized but don't know if it will succeed. At least I can strife for it. Johan, I've bothered you long enough with my problem. Warm greetings to your parents and sister and also Thijs, and of course yourself: warm greetings from your friend, Harry. P.S. Please, share this letter with Annie + Jo.

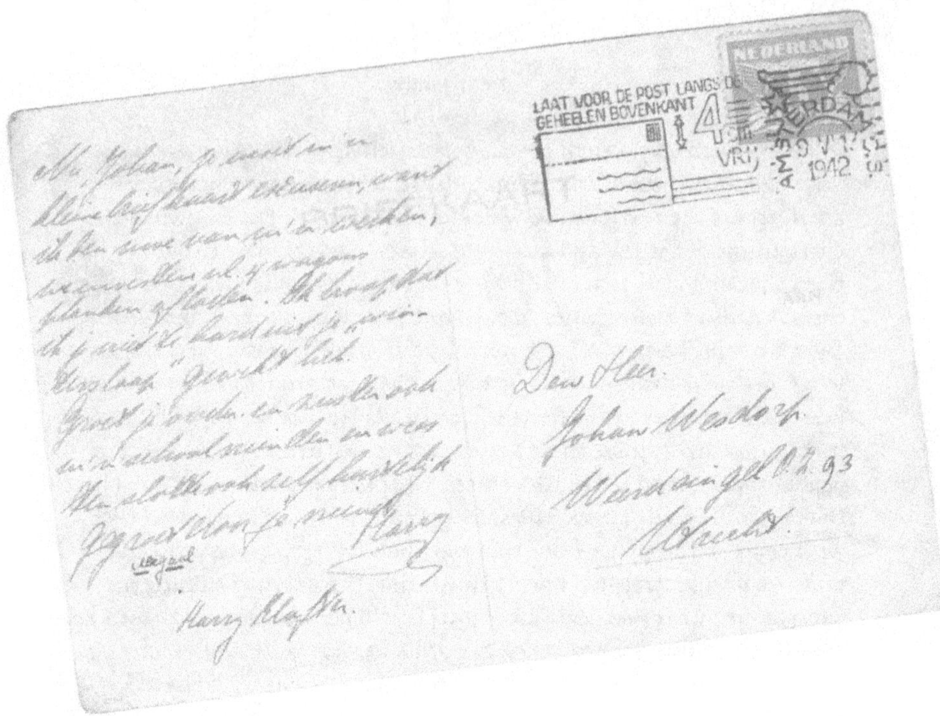

7-6-1942 (note card)

Dear Johan,

Why didn't you write me for such a long time? I hope you are not ill?
Did you receive my letter that included one for Annie and Jo? Have you
already forgotten me? Beginning Monday I must work outside, but
only for half days, making it possible to keep studying. I don't want
to quit and continue with my studies. I hope you had good grades.
When you write me, please let me know your grades. How is my laboratory? The swamps surrounding the camp breed lots of blood-sucking
mosquitoes. Sorry about this short note card, but I'm tired from working. We had to unload four lorries of planks. I hope that I didn't awak-
en you too roughly from your 'winter sleep.' Greet your parents and
sister and my school friends, and yourself: warm greetings from your
friend Harry.

CHAPTER 5
1942
Polizeiliches Judendurchgangslager Westerbork

On July 1st, 1942, the new commanders of the camp, the *Schutzstaffel* (SS), changed the former absorption camp with 1,200 inhabitants into a *Polizeiliches Judendurchgangslager* - a Political Jewish Transit Camp. Those of mixed marriage were ecstatic with joy upon hearing they were allowed to return to Amsterdam.

During morning roll-call on July 13, *Sturmbahnführer* Dr. Deppner announced that all the men were to report the next morning in the small hall. *"Zum Arbeitseinsatz"*- to work - they were to undergo a medical examination. That same day ,a transport would arrive from Amsterdam to Hooghalen. After registration, these people, together with one hundred from Westerbork were going to Germany *"zum Arbeitseinzatz"*.

In the afternoon of July 14, I waited in line to enter the hall. Deppner, sitting at a table used for religious services by the chazan or the pastor, studied a list that was compiled the night before. It contained names, ages, and the type of work these people did. Schol stood behind him. The person who entered said his name and number.

"Beruf? Arbeit? (Job)."* Deppner asked. Depending on the answer he decided, *"bleibt"* (stay) or *"geht"* (goes). Occasionally, he asked Schol something, who then responded: "You'll hear from me."

As my friend told me that Auschwitz was a work camp with better living conditions, I wanted to join them.

"Don't even think about it!" Mother said.
No one was allowed to address a Nazi, therefore Mother waited near the podium until Deppner noticed her.

"What do you want?" Deppner snarled.

With a strong voice, my mother said. *"Bitte, Herr Sturmbahnführer,* can my son please be exempt from the upcoming transport? I need him here. My husband is in prison and I cannot be left behind alone. I would like to wait for my husband to join us and then the three of us will depart for Auschwitz."

It was quiet for a moment. "Permitted," Deppner said.

That evening, in the big hall long rows of tables and chairs were made ready for the registration of the expected transport from Amsterdam. In the smaller hall, people were to receive a mug of coffee and bread with cheese. Throughout the night the women worked to prepare the bread and cheese sandwiches.

The morning of July 15, the camp was restless because there were 'only' 950 people from Amsterdam on the train. Even though Deppner already had chosen 150 men from Westerbork, the Nazi quota was not full.

Salo Carlebach

Deppner found the solution to this 'problem' by adding 50 orphans to this transport.

"Auschwitz also has a *Kinderheim*," he told the protesting house parents. Teacher Salo Carlebach[1] volunteered to join the children.

I noticed that there were only men on the Amsterdam transport. Pale and tired looking, they gratefully excepted the coffee and sandwich after being registered. They were shocked to learn they were to walk the same distance back to the Hooghalen train station. In front of them walked the men and boys from the Camp, each with his rucksack and blanket. The orphans were transported by lorry. That first transport from Westerbork to Auschwitz consisted of 1,137 persons.[2]

[1] Siegfried Salomon (Salo) Carlebach, originally from Leipzig, was a teacher in Amsterdam. The Jewish Council sent him to Westerbork to teach the children and help with the Youth Group. He organized many things in Westerbork, even special parent evenings to talk about their children's problems. The children trusted him and he was much loved. When Salo told Deppner he wanted to join the children on their journey East, Deppner asked why. "I want to stay with them because they are important to me," he said. Leo Bluhmensohn took over Salo's work in Westerbork.

[2] My friends never had to work – on arrival in Auschwitz, they were sent immediately to the gas chambers. The orphans too were immediately gassed on arrival. Salo was murdered between September 25 and 30, 1942.

By now we understood fully what the purpose was of those large barracks. If you only were to stay one or two nights on your way to the East, there was no need for comfort.

October 1942, the command of the Camp was taken over by *SS-Ober sturmführer* Albert Konrad Gemmeker. The Camp was surrounded by a two-meter high barbed-write fence and seven watchtowers. The entrance to the Camp was guarded by the SS.

Interior transit barracks

Watch-towers and barbed wire

The Dutch military policy, assisted by the OD (ordedienst) had to keep order in the camp.

To prevent policemen becoming too 'attached' to the Jewish prisoners, every two months the regiment was changed.

Between July and December 1942, every Monday and Friday a train departed from Station Hooghalen to Auschwitz. In 1943, Tuesday became the day of transport.

"When it happens, it leaves a big impression and you think you'll never be able to forget it. In truth, so much is happening that the next incident supplants the previous."

Mirjam Bolle

That is exactly how I've experienced it.

CHAPTER 6
Durchgangslager Westerbork

Railway tracks inside the Camp - right the chimney of the boiler house

On November 2nd, 1942, a new railroad was inaugurated from Hooghalen station right into the Camp. The rails were parallel with the Camp's long, straight main avenue.

From that moment on this so-called Boulevard des Misères became the arrival and departure point for many people.

This avenue was also nicknamed the *'Rachmones-Allee'* or *'Tsorres-Allee'* (Misery street). A second railroad line with two shunting switches and a stop block ran past the potato cellar just outside the camp.

My father, who had been in prison for over a year, regularly wrote on the Wolvenplein prison paper – the *Deutsche Untersuchungs- und Strafgefängnis.* Much of his correspondence had been preserved. To scribble as much as possible on that little piece of paper, Father often used abbreviations. With the passing of time, he began to write smaller and smaller. Since the Germans presumed that Father still had more assets, he regularly had to appear before a judge. In this letter, he mentions such a trial.

An: E. Klafter-Mok
Lager Westerbork B.12, Hooghalen (O)
Absender: Isak Klafter, B 134U   Wolvenplein 27, Utrecht

Date: 23.12.42

My darling wife! Perhaps you are right, considering the adjournment
now set for January 6. Let's hope for a good ending. What is more important to me is that you are still there, but I hope I don't have to worry
too much about Harry's cold. It pains me to hear you are allowed to
receive fewer packages. As long as you are allowed to keep on living.
We must carry our lot. You are correct by saying that you have to
learn to live with less and you still look fine. Harry, take care of your
health. Downhill goes faster than uphill. Thanks for the dates, is
enough. My memory is still functioning. I even remember when you
said upon returning from the big trip: "If we go, TP also has to leave,"
because I meant to keep TP until everything was running smoothly in
Palestine. Yes, you are such a strong sweet little animal! I learned that
I won't be eligible for Celle (Bergen Belsen) because I will receive an 'S'
on my papers after being released from prison. Don't be sad. He who is
born for a dime, will never be worth a quarter. I can imagine what you
go through, but we are from strong stock, and so are you. Persevere,
little one, like so many thousands. At the moment, it's not too bad
because the days are short and I go to bed at 7 p.m. Being able to lie
down 12 hours and sleep 10 of them – wonderful. I keep wondering
when I will be able to embrace you again. I think it will take at least 6
months and then the question will be if you are still in W. Don't cross
bridges before you come to them. I no longer torture myself with illusions or feed my wishes with idle hope – they go up in smoke. So, we'll
wait. Today and the next 7 days I only think about the Chanukah
lights. And who knows next Chanukah? One year will pass and perhaps then it's possible. I'm full of courage. Many years in free and
better circumstances. That is what I want to wish you my dear, sweet,
courageous wife! Many kisses, I embrace you, your loving Izaäk."

Finally, in 1943, the work detail was finally given thick blue coats to wear over our overalls. We had work shoes but no rain coats and no gloves. Due to the shorter winter days, we worked fewer hours. Snow blew around the barracks and icicles hung from leaking rain pipes. Due to lack of coal, the stove didn't work. When it didn't snow, all you could see outside was brown heathland, cut by an unpaved road. At the horizon was a dark pine forest.

I had to repeat the 3rd class of the HBS and knew that, if I wanted to have a job after the war, I had to become a serious student. Thus, I decided to become a *'Selbststudent'* and asked Freddy to send me my final exams study books from his hiding place. When I didn't understand a math or chemistry problem, there were plenty of teachers nearby to ask. Very soon I caught up with the studies, but needed a quiet place to concentrate. In my barracks that was impossible, so I asked the Breslauer family if I could use their room during the day. At night, I sometimes sat close to the heater in the central part of the barrack with fine weather I was outside in the field.

While working in the hospital laboratory, I got to know Dr. Dries Querido.[1] Chaim Weizman always had been my idol, but now Dries Querido was my big example. He taught me about vitamins and the discovery of vitamin B1. A new world opened for me and I was thrilled when I could assist Dr. de Vries, a famous Amsterdam hematologist in the laboratory.

I shared barrack 21 with some German youngsters. Being not allowed to be outside after curfew, many evening activities were organized. By the light of a flashlight, someone read from *the Forty days of Musa Dagh* by Franz Werfel[2]. The story of the Armenian genocide and the resistance of this small group against the Turks made a deep impression on me. Even though I didn't understand everything art historian Lenz shared, I absorbed his teaching like a sponge.

---

[1] After the war, Dr. Querido became an endocrinology professor in Leiden. He was married to Heleen Pimentel, a famous actress.

[2] *"The Forty Days of Musa Dagh"* - Later, when I was a surgeon in Jerusalem, I often recommended this book to German medical students who interned at my department.

Once a week the train now departed from within the camp, and everybody knew what was happening. On Monday-evening, the antique two-axle railroad car from before WWI entered the camp. Its twenty cattle cars were being transformed into a transport train. Each carriage had its own toilet barrel, specially fabricated by the Westerbork cooper. The carpentry workshop built rough benches while the painting workshop delivered the destination board: Westerbork-Auschwitz.

Occasionally, I had to help the *Notbereich* when the OD and the *Fliegende Kolonne* couldn't handle the big transports. Wearing a special "NB" arm strap, I had to assist incoming and outward bound transports, helping with the unloading and loading of the luggage and escorting people.

Assisting an incoming transport was nothing compared to escorting people in the opposite direction to the deportation train. Sometimes sick people were brought to the platform on stretchers.

I joined this desolate procession that plodded to the waiting train, carried their luggage or helped people with small children. Holding the number that corresponded with the one on the carriage, everybody quietly waited until their turn came to board the train, helped by the OD.

It was harrowing to witness family members being separated and how the OD kept pushing until everybody was inside.

For the transports to Auschwitz and Sobibor cattle cars were used — 74 people were packed into one carriage. After the sliding doors were closed, a quick count was performed and the number of people inside was written on the door with a piece of chalk.

Because Gemmeker didn't want any hysterical departure scenes, the area surrounding the railway was off limits to the rest of the prisoners. Everybody had to stay inside the barracks until the train departed. Gemmeker, his SS staff and the Jewish department heads stood on the platform, passively watching and waiting until at 11 a.m. sharp the sign was given. After a long whistle, the train jerked and began to move.[3]

The moment the steam whistle sounded of the boiler room we knew the transport had left the camp. All restrictions were lifted and everybody could walk around freely. 'Normal' life returned to the camp. Until the next transport. How I dreaded those transport duties. Especially when I knew family members were among the deportees.

In general, nobody knew what came after Westerbork. There were rumors about gassings, but nobody believed them. It was incomprehensible.

"We just thought we had to work in factories, for the war industry... But we probably didn't want to think about the question what those ill people had to do in the East, and what the task would be for those weak people. We thought: who knows, perhaps they have to peel potatoes or work in the kitchen," Jules Schelvis wrote.

3 The train travelled from Hooghalen to Assen, Hoogezand, Sappemeer, Zuidbroek, Winschoten to Nieuweschans and then crossing the Dutch-German border, towards an unknown future.

Jules Schelvis, who survived the hell of Sobibor, wrote how the Jews kept going during these century long persecutions.

"I also thought: I'm only 23, young and healthy. I must work, but that's not too bad... What can happen to me? Each time this special Jewish mentality emerged: arrange yourself after each disaster and adapt. That all Jews were to be literally eradicated, nobody would ever believe that."

Of course, I sometimes wondered whatever all those old people, children and sick people were doing in a work camp. The only way to survive this uncertain hell was not to think too deeply.

My fellow students in Westerbork 1942, before the deportations began.
Rabbijn Augapfel is the one holding his hat.

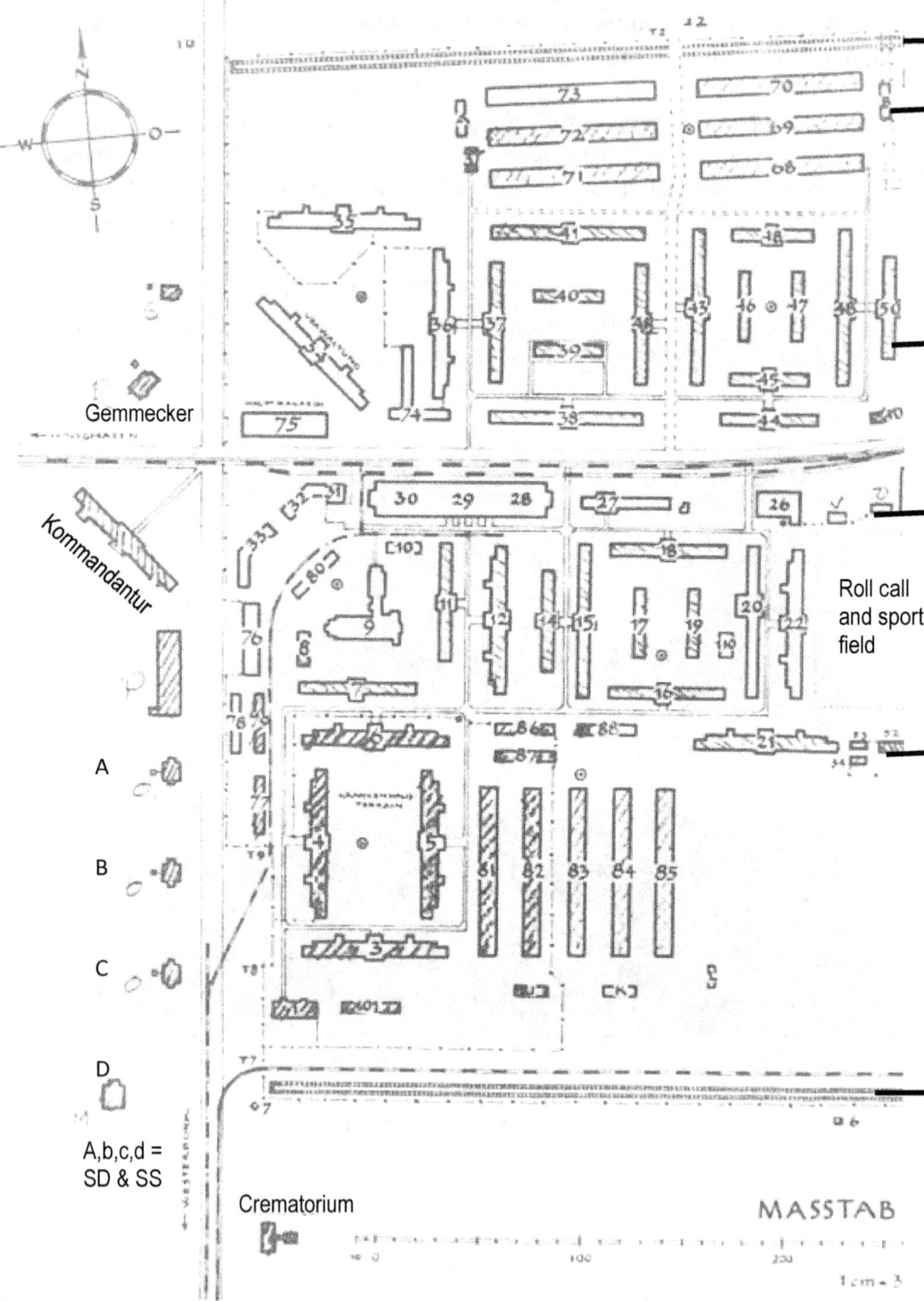

N
W O
S
Gemmecker
Kommandantur
Roll call and sports field
A
B
C
D
A,b,c,d = SD & SS
Crematorium
MASSTAB
1 cm = 3

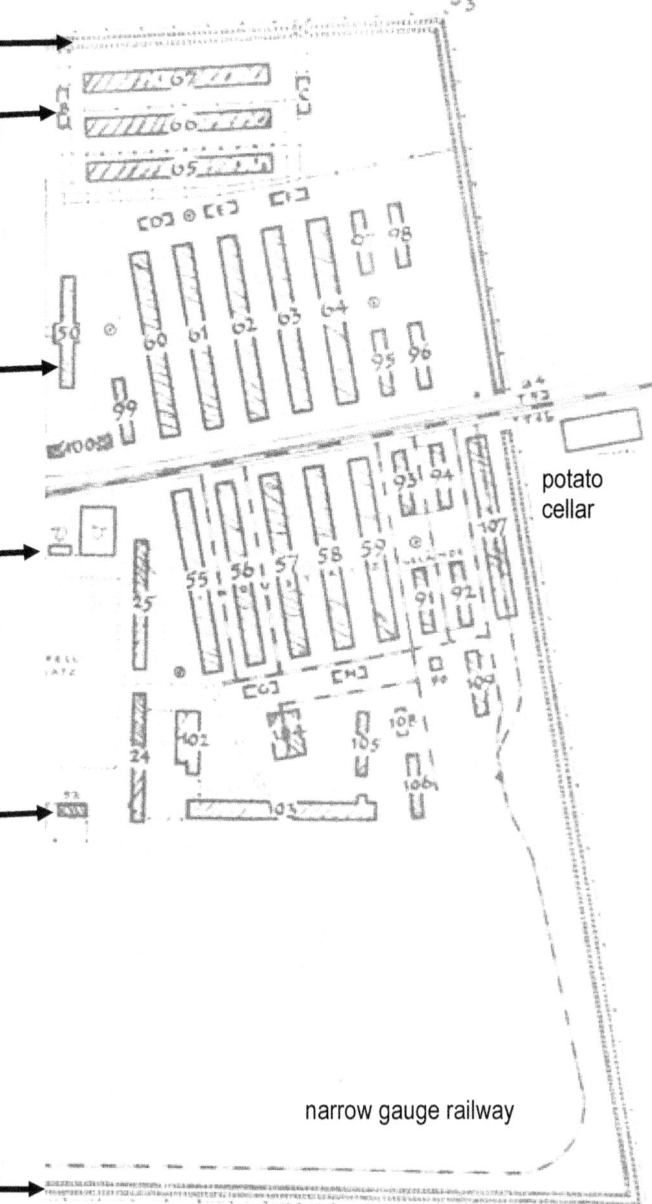

MAP WESTERBORK

1940-1941

9 = previous big and small hall
15 = Family barrack
22 = Singles barrack
28-29-30 = central kitchen

From 1942

3 = school
4,5,6 = hospital
20 = Laundry
21 = Youth barracks
22 = OD/fire brigade
24 = carpentry workshop
25 = foundry
26 = boiler room
27 = bath house
35 = orphanage
36 = Quarantine
38 = LAWA/LAKA
55,56,57,58,59= industry
60,61,62,63,64 = industry
91-94 = industry
95-98 = industry
6566,67 = punishment bar-racks
83 = big barrack
84 = latrine
85 = Barneveld barrack

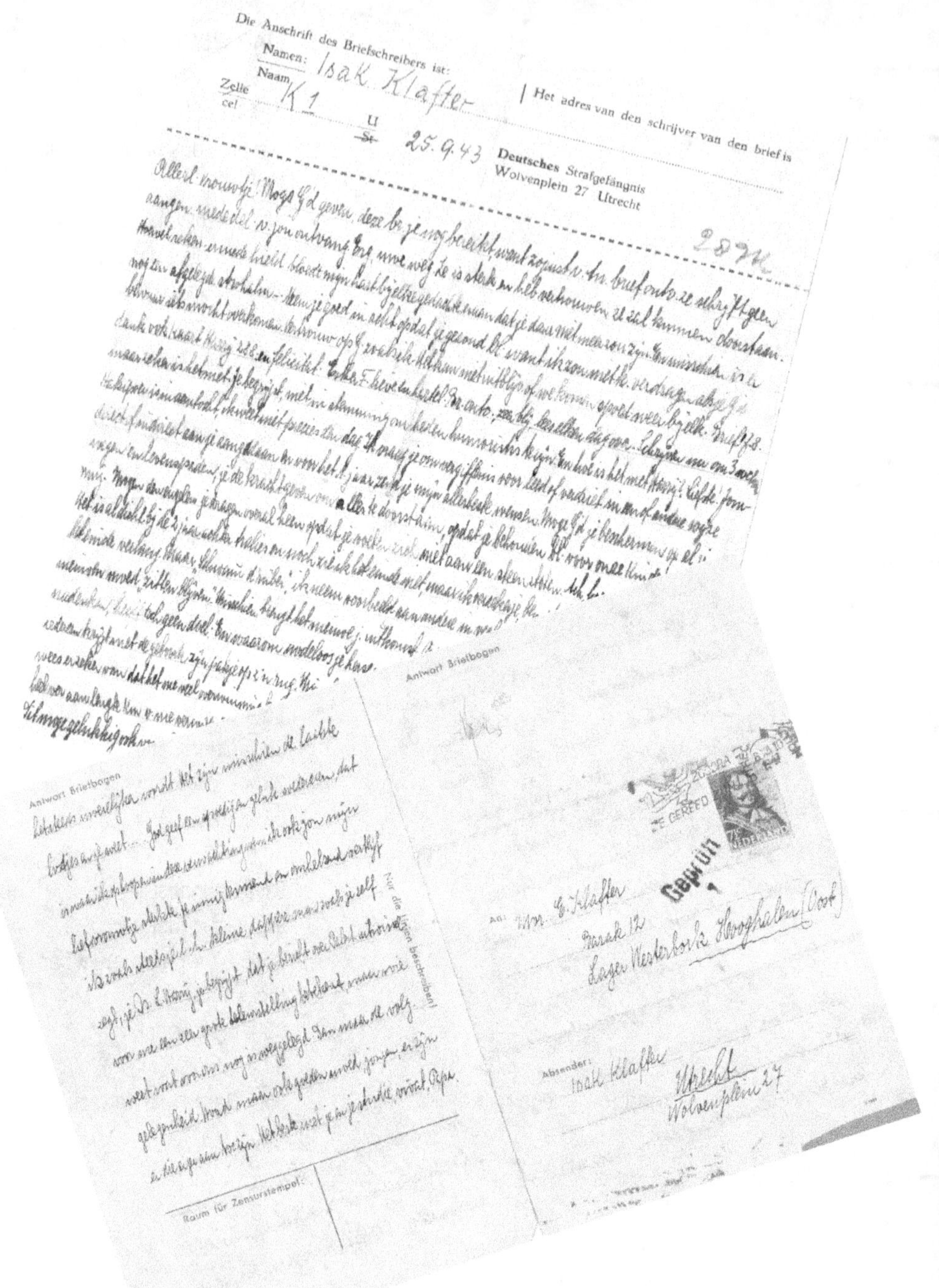
Die Anschrift des Briefschreibers ist:
Namen:
Naam: Isak Klafter
Zelle
cel: K 1
U
S 25.9.43
Het adres van den schrijver van den brief is
Deutsches Strafgefängnis
Wolvenplein 27 Utrecht
Antwort Briefbogen
Nur die eigene beschreiben!
Raum für Zensurstempel:
Aan: Mr. G. Klafter
Barak 12
Lager Westerbork Hooghalen (Oost)
Absender: Isak Klafter
Utrecht
Wolvenplein 27

Kamp order February 5, 1943

When someone flees, 10 randomly chosen co-occupants
will be put on the punishment transport; probably also
the barrack leader will be punished.

Reprisals were a psychological weapon, because the maximum amount of people on the transport list was already determined beforehand. Sending ten 'S' (*straf*) punishment prisoners as a reprisal meant respite for ten others.

It was imperative to find yourself a job that made you 'needed,' so you were put on the *Sperre*-list, exempting you from transport.
New arrivals looking for a job had to start at the bottom: cleaning the barracks, cleaning the toilets, picking up the food, camp worker, administrative worker or registration services. One step higher came the: barrack leader, administrative leader with adherents and responsible duties.

Kurt Schlesinger

Over these stood mainly the original refugees, German Jews who decided who was and wasn't going on a transport. "King" Schlesinger was at the very top.

To reign the camp, in fact, meant: preparing for the next transport.
The bureaucracy, the lists and the jobs made it possible for an individual to receive temporary respite from transport. Most people however, especially the Amsterdam proletariat, seldom stayed longer than a few days and left with the next transport.

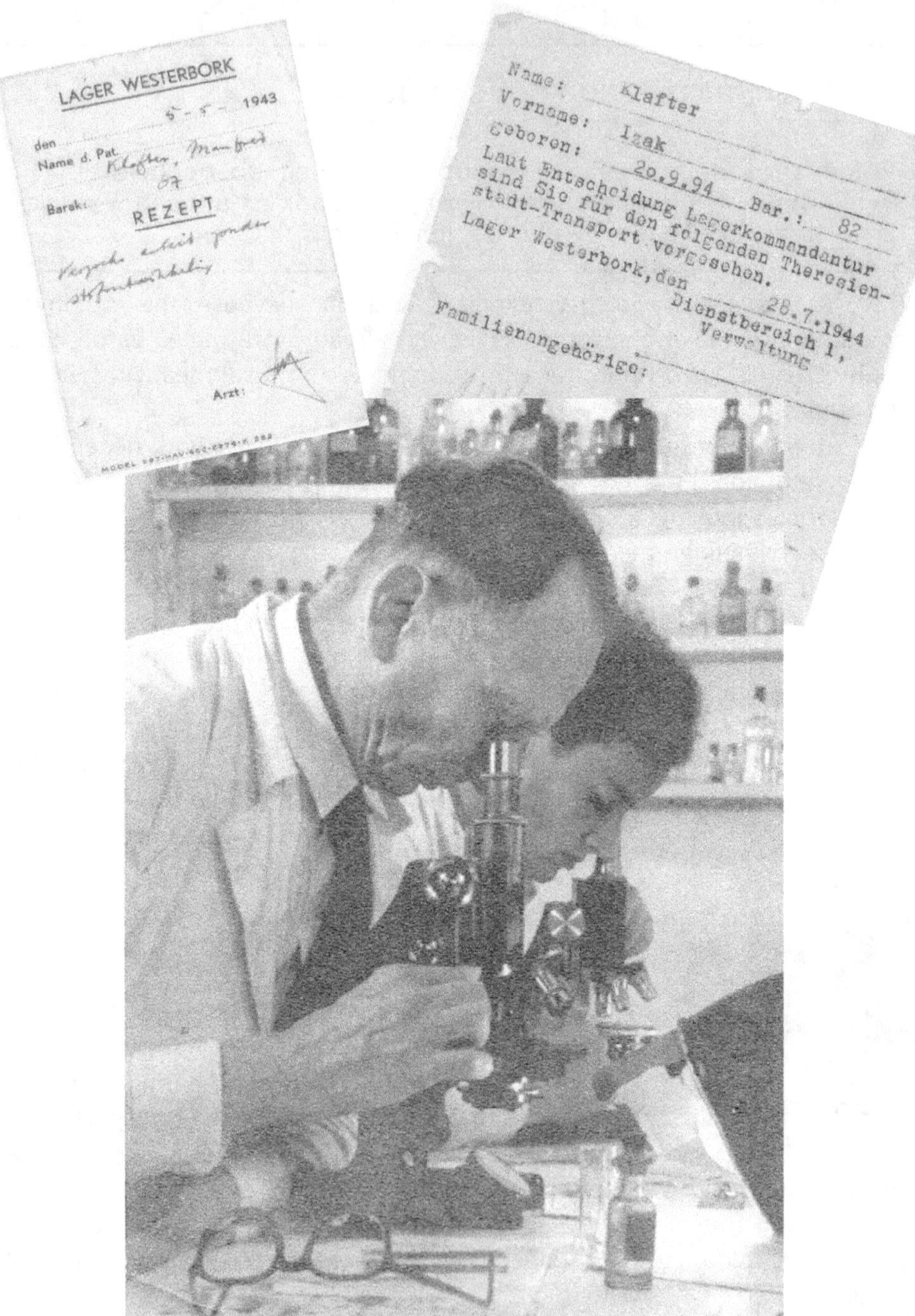

In the laboratory with Dr. Grünbaum

CHAPTER 7
1943
Durchgangslager Westerbork

It was the year 1943 and I already lived in Westerbork for more than a year. On a regular basis, I could be found in the camp hospital in barracks four, five and six. It even had an operating theater, outpatient clinic, laboratory, pharmacy and dentist. The hospital had more than enough personnel because so many Jewish doctors and nurses had been deported to Westerbork. Together they tried to keep their patients for as long as possible in the hospital, thereby exempting them from deportation.

Mother and I were relieved when grandma Mok was taken off the transport list because she had to undergo a hernia operation in the Groningen hospital. However, her respite was short lived, for the moment she was deemed 'fit,' grandmother was sent to Auschwitz.

"Auschwitz must be a good place," many people reasoned. "Otherwise they wouldn't send only healthy people there?"

By now, I had learned my HBS curriculum and was ready to take my exams. The problem was that I had to travel to Amsterdam to do so. If you had a specific job, some people from Camp Westerbork could travel. In general, Kurt Schlesinger and his 'disciples' decided whom of their friends was allowed to do an outside job or even get a furlough.

In Westerbork one needed a patron to get something done, so I asked Breslauer, who by now was Gemmeker's official camp photographer, if he could put in a good word for me. Only because my father was still imprisoned and my mother stayed behind in Westerbork as a 'hostage,' I received permission to travel. Someone from the OD was to accompany our group.

On May 26, 1943, I received my travel permit which was also my train ticket. In Amsterdam, I ended up in the middle of a major round-up. German soldiers and Dutch policemen closed off streets so Dutch policemen could pull out the Jews from their homes. Later I heard that thousands of Jews had been deported to Westerbork that day. When they grabbed me I showed the policeman my *ausweiss*.

"I've just come from Westerbork," I protested. "Here is my permit to take my exams."
Seeing the paper, *SS-Sturmscharführer*[1] Franz Fisher immediately released me and I continued my journey to the Joodse (Jewish) Lyceum[2].

That day, I was one of the last students to take oral exams HBS/ Gymnasium at the Joodse Lyceum. On receiving my diploma, that same day I returned by train to Westerbork.

The summer of 1943 was dry and hot; sandstorms whipped sand in my eyes and I felt it grinding between my teeth. The *Ordedienst* regularly had to pull out to extinguish a heath fire and returned blackened by soot. Sudden downpours turned the dirt tracks into mud pools, but it continued to be sweltering hot in the wooden barracks.
Mother's bed was still in the little corner of the women and children's barrack. It was never quiet – day and night children cried, there was no privacy and no hygiene. Many people had fleas and lice and the camp stank. When a fly infestation occurred, each person was instructed to catch 50 flies and hand them to the barracks leader. Although those problems were nothing compared to the continuous tension throttling us.

I held different jobs. Sometimes I worked in the hospital laboratory, but also in the workshop at the boiler room where cables were cooked in big caldrons. These cables were broken up because of their tar, which I had to scoop out with a big ladle. As the Germans needed raw materials, we also extracted manganese from discarded batteries.

My work hours were from 7.00 – 12.00 am. And from 2 – 7 p.m.
At noon break and after work, I picked up food at Mother's barracks. Often, this was supplemented by food packages my brother sent us.

---

[1] **SS-Sturmscharführer** was a Nazi rank of the *Waffen-SS* that existed between 1934 and 1945. The rank was the most senior enlisted rank in the *Waffen-SS*, the equivalent of a regimental sergeant major, in other military organizations.

Gemeentelijke Inhalingscursus voor
Ondergedoken Leerlingen van U.L.O. en M.O.

Ondergetekende verklaart hierbij, dat H. K L A P T E R
in Mei 1945 het eindexamen H.B.S. - B. met gunstig gevolg
heeft afgelegd en dat hem de volgende cijfers zijn toegekend:

Reken- en stelkunde en
driehoeksmeting 5

Stereometrie en
beschrijvende meetkunde...............7

Mechanica.............................7

Natuurkunde...........................9

Scheikunde............................5

Plant- en Dierkunde...................8

Aardrijkskunde........................7

Geschiedenis..........................7

Nederlandse taal en letterkunde.......7

Franse taal...........................7

Engelse taal..........................8

Hoogduitse taal.......................7

Cosmografie...........................-

Handelswetenschappen..................6

Lichamelijke oefening.................6

De Directeur

My final exams grading list

Demolishing old batteries in Westerbork

2 From October 1941, Jewish students had to study at the Joodse Lyceum in Amsterdam. After the war, Jacques Presser, one of the teachers wrote several books. Until they went into hiding in July 1942, Anne and Margot Frank were also at this school. Minutes from the teacher meetings showed how it was decided which student was permitted to continue studying for their exams and who would not. Those students were deported. From the 489 students, 45% were murdered, 40% survived the war, and from 15% their fate is unknown. After the last round-up in September 1943, the school was closed because there were not enough students and teachers left to continue.

Westerbork football team, coached by Ignaz Feldmann (right)

Those who had a 'job' were expected to work hard in Gemmeker's 'work camp.' Thankfully, he also made sure we had some leisure time. On Sundays, I often joined the football team playing on the roll-call field. We created portable goalpost and wore home-made football shirts. There were also boxing matches and athletics. I loved to participate in the sprint races.

Everybody wearing a uniform had to be greeted by taking off my hat or cap. Without a doubt, every higher authority, including the Westerbork aristocracy, had to be obeyed. Violating a strict camp rule meant imprisonment in the punishment barrack – no. 65. People who ended up there wore a blue overall with red shoulder pieces, a red/blue cap, wooden shoes and an arm strap with 'S'. Those who committed a severe crime, or if you had been in hiding and were betrayed, your hair was also shaven. People from barracks 65 were not allowed to work in the agricultural fields and were often quickly deported. Until that time, they had to do dirty jobs like taking batteries apart. Only with help and 'Vitamin R' – relations, once in a while, it was possible to remove an 'S-case' from the next Auschwitz transport. Once they were off the list, things often worked out well.

In August 1943, all the women between 16 and forty had to help with the harvest. I was grateful Mother was too old for that. When the harvesting was done, not much was left for the Camp, as three-quarters of the grain went to Germany.

The following letter Father wrote in honor of their 25th wedding anniversary. He always had a few inspiring words for me.

Klafter-Izaak -Zelle K1, Wolvenplein Utrecht -   Date: 22.8.43
"My beloved wife! Imagine you will receive this on Saturday 28. Day of
remembrance, 25 years ago happiness befell us... Physically separated,
but our souls are together. When I make a trial balance I realize how much
you have meant to me all these years: a buddy and wife from top to toe.
Thanks to you I have two fine boys whom you have raised with sacrifice,
love and dedication. They could not have had a better mother! Stay
healthy... Live in the present, don't worry about tomorrow. Remember:
there is no reason to be gloomy. How much longer? A few months...
Harry, be tenacious and persevere, that's what will bring you through.
Even though it's hard at times, remember, it may be not as bad as it looks.
I know that you are man of character. Your loving papa."

We lived from 'Tuesday till Tuesday,' from transport to transport. Camp life blunted every one. When you were not immediately transported, one quickly got used to the daily routine. If it didn't affect someone you knew personally, it seemed those weekly transports just passed you by.

Of course, it wasn't all gloom and problems in Camp Westerbork. Many weddings took place and Westerbork village's the registrar's office even opened a branch at the Camp. Rabbi Augapfel blessed the weddings under the *Chupah*. If people wanted a church wedding, a pastor or priest came to bless the marriage. Neither my cousin, David Reichman, wanted to wait any longer, so he married his fiancé Inge in Westerbork. Since he belonged to the work detail, his friends made a triumphal arch from their shovels for the bride and groom. This picture was taken in front of the administration barrack.

In Westerbork camp, children were born but people, young and old also died. Until 1943, they were buried in the Jewish cemetery in Assen. When the Germans no longer permitted outside burials, their bodies were burned in the crematorium, just outside of the Camp, on the farm road.

On September 6, 1943 there were rumors that the camp would be liquidated around November 1st. The Jewish Press Agency (JPA) or rumor circuit, was a mix of knowing and wishing, more trustworthy when you were closer to the source. During this uncertain period, I had to undergo a tonsillectomy. An ENT specialist from Amsterdam had to travel all the way to Westerbork to do the procedure. While a nurse held my head, the doctor removed my tonsils under local anesthesia – a traumatic and painful experience.

That year, it seemed the Jewish holidays had an even deeper meaning: *Rosh Hashanah* first and then *Yom Kippur.*

Father's fear that one day Mother would be on the transport list is evident in his letter from September 25, 1943. Some family members already made the journey into the 'unknown.' Here is an excerpt:

25 September 1943

"But she [family member] is strong and I am sure she will be able to bear it," he writes, referring to the deported person. "Make sure you take good care of yourself and stay healthy. I would not be able to bear it if, G-d forbid, something would happen to you. Trust G-d, like I do. It could not fail to occur or we soon will meet again. We now write very 3 weeks but nothing is certain. You understand I am not in the mood to be funny. And how is Harry? Dearest, Yom Kippur is approaching, but I don't know exact which day. I ask forgiveness for sorrow or pain I have given you one way or another, direct or indirect, and for the New Year I sent you my best wishes. May G-d protect you in all your ways, give you the strength to endure everything, so you may be saved for our children and for me. May angels carry you, so your feet won't bump against a stone... It's near – the two years behind bars. Still I don't see the end, but assure you, I am strong, even though I long for it to end. Others who are worse off are my example... Perhaps the New Year will bring a solution. I don't want to think about anything else – it doesn't serve any purpose. And why should I torment my brains with gloomy thoughts?... At birth, each one of us receives his own ruck sack...

Dear Harry, thanks for your notecard... I hope you are completely healed after the operation and that there are no adverse effects. Are you allowed to study? I hope you are still there. Write me more often, you make me very happy... [furthermore he uses telegram style greetings to many family members who are also in Westerbork.] papa."

Autumn arrived with lots of wind, rain, mud and sandstorms. Inside the barracks, it was ice cold because the leadership thought it to be too early to start using the heaters. I felt the humid cold seep into my bones. On September 29, 1943, a large transport arrived from Barneveld. From that day on, Barracks 84 and 85 were dubbed the "Barneveld barracks."

Those arriving in Westerbork first had to be registered in the registration barracks. In the evenings this same hall was used for concerts and shows. I was among the work detail of seven youngsters
whose job was to clean that big hall. Despite the water we first sprinkled on the floor, sweeping the hall was still a dusty job. Until this very day I detest offices, probably because I continue to associate the sound of typewriters with the Westerbork registrations.

Soon I made contact with a few academics from the Barneveld Baracks.[2]

Professor Schneider, a German philosopher was part of the cleaning work detail. By using a stick with a nail, he collected cigarette stumps from which he made new ones. Often, I accompanied him on his rounds through the camp, listening to his recitations of Spinoza and Hegel. I found this to be so interesting and gratefully made use of this private university. The academics living in the Barneveld Barracks were always willing to help a *Selbststudent*.

[2] BARNEVELD According to Plan Frederiks about 660 Jewish Dutch people would be spared deportation because of their 'merits to Dutch society.' They were housed in a Barneveld castle, "De Schaffelaar" and a villa, "De Biezen." That too proved to be a false promise.

On October 4, 1943, Amsterdam was declared *'Judenrein.'* The last workers of the Jewish Council were shown their beds in one of Westerbork's big barracks. Jewish life in Utrecht also ceased to exist. Thanks to the perfect Dutch administration AND the great cooperation of Dutch government offices the well-prepared Nazi plan to destroy the Jews was efficiently realized.

There were rumors that miss Schlottke would come to Westerbork to select people for a possible exchange. Since Mother worked in the sewing department, her name was on the *'Sperrliste."* Even that was no guarantee when the weekly quota had to be reached.

Excerpt letter October 3, 1943 from Father to Mother

"My dearest Esther. Occasionally someone can have a lucky break, and you see, my darling, the New Year starts good, and who knows?... When you receive this letter the fast will be behind us. G'd willing, I'll fast, but if you can't do it, don't. Health before everything! I'm very moved about aunt K and please G'd, may she be able to endure everything. I'm so grieved about it. I can handle everything, come what may, as long as you stay healthy. I never lose courage and even have the strength to encourage my cell mates... Thanks for your new year's wishes. May they be fulfilled for all humanity. How do you look? As beautiful as ever? How slim you will have become. And which blouse do you usually wear? Give me an extensive description, so I can visualize you... Not too sentimental, my boy (I give myself a pat on the cheek). Anyway – we keep up our courage! I'm resigned and wait, which is easier knowing that I have such a courageous and sweet wife, who is able and willing to adapt to all circumstances. I kiss and embrace you always, your loving Isaak. Dear Harry, thanks very much for your wishes. Are you completely ok? Good to know you are content. You see, keep on persisting. No decision about the continuation of your studies? And where? Would it be possible to send me a postcard occasionally? Mama's letters always take such a long time. See what you can do. Warm greetings and best wishes of your loving Papa."

Lagerbefehl Nr. 52–13.October 1943

Relates to: punitive measure taken in case of escape.
Yesterday, camp resident Hartogvan der Goen, Barrack
64 escaped while working in a work detail in
Hooghalen. As punitive measure, I have decided that
the mother and sister of the escapee,Rosine VAN DER
GOEN-TROMP B. 64; Vrouwtje VAN DER GOEN, B. 64 as
"S"-cases will be transferred to Barrack 67 and
therefore will be added to the punishment transport.
I explicitly emphasize that in future similar punitive
measures will be taken after each escape, without
regard to any possible reason for clearance.

Der Lagerkommandant, Gemmeker, SS-Oversturmführer

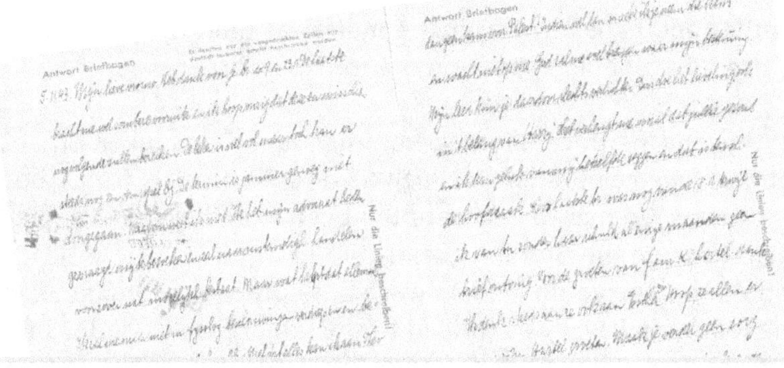

In November 5, 1943 Father wrote a letter in which he hints about Mother's possible deportation:

"My dear wife. Thanks for the letters of October 9 and 23. That last one made me somber. I really hope this letter and perhaps the next one will reach you in time. The cup is full, but still can hold another drop. Unfortunately, the trial was cancelled. Why, I don't know. I've asked my lawyer to visit me and will decide to do what we possibly can. But what good can it do? Better not get into philosophical observations but resign myself and await my fate... I so much looked forward to December 2nd, but situations always turn out differently than one expects. Do you mean that your turn will come? Didn't you have chance for Palestine? If you do, I beg you, grab that chance and don't wait for me. G-d will bring me to my destination. You will only lighten my sorrow. So please, my darling: do it, also for the wellbeing of Harry. I'm especially happy you are in good health and thankfully can say the same about myself and that is what matters most.... Don't worry about me, my darling. As long as you are alive I will be able to conquer both psychologically and physically. I continue to be hopeful, even though it becomes harder. The last bit always seems worse and who knows... G-d soon will grant a happy reunion. That is what I hope for and this expectation I also wish for you, my darling wife, strength. Kissing and embracing you deeply I continue to be your loving, short, courageous husband, like you said yourself. Your loving Izaak.

Dear Harry, you understand that your message about the Palestine exchange was a great disappointment to me, but who knows what will be in store for us. Perhaps the next opportunity.

Keep up your courage, dear boy! Many are worse off. All the best, also with your studies. Your loving Papa."

Mother and I knew it was just a matter of time when her name, and perhaps also mine, would appear on the transport list.

At the end of December, SS-commandant Gemmeker organized in Westerbork a *Yule* celebration for high SS and SD officials from The Hague and Amsterdam. We had to decorate the big hall and in the evening Jewish waiters had to serve the German guests.
At the same time, the youth leaders were busy preparing for *Chanukah*.

The following day, I was thrilled to see hundreds of allied planes flying towards Germany. Behind them came hundreds more. The whole camp stood outside, watching the spectacle.

"The sky is so full that the birds have to walk," somebody joked.

I had so much looked forward to *Chanukah* but suddenly Gemmeker forbade all meetings and our celebration was cancelled. This meant no *Chanukah* party for the children and no cultural evenings for the adults.

"Could it be a sign that the war isn't going well for Germany?" I wondered.

Ausweis sample. This certificate allowed the owner to leave Westerbork to work in the *Lagerkommandantur* or German houses.

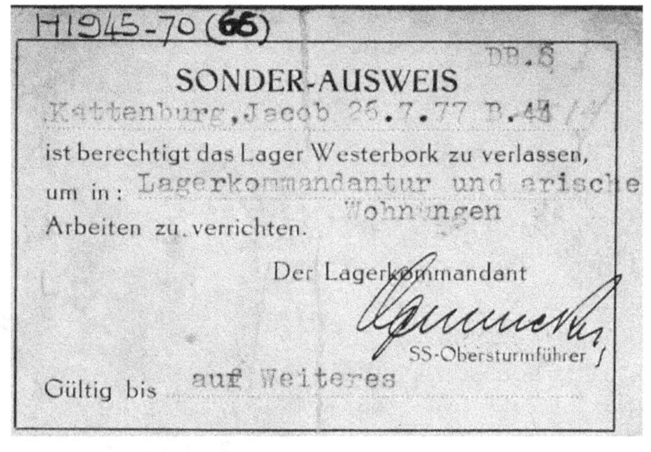

Map of the Netherlands during WW II with Nazi:

Concentration camps (1)

Transit camps (2)

Work camps (3)

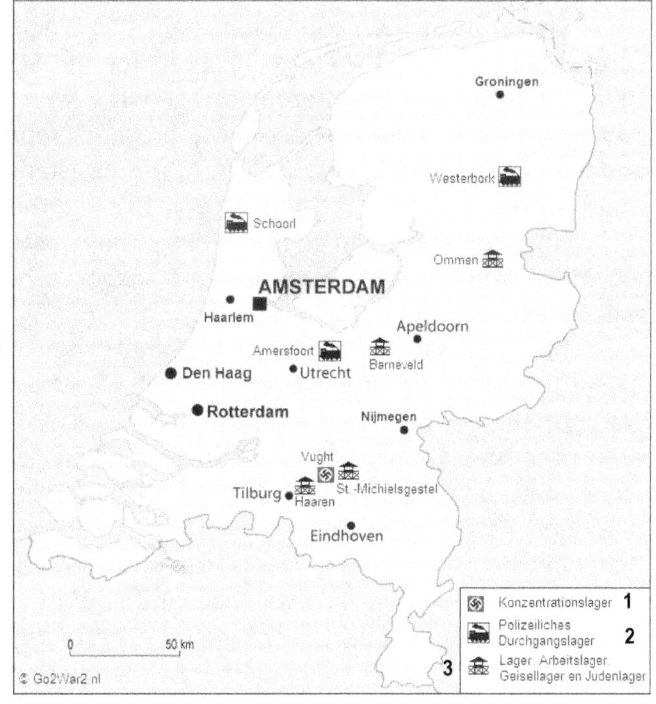

CHAPTER 8
Westerbork 1943-1944

On a regular basis, work details from Westerbork had to assist during round-ups or other activities in cities around the country. Moving houses was also the work of the *Fliegende Kolonne* and the OD – the stewards. One day, a group of men

The *Fliegende Kolonne* in action

and I were travelling to Zeist in a German lorry.

There are many beautiful villas in this wooded area, and the Nazis confiscated several of them to be used for the SD and the Gestapo. The HEMA manager, mister Bezem and I were to clean one of the villas. Suddenly two women appeared. My brother Freddy knew Mijntje Koster and her daughter Willy very well from the Resistance. After having learned that a work detail from Westerbork was in Zeist, the women told me to use this chance to escape and go into hiding. Knowing that Mother immediately would be deported on a punishment transport when I escaped, I declined their offer.

Most of that day, mister Bezem and I spent doing nothing. The new owner was expected to arrive at 4 pm. so at 3.30 p.m. I emptied a bucket of water on the floor and we began to 'work.'

When the SS-man arrived, I was amazed when he addressed us. "Enemy planes have bombed the German city I live," he said. "I'm anxious about the fate of my wife and children."

I couldn't believe my ears! The bosses of this Nazi were sending trains to Auschwitz, they ripped families apart and now this man shared his worries with two Jewish prisoners! *Perhaps he expects pity from us?* I wondered, inwardly rejoicing in the calamity that happened to his family.

Just before we were to return to Westerbork, I heard that another German driver had to deliver a load to St. Michelsgestel[1].

Since Father regularly changed prisons, I didn't know where he was at that moment. Perhaps in St. Michelsgestel? I wondered. To my surprise, the leader of the work detail gave me permission to go there. The German soldier liked the company, so together we drove to the south of the country. To my disappointed Father wasn't in St. Michelsgestel, so I returned to Westerbork.

After having been in Westerbork for two years, Esther Klafter's name appeared on the transport list. I wanted to join her, but she was adamant.

"You MUST stay in Westerbork. Papa will soon be released and you must wait for him. Harry, you'll be the contact person of our family!"

"But Mama, you need help!" I protested. "I don't want you to travel all by yourself." I grabbed my rucksack containing the few belongings I had. Taking the rucksack from my hand, Mother said in a stern voice, "Leave it and help me pack my luggage."

On January 18, 1944, I helped Mother depart to the Theresienstadt ghetto. Even though there were still thousands of people in Westerbork, I felt totally alone.

With Mother gone, I didn't have to share my bread ration anymore. Every three days, I received one-quarter of bread, and the other days half a bread. They also gave us a little margarine, cheese, sausage or marmalade and once a day a warm meal. Because there were no cupboards in the large barracks, many people hid their belongings and bread under the mattress. Of course, there was a lot of theft and I was so grateful for having a cupboard.

Some of the letters Mother received in Theresienstadt survived the war.

---

[1] In May 1942, academics and students of the Leiden University protested against the dismissal of Jewish professors and teachers and the introduction of the Yellow Star. The Germans responded by arresting 460 non-Jewish high profile Dutch people, among them politicians, mayors, professors, spiritual leaders and lawyers. Until the end of 1944, they were imprisoned in Camp Sint-Michelsgestel.

Freddy sent this postcard from his hiding place in Amsterdam.

From Louwaard (Manfred-Freddy) to Mother
transport 18/1/44 to Theresienstadt.

"Dear Mrs. Klafter, everything is fine with your husband and son. Your son suffers from a light case of diphtheria but is healing well. There are no changes in your husband's circumstances. I spoke with him last week. Also saw your cousin. Everyone here sends you their best wishes and greetings. We hope to hear from you soon." Signed, Louwaard.

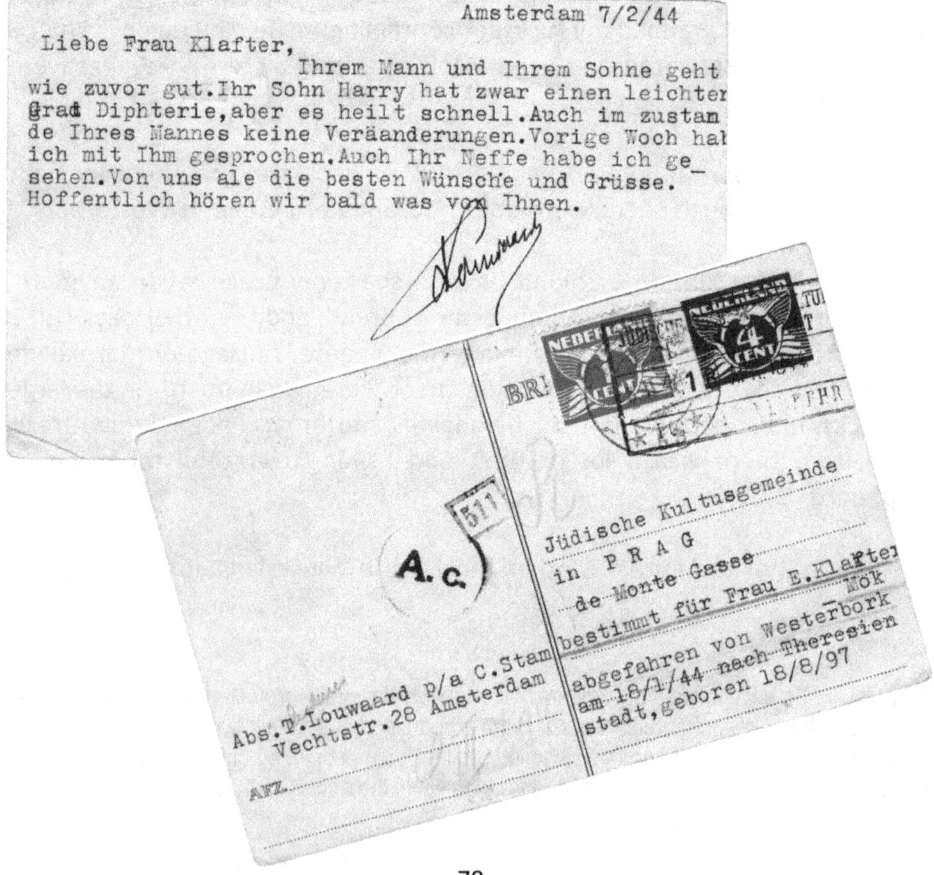

Diphtheria was a contagious disease spread by coughing, contaminated milk or food. After an incubation period of two to five days, the patient began to complain about a sore throat and fever. The disease could damage the lungs, heart and nervous system and many patients had trouble swallowing because of the swollen throat. With such a big concentration of people, a diphtheria epidemic was just a matter of time in Westerbork. Dr. Buis voluntarily came to Westerbork from Amsterdam to treat the many patients. The Nazis 'thanked' him for his service by gassing him in Auschwitz.

When I contracted the disease, the injected horse serum gave me an allergic reaction: my whole body was swollen and the itching drove me nuts. In Westerbork, many people also suffered from a light case of icterus. As it wasn't serious enough to be admitted to the hospital, there were many 'yellow' Jews walking around in the Camp.

The next letter I wrote to Mother:

23-2-1944

My dear little Mama, I can ask you so many things, but won't receive an answer. You understand I'm anxiously waiting for any news from you to know how you are doing. I cannot write about everything I hope, it's no use. Everything about you will interest me, from the moment you left Westerbork until now. One cannot change his lot; everything one experiences has a meaning. Life is a play, each plays his own role and receives his part. Don't be discontent; we have to look at the big picture. Discard all the unimportant things and look for the most important and only think about the end of the war. I'm doing very well. Ellen* is a darling, she now has her own room and I spend my days with her and eat there as well. Sometimes I'm with the girls*. Don't worry about me. Breslauer* washes and dust. Mrs. Friedman also feeds me and David gives me extras. I don't have any stock, but live from handouts and that's the reason for this little package I'm sending you as well. Did you look up all the addresses? Greet all our acquaintances. Did you write Katscher*?

Try to contact them, who knows they are in Theresienstadt. And now the most important information for you: Papa's verdict was postponed because they said they needed to interrogate more witnesses. Fred is o.k. too (all Yiddishe children). I hope to hear from him soon. Esther* went to Celle, she was very brave.

I read and continue to study and everybody is very friendly to me – I'll manage and will survive this time, will come out stronger than I entered. The newspapers are very optimistic and we see enough planes. I'm still working at the laboratory but don't have a lot do there. The camp empties out. You would be frightened if you saw it.

Mama, you know me, I never write long letters and neither I'm sentimental. I'll end now.

Soon I hope it will be a healthy reunion. All the best and I hope you continue to use the strength that helped you get through these last two years there as well. And that nothing will get you down. The three of us will bring you back from there! Also, greetings and best wishes from Uncle Jacob and Aunt Lonnie*. Lots of love and a kiss on both cheeks (a pity you can't return them) your loving Westerbork son, Harry.

* Ellen cooked for the commandant and helped me (and later also Freddy) greatly. "The girls were my cousins, Gretl, Judith and Ruth. "Breslauer" was Mrs. Breslauer, she did my laundry and repaired my socks. "Katscher" was Ergica, the foster daughter. "Esther" was Mother's niece.

My friend Bobbie Strauss and his brother probably had been betrayed while in hiding, for I saw them coming in with a penalty transport. Our eyes locked through the barbed wire, but we were not allowed to talk to each other. Both knew his situation was hopeless, so we wordlessly said goodbye to each other.

Westerbork punishment barracks

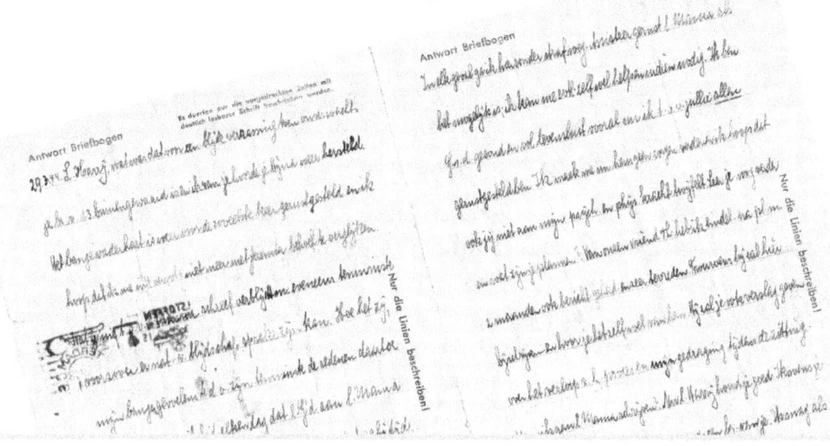

Letter from Father

Date: 29.3.44

An: Harry Klafter, Lager Westerbork B 21, Hooghalen (O)
Absender: C. Stam, Vechtstraat 28, Amsterdam

D. Harry, this was such a happy surprise to receive your l. fr. 11.3 and I learned you are almost recovered. Again, my fearful father heart was put at ease and I hope in future you won't have to compare me with Jeremiah. I'm relieved and pray each day that our dear G-d will give Mama the strength to endure, so that she may return in our midst. We can be so proud of dear Mama. No use waiting for me as I may have to stay here at least another six months. The court case has been postponed and the judge says there is not enough evidence to convict me. In any case, possibly I'll leave without punishment. If needed I'll be able to look after myself.

Thank G-d I'm healthy and full of gest for life, especially now when I'm reassured about all of you. I no longer worry and hope you won't doubt my psychological and physical strength.

Do you continue studying? What are your plans? Our friend Theo also sent me a note. He'll fill you in on the progress of the trial and how I behaved during the court case… Dear Harry, be well. I wish you a full recovery and hope to hear from you soon. If all goes well, I'm allowed to write every four weeks. Greeting you warmly, your loving Father.

Hang in there, live in the present, not in the past. Your future is before you!

Letter from "Theo Louwaard" - Freddy's alias.

3/4/44

Dear Harry, I don't think you can complain about my letters, but we do about yours. I'm longingly looking forward to receive a letter from you, for the uncertainty about you is awful.

So, if possible, please, keep me up to date. The Holidays are approaching and melancholically I think about five years ago. How time flies. Happy holidays! Until now I didn't hear anything from Mother, which is strange. I wrote her today. Father's lawyer told me he doesn't look bad but you can imagine his patience begins to wear thin. Warm greetings and I hope to hear from you soon. Theo.

6-4-1944 letter written on the official Lager Westerbork paper to uncle C. Stam in the Vechtstraat 28 – (Freddy's correspondence address)

Dear Theo, first of all: the package was delicious and secondly, I was very pleased with the TWO letters! Both were given to someone who joined last Wednesday's Theresienstadt transport to give to Mama. I wish you happy Pesach. I will attend two very nice Seder evenings. One withLeo Seligman and the other with Dr. Lutten from Gouda. Slaves we were in Egypt. Slavery, it seems to be our People's consciousness. And now? What will this bring us? You read about the persecutions we experienced then. And now we are in the middle of them and have gotten used to them. The danger is to be swept away without protest. They soften you up. In Palestine, we will be at rest and won't have to waste our energy on fear and be ready for the 2,000 year journey. Perhaps from there we can create a world of peace and higher ideals than industry and economy. That is so needed. Nowhere have you seen progress, new inventions and better technology. People have not become happier. Most don't understand it, are not aware of life. So much is absurd. I can go on and on but it will bore you. Perhaps it's my age. [Harry is 18 years old when he writes this]. Next time I'll write to Father. If you write him, give him my greetings. Warm greetings and all the best, Harry.

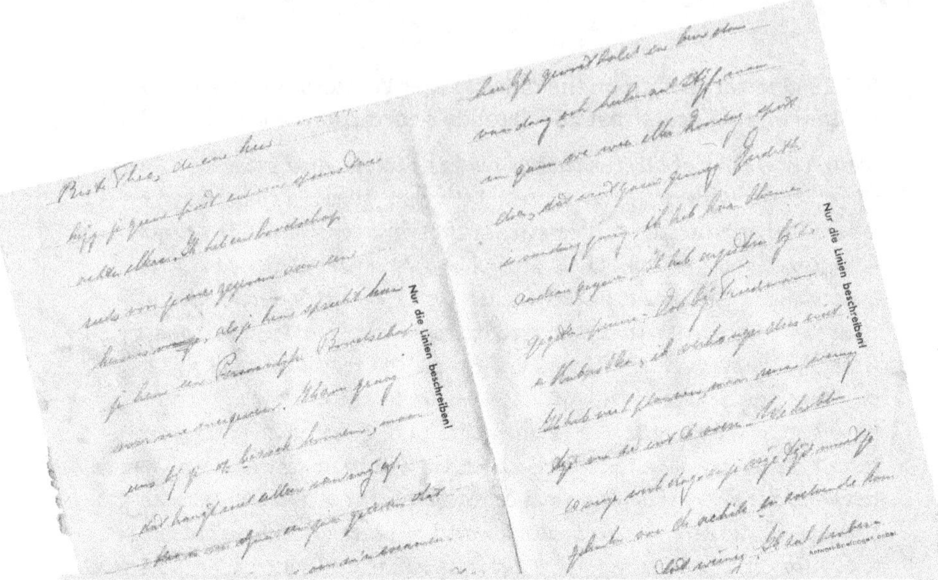

This letter I wrote under an alias— Manfred Schwab – so I could write more letters per month, to my brother who lived with an uncle, Mr. Stam.

Date: 11.4.44

An: Men. C. Stam*, Vechtstraat 28III Amsterdam –Z.
Absender: Manfred Schwab, Baracke 21, geboren: 17.5.25

Dear Theo,
One day you don't receive any mail and then suddenly one after another. I already gave you the message through an acquaintance, so when you meet him, you can give him a personal message for me. I would love to visit you but that doesn't depend on me. Almost a year ago I was in Amsterdam for my exams. So much has happened since then and so fast! Yesterday I played football and today feel stiff, but now we have sports every Sunday, so I'll get used to it. Judith celebrates her birthday today, I gave her a bunch of flowers. A day before yesterday, I had dinner with them. Great. Also at the Friedmans, so I won't die from hunger. I have many plans but little time to actually do them. We work 10 hours each day and I must use my free time to study. There isn't much time left for other things. I'm trying to change this. I have to go to work, the whistle just blew. Next time a little more. Our warm greetings, also to Annie and the children. Until next time, Harry.

Letter written under the alias of Paul Sonnsberg, to my brother in Amsterdam.

Date: 25-4-44

An: Men. C. Stam, Vechtstraat 28 III, Amsterdam-Zuid.
Absender: Paul Sonnsberg Baracke 21, born 5.7.25

Dear Theo, impatiently I await your next letter. I hope you received my previous two letters and my messages. I don't understand that I haven't received an answer from you yet and begin to worry. Every evening I hope to find mail on my bed when I come home. Yesterday I wrote Father…. It seems they receive packages in Theresienstadt… We had another fantastic revue, the best ever. Sunday evening our youth group enjoyed a Chopin evening and despite this, I've had more than enough of it all. I've heard there are talks in the outside world, they don't sit still, it must succeed. It will be our only hope, for Europe is no use to us. Both of us have been lucky. Judaism is finished. Jewish youth surviving this period and set-tling in Palestine will be the strongest. They are enthusiastic but also see the need because of everything they have been going through. I hope to receive a reply soon. Warm greetings, Harry.

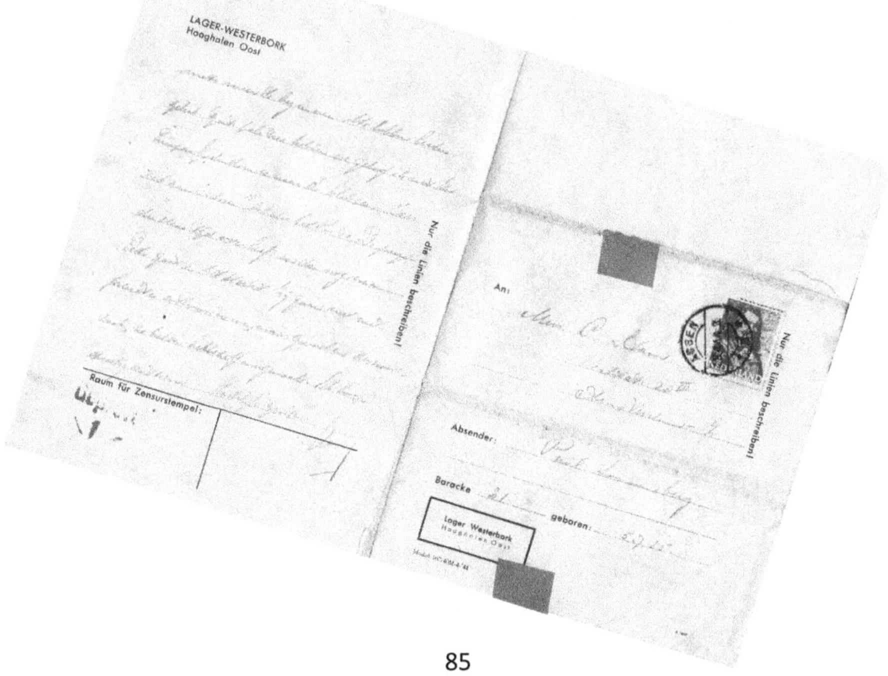

Because there were so many artists and musicians in Westerbork, Gemmeker gave permission to create an orchestra and theater group – the *Gruppe Bühne*. Kurt Gerron, a famous impresario who directed Marlene Dietrich's movie Blue Angel, was in charge of the theater group. The constructed stage was portable, so when the hall had to be used for registration they just fitted the orchestra part into another part of the podium. Ticket sales were at the *Dienstbereich* but most of the time they were sold out in record time.

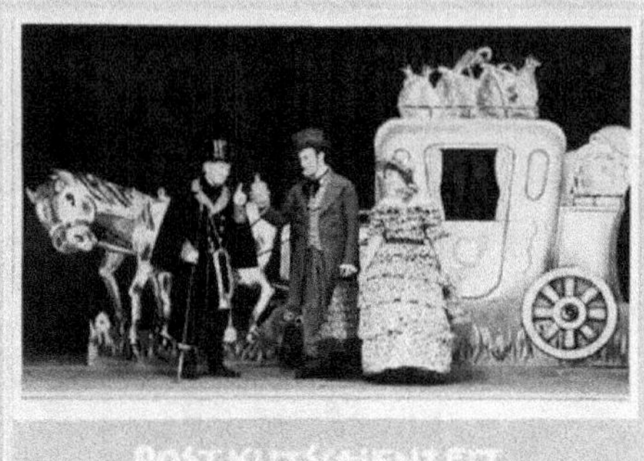

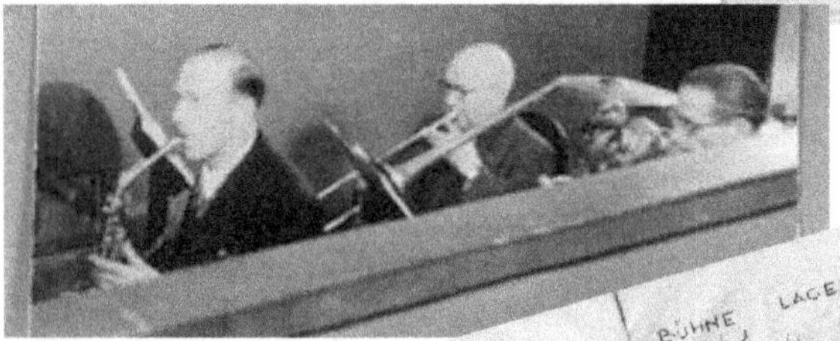

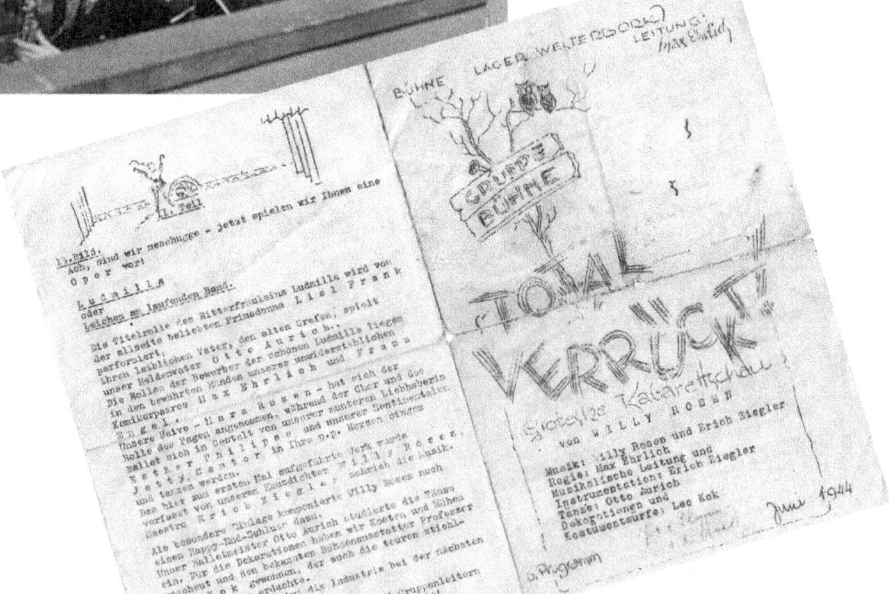
II. Teil

11. Bild.
Ach, sind wir meschugge – jetzt spielen wir Ihnen eine
O p e r vor!

L u d m i l l a
oder
Leichen am laufenden Band.

Die Titelrolle des Ritterfräuleins Ludmilla wird von der allseits beliebten Primadonna L i s l F r a n k performiert,
ihren leiblichen Vater, den alten Grafen, spielt unser Heldenvater O t t o A u r i c h.
Die Rollen der Bewerber der schönen Ludmilla liegen in den bewährten Händen unseres unwiderstehlichen Komikerpaares M a x E h r l i c h und F r a n z E n g e l.
Unsere Naive – M a r a R o s e n – hat sich der Rolle des Pagen angenommen, während der Chor und das Ballet sich in Gestalt von unserer munteren Liebhaberin E t t h e r P h i l i p s e und unserer Sentimentalen J e t t y C a n t o r in Ihre u.P. Herzen singen und tanzen werden.
Das hier zum ersten Mal aufgeführte Werk wurde verfasst von unserem Hausdichter W i l l y R o s e n, Maestro E r i c h Z i e g l e r schrieb die Musik.

Als besondere Zulage komponierte Willy Rosen noch einen Happy-End-Schluss dazu.
Unser Ballettmeister Otto Aurich studierte die Tänze ein. Für die Dekorationen haben wir Kosten und Mühen gescheut und den bekannten Bühnenausstatter Professor L e o K o k gewonnen, der auch die teuren stiechten Kostüme erdachte.
Das Material dazu wird die Industrie bei der nächsten Inventur vermissen ...

Allen verehrten Gönnern, Dienst- und Gruppenleitern ergebensten Dank für die geneigte Mitarbeit!

LAGER WESTERBORK
BÜHNE
LEITUNG: Max Ehrlich
GRUPPE BÜHNE
TOTAL VERRÜCKT!
Groteske Kabarettschau
von W I L L Y R O S E N

Musik: Willy Rosen und Erich Ziegler
Regie: Max Ehrlich
Musikalische Leitung und
Instrumentation: Erich Ziegler
Tänze: Otto Aurich
Dekorationen und
Kostümentwürfe: Leo Kok

Juni 1944

6. Programm

CHAPTER 9

"A Continuous, Heavy Pressure on Your Chest."
Mirjam Bolle.

When Father was arrested in 1941, Freddy no longer had funds to continue his studies. He decided to become a salesman under a new identity, "Theo Louwaard" and even carried a baptism certificate. On Good Friday 1944, the Germans were hunting for downed Allied pilots. During an inspection in the train to Leiden, the soldier thought that the watermark on Freddy's identity card resembled those of English pilots. He ended up in jail where they interrogated him for several weeks. One of the interrogators was the infamous *SS-Sturmscharführer* Franz Fisher. [The same Harry encountered in Amsterdam.] When it was clear that Freddy was neither spy nor pilot, they sent him as an 'S-case' to Westerbork.

I already heard that my brother was on his way to the Camp. Even though it was very difficult to contact someone in the punishment barrack, I managed to get in touch with him.

"How are you doing?" was Freddy's first question. "And how are our parents doing?"

He was startled when I told him about Mother. "Listen carefully, Harry," Freddy began. "From Westerbork, they do not send people to a better camp, only to a worse camp." From what he told me I understood our parents were in mortal danger. "All that nonsense about work-camps, it's all lies!" Freddy said. "Trust me; those trains only transport people to their deaths!"

Occasionally, we had heard rumors but they came from individuals. As everybody agreed that Westerbork wasn't an easy place, nobody could believe it could get any worse. I could not deny the terrible news my brother, whom I trusted for 100%, just told me.

However, my priority was to get Freddy out of that punishment barracks as quick as possible. Time was short, for his name was already on the next Auschwitz transport list.

I enlisted the help of my cousin Judith. She was nurse who worked with Dr. Spanier.

The doctor in charge ordered his colleague, Dr. Zeldenrust to give Freddy a certain injection that caused his temperature to become sky high. Of course, my brother was immediately transferred to the camp hospital, where Dr. Spanier advised the Camp commandant to keep Manfred Klafter in the hospital until his health had improved. Freddy's name was taken off the Auschwitz transport of June 3, 1944. This transport consisted of captured people in hiding and botched escapes. There were many hiding places in the province of Drenthe, but not for Jews. Most people were either afraid or not interested in helping escaped Jews. Jewish people in hiding that had been betrayed continue to arrive in Westerbork.

Den Baracken- u. Gruppenleiter sofort vorlegen u. als Ausweis ständig bei sich tragen.

Name: _Klafter_ Bar.: _82_
erhält _4_ Tage dienstfrei
Bettruhe
Datum: _31/5_ 1943.
Unterschrift d. Arztes: _____
ges.: { _____ Barackenleiter.
{ _____ Gruppenleiter.

Freddy's Ausweis

When Freddy was healed from his 'mysterious' illness they gave him a bed in Barack 82. Determined not to be sent against his will over the border, Freddy began to look for ways to escape.

The *Alte Kampinsassen,* those who trusted in their *Sperre* stamps and 'protection' were not willing to take the huge risk of trying to escape. At first neither did I approve of Freddy's 'wild' plans.

June 6, 1944 – D-Day. The Allied invasion renewed hope that the war would soon be over. There were hardly any transports East and life in the camp went on as usual.
Considering the 'summer-time,' the days were longer, meaning we also had to work till 6.30 p.m. At least curfew was adjusted accordingly. On Sundays, there were many football matches.

Someone told me that barracks 60 was full of confiscated radios. After they had been repaired, these radios were sent as *'Liebesgabe'* (love-gift) to Germany. Wanting to hear firsthand what was going on in Europe, and not via the IPA (*Yiddische Press Agentur* - or grapevine*)* my brother and I decided to 'organize' a radio. "Organizing' was a camp language for borrowing without asking.

While a few friends kept watch outside, I entered the shed and quickly chose a suitable radio. Bound with a rope, I lowered it into the space between the workshop's wooden- and stone wall.

"Done!" we quickly ran back to our barracks.

A few days later, under cover of darkness, Freddy and I sneaked into barracks 60. While one of my friends kept watch, I carefully pulled the radio from its hiding place. Due to lack of antenna, I put my finger in the hole, while Freddy with his ear against the radio, searched for the right frequency. What the BBC told us was almost unbelievable: The Allied Forces already reached Paris. "That's in the direction of the Netherlands," Freddy whispered. "The War will really be ending soon now."

From Father's letters, we understood that he would be released soon. Also, his brother Jacob[1] had been apprehended in Amsterdam after Father had been arrested. At first, the brothers didn't know they were being held in the same prison.

After being incarcerated for two-and-a half years, the Nazis realized that Father had been telling the truth after all, and that he didn't have any more money. Seeing that he had been falsely accused of currency smuggling, and thus had violated Dutch law, he fell under Dutch and not under German jurisdiction. However, the moment Father was acquitted, he was handed over to the Germans, whom promptly deported him to Westerbork.

As Freddy already prepared escape plans, I suggested that the three of us would try to escape. That was until we saw our deathly pale, very skinny father again after all these years. He had become an old man who could only shuffle. *Papa must be admitted to the hospital,* I knew.

"How much you have grown, my boy," was the first thing Father said. He looked around. "Where is Mother?"

"Mama was sent to Theresienstadt, papa." My heart fell when I saw this news turning off the lights in his eyes.

---

[1] Jakob Klafter (my uncle) was arrested because of so-called tax evasion. In truth, the Gestapo wanted to find out if Father had more money and investments elsewhere. A prison guard told Father that his brother was being kept in the same prison. (This fact later would play a crucial role in finding the woman in Assen who sheltered us after our escape.) For a period, Father was also held in the Scheveningen prison and the one on the Amstelveense Weg in Amsterdam.

Thanks to the good care Father received in the Camp hospital, he was regaining his strength and allowed to join Freddy in Barracks 82. My brother and I knew we had to abandon our escape plan because our weak Father would put all of us in jeopardy. Tense, we waited for the day the new transport lists were presented. Thanks to my good connections, Father was taken off the Auschwitz list and put on the Theresienstadt of July 31, 1944.

Too soon, the moment arrived that Freddy and I had to say goodbye to our father.

The evening before the transport, we quickly wrote a letter to Mother that he would give her.

Not being allowed on the platform or near the train, we said our goodbye on the evening before the transport. That was the last time I embraced my father.[2]

Freddy, Father, myself and Mother in Utrecht

2 Father did see Mother in this Czech 'model-camp.' By reason of an inner ear infection, he was taken off another transport list, but eventually sent to the extermination camp Birkenau in Poland, where he was murdered.

Dearest Mother,

I cannot tell you how happy we are, knowing that you and Papa will be together again after such a long separation. We preferred this reunion to have taken place on Dutch soil, but we already had so many unfulfilled wishes that we decided to let it go. The main issue is that you have Papa back, in good health. And you are responsible that he stays this way!... We hope you are still strong and healthy. In short: OUR mother, as we know you. We are well, well in the true meaning of the word. Hope it stays this way. Papa will tell you everything about our experiences. Thankfully, we have many friends and it won't be long until all the suffering will be over. A thousand embraces from your oldest, Freddy.

Dear Mama, as we are prevented to come in person, we decided to send Papa to fetch you. I hope you are o.k. with that. We are doing very well. Papa's eye witness account will convince you of that. We were wondering why we still didn't receive any mail from you. Ellen takes good care of us, and also helped Papa tremendously. We hope to see you very soon. Lots of greetings and a kiss from your youngest, Harry.

The July 31, 1944 transport was actually a double transport: 200 people were deported to Theresienstadt, including Father, and 200 people went to Bergen-Belsen. Freddy and I were amongst the 3,500 Jews who stayed behind in Westerbork.

Between April and the end of July, more than 2,000 Jews had been deported to the East. This created more space in the barracks. August 1944 was a special month: we heard good reports about the Allied advances, and the weather was beautiful. The most beautiful of all was the fact that there were no transports.

Almost daily we saw Allied planes flying in the direction of Germany. Probably because of the watchtowers and the barbed-wire from the air Westerbork must have looked like a military camp. One day, my friend and I were walking outside when suddenly bullets from an American Lockheed Lightning flew around our ears. In a reflex reaction, I fell backwards.
My friend, however, threw himself face down and was instantly killed.
In Barracks 85 two people were wounded and one dead.

August 3, 1944, the Camp inmates learned that from now on, all cultural camp activities were forbidden. "The camp is being liquidated," somebody whispered.

When the SD appeared in the Camp with dogs, I knew this was serious.

"Will the transports begin again?" I wondered.

Scrapyard with Johnny and Jones, two singers. Drawing by Leo Kok.

351.	Kaufmann	Moritz	17.10.03	Buroangestellter
352.	Kaufmann-Anfaenger	Bertha	4.8.01	Angestellte
353.	Kaufmann	Ernst	21.9.31	ohne
354.	Kaufmann	Rudolf	6.6.12	Lehrer
355.	Kaufmann-Randerath	Charlotte	22.1.15	ohne
356.	Kaufmann	Noemi	7.12.41	ohne
357.	Kauffmann	Walter	30.5.09	Angestellter
358.	Kauffmann-v.d.Wall	Eva	13.4.08	Wacherin
359.	Kempler	Ignaz	22.1.22	Schneider
360.	Klafter	Harry	1.11.25	ohne
361.	Kleeblatt	Walter	25.6.22	ohne
362.	Kleinkramer	Gerrit	7.9.98	Angestellter
363.	Klijnkramer-Peingersch	Marie	21.10.11	Landarbeiterin
364.	Kok	Leo	7.1.23	Reklamezeichner
365.	Kok-de Wijze	Kaatje	21.8.24	Pflegerin
366.	Kool	Flora M.	28.1.14	Steno Typistin
367.	Kopelman	Dawid	5.7.98	Pelzarbeiter
368.	Kopelman-Waldinger	Mirla	15.4.06	Kontoristin
369.	Kooperberg	Lien	3.6.19	Med.Analystin
370.	Kornfein	Gustav	16.9.03	Agent
371.	Kornfein-Heller	Hedwig	10.8.04	ohne
372.	Krakauer	Leo	5.9.16	Administrateur
373.	Kral	Walter	6.9.26	Metallarbeiter
374.	Kramer	Erich	11.1.93	Fabrikant
375.	Kramer-Wagner	Ruth	16.11.07	ohne
376.	Kramer	Walter	11.7.29	ohne
377.	Kranz	Meier	19.10.10	Zuschneider
378.	Kranz-Brunner	Henne	10.5.11	ohne, Stenotypistin
379.	Kywi	Bernd	8.10.21	Schuhmacher
380.	Kywi	Kurt	11.2.95	Kaufmann
381.	Landau-v.Creveld	Susanne	6.6.12	ohne
382.	Landau	Renee	28.11.38	ohne
383.	Lange	Isaac	10.3.97	Buchbinder
384.	Lange-Cohn	Martha	16.9.09	Erzieherin
385.	Lange	Michael	5.1.37	ohne
386.	Laufer	David	17.10.96	Kaufmann
387.	Laufer-Koppel	Dora	31.7.91	ohne
388.	Laufer	Frits	5.2.18	Elektriker
389.	Laufer-Schick	Franciska	30.4.21	ohne
390.	Laufer	Gert	5.5.41	ohne
391.	Laufer	Edith	21.10.42	ohne
392.	Laufgang	Hermann	16.6.13	Verkaeufer
393.	Laufgang-Santcroos	Esdnasa	16.10.18	Kindergaertnerin
394.	Laufgang	Mendel	1.2.44	ohne
395.	Leser	David	17.9.09	Monteur
396.	Leser-Flesschedrager	Elisabeth	20.5.14	ohne
397.	Leser	Bertha	7.11.37	ohne
398.	Levy	Albert	5.11.05	Lederwarenfabrikant
399.	Levy-Weisz	Jenny	22.4.02	Prokuristin
400.	Levy	Stefan P.	21.1.43	ohne

Copy of my transportlist. I'm number 360

201	Jacobson	Jacob L.	28. 9.01	Buchbinder
202	Jacobson-Lobatto	Judith	20.10.04	ohne
203	Jacobson,	Paul	2. 1.14	Lasser Elektr.
204	Jacoby,	Karl Franz	18. 5.02	Handweberund Spinner
205	Jessurun Lobo,	Elisabeth	9.12.18	Laborantin
206	De Jong,	Maurits	20. 7.71	Techniker
207	Judels,	Rosette	10.3.86	Haushalthilfe
208	Kaiser	Ite	25. 9.78	ohne
209	Kaminsky-Heymann,	Lucie	29. 3.01	Medizin
210	Kan,	Herman	29. 8.61	ohne
211	Kan-Kaufmann,	Johanna	7.11.79	ohne
~~211x~~	~~Kan~~	~~Karma~~	~~21. 3.61~~	~~ohne~~
212	Kan,	Rosette	16.11.14	Studentin
213	Kanstein-Hohen,	Bertha	13.10.64	ohne
214	Kanstein,	Frederik	9. 6.91	Ingenieur
215	Kanstein-Koperberg,	Agnes J.	23. 5.94	ohne
216	Kauffmann,	Gerhard	22.12.23	Student
217	Kauffmann,	Ingeborg	25.11.27	Zahnarztassistent
218	Kauffmann,	Marion	2. 9.27	ohne
219	Meijl-Breijer,	Marianne	14. 5.22	Büro-Angestellte
220	Keiyer,	Betsie	21. 6.06	Haushaltshilfe
221	Kelk-Drukker,	Martina	1.11.65	Krankenschwester
222	Kessler-Salmon,	Nastje	10. 7.75	ohne
223	Killmar-Löwenstein,	Irmgard	14.12.97	Näherin
224	Kindler,	Heinrich	9.11.92	Anwalt
225	Kindler-Fleischer,	Margarethe	16. 6.01	ohne
226	Kirstein-Oetwald,	Helene	17. 2.73	ohne
227	Klafter,	Manfred	4. 9.19	Textiling.
228	Klein,	Artur	15. 5.94	Kaufmann
229	Klein-Aron,	Ruth	2. 6.12	ohne
230	Knegje,	Roosje	9.10.06	Hebamme
231	Koskebakker-Bosman,	Francisa	12. 8.80	ohne
232	Kok,	Jan	17.12.02	Bäcker/Koch
233	Kok-Groenveld,	Hendrina	3.12.03	Schneiderin
234	Kolthoff,	Hanns	8. 1.32	ohne
235	Kugnitzky,	Hans Arthur	29. 8.01	Kaufmann
236	Landau,	Samuel	29. 9.20	Pelzarbeiter
237	Landau-Schönberg,	Gertrude	29. 3.25	Hausobinenstioerin
238	Landau-Landau,	Rita	24. 6.92	Näherin
239	Landauer,	Gerty	19. 9.22	ohne
240	Landauer,	Gustav	12.10.87	Fabrikant
241	Landauer-Schuster,	Margarethe	18. 2.95	ohne
242	Lang,	Ludwig	9. 1.83	Elektrotechniker
243	Lang-Wechsler,	Stella	16. 2.88	ohne
244	Lassally-Schäfer,	Else	10. 9.94	ohne
245	Lassally,	Irene	12. 1.28	ohne
246	Lassally,	Peter Gerh.	14.10.52	ohne
247	Lauinger,	Andreas	30. 7.27	Student
248	Lauinger,	Hanna	25. 1.23	Kinderpflegerin
249	Lauinger,	Thomas	7. 3.25	Schreiner
~~250~~	~~Visser,~~	~~Dirk Eduard~~	~~31. 7.16~~	~~Koch~~

Copy of Freddy's transportlist. Because of his false identity, Manfred was on the "Protestant" list (number 227)

CHAPTER 10
September 1st, 1944

From the podium in the main hall, SS-Commandant Gemmeker announced that much to his sorrow, Lager Westerbork was to be evacuated.

"Sunday, September 3, 1,000 inmates will depart to Auschwitz," he said. "For Monday, September 4, 2,000 inmates are on the Theresienstadt list. This includes the Group Barneveld, those that are baptized, the main registered list and the *Alte Kampinsassen*." He looked at the assembled people. "I regret to tell you that we don't have railroad cars available for the Theresienstadt journey. These also will be a transport to Bergen-Belsen. Only 300 inmates will stay behind in the Camp for maintenance."

It was as if lightning had struck the camp. Suddenly the FK and OD realized they had to help themselves into the train. Curfew was delayed to prepare for the transports of September 3 and 4.

Freddy and I were on the list for Theresienstadt. We hastily began to discuss our escape plan. Ellen, the Commandant's kitchen maid, had helped us find a suitable hiding place in the loft of one of the barracks. Ellen would smuggle food to that hiding place so we could stay put for a few days after the camp had been evacuated. At the last moment, Ellen aborted this plan, so we had to come up with a new one.

As I had lived in Westerbork for several years, I knew the area very well. On three sides it was surrounded by barbed-wire and channels, also near the watch towers. There was only one 'dry' corner and that was to be our escape route. I asked my friend Hatch Nijstatt, who worked in the metal workshop for a wire-cutter.

"Why do you need a wire-cutter?" he asked.
After telling him of our plan, I suggested he join us.

"No, thanks, too risky," Hatch responded, but handed me the wire cutter.

I walked around for hours, waiting for the right moment. The wire cutter burned in my pocket. The moment the guard patrolling the road was out of sight, I quickly cut the barbed wire. My heart beating in my ears, I waited at a safe spot to see if the guard would notice the cut wire.

Nothing happened. I covered the cut with some grass and ran away. Freddy was surprised to hear that I managed to cut the wire.[1]

"Tonight, we make a run for it," he decided.
I tried to convince some friends from the *hachsjara* group from Loosdrecht[2] to join our escape.

"No way," one of them said. "After the war, we all go to Palestine. It won't be so bad. We chose to stay."

The road outside the Camp

Sunday evening, September 3, the usual roll call was at 9 p.m. in the barracks. Freddy and I hid behind a barn near the cut wire. It drizzled and there was no moon that evening. The moment the siren pierced the quiet night we ran towards the fence. "Success!" Freddy yelled.

As we discussed beforehand, I held the barbed wire to let Freddy crawl under it first. Then, Freddy helped me. We began to run. In the pouring rain, we shot over the road, between the houses of the SS guards, towards the moor. The soldier guarding the road saw a movement and began shooting. Running back to the camp to raise the alarm, he unintentionally gave us quite a lead.[3]

1 In 1980, nurse Nieweg told me that on that particular afternoon I had run into the hospital, yelling, "Hide me!" She quickly dropped a heap of dirty sheets on top of me. A little later a few German soldiers entered the hospital. I couldn't remember anything about this situation.
2 The Loosdrecht group: upon arrival in Auschwitz most of those youngsters were murdered.
3 In 1990, while in Geneva, somebody tapped Freddy on the shoulder. "Hey! You're supposed to be dead! How can you be here?" To prevent further escapes, the Camp leadership said we had been shot. Two days later, four youngsters were shot while trying to escape.

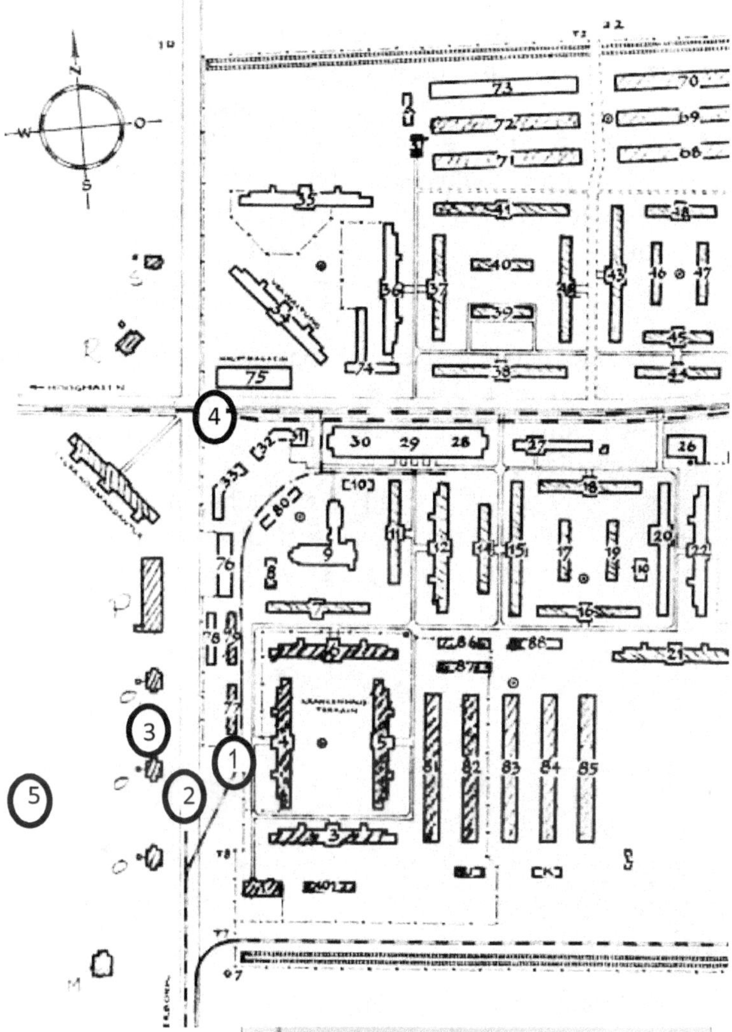

1 Escape through the fence

2 Crossing the road

3 Guards raise the alarm

4 Main entrance to the Camp

5 Heathland

Barracks with heathland

The following details are taken from Freddy's story, as I couldn't remember much of that terrifying night.

Shots were coming from all sides. When we heard shooting coming from the left side, we ran to the right. When shots came from the left, we ran to the right. Being an asthma patient who was usually out of breath after running 20 meters, Freddy suggested we return to the camp and act as if nothing happened. This time I was adamant. "No way! Come one, Freddy. Let's at least try!" Again, we began to run. For our lives.

Sound carried far on that barren, outstretched Drenthe moor. During our flight, one of us lost a scarf, which aided the search dogs who probably picked up our trail. Because the rain had washed away our scent they thankfully didn't find us.

Freddy and I jumped over ditches and elbowed our way through nettles. Considering that it was pitch black, we had no orientation and didn't have a clue of which way to go. Until our thighs, we sank in the muddy swamps.

It was despairing, and each time one encouraged the other to continue. After running around for about two hours, we found ourselves again near the watchtowers at the back of the camp. My heart sank, but at that moment, above the noise of the sirens and the shooting, I heard a train whistle. Exactly at that moment the train stoker added coals to the fire, creating a fire line through the darkness in Northern direction.

Without hesitation, we began to run in the direction of Assen and almost into the arms of the German soldier guarding the railroad crossing. We immediately turned around and ran in the opposite direction. That night we ran almost seven hours, non-stop.

Later, Freddy told me that at that moment he realized it was his birthday. It felt like a re-birth to him.

Today, the province of Drenthe looks entirely different from the province in 1944. There were no forests then, only barren peat moor. As this area was one of the poorest in the Netherlands, many Drenthe farmers were pro-German and members of the NSB. On the other hand, compared with other agricultural provinces, this province also had the highest percentage of resistance fighters. During the war, the very active Drenthe *Landwacht* closely worked with the *Sicherheitsdienst.*

We were always extra careful when approaching a farm; the moment a dog began to bark we quickly left. Danger was everywhere. Near the railway, we ran the risk of encountering a German patrol, and we intuitively knew to stay away from there. Later we learned that the *Landwacht* had been informed to lookout for us. Since the Germans controlled the bridges, we were forced to find alternative routes. At dusk, we had reached the outskirts of Assen. We were exhausted but had to go on. When we passed a building with a lot of bikes, Freddy suggested to 'organize' one.

"Too risky," I said. "Let's continue on foot."
We were terribly dirty and scratched, looking at my muddy brother, I realized we were still wearing our yellow stars.

"We immediately have to get rid of them!" Freddy said.
I pulled the hated mark from my sweater and threw it into a small pond.
By now it was 4 a.m. "Somebody's coming!" I warned.

"Let's say we are looking for a vicar," Freddy suggested.

It happened to be a school teacher, on his way to the city of Meppel. The man seemed trustworthy, so Freddy told him we were looking for the Steendijk in Assen. Friends told him a mixed couple lived there, the Beer family, but he didn't have a clue how to get there. The teacher offered to show the way and brought us to the front door of the house on Steendijk. He quickly said goodbye and left.

Freddy knocked on the front door, and with thumping hearts we waited for somebody to open the door. When nothing happened, we walked to the back of the house and softly knocked on the window. No response. Suddenly a door opened.

"Come inside, quick!" a woman holding an infant whispered.

Without asking any questions, she kindled the stove, made coffee, and cut bread we greedily ate. When we had somewhat come to our senses she said, "Now tell me what's happened."

As Freddy was close to having an asthma attack, he let me tell the story.

While the woman cut us some more slices of bread, she told us how lucky we had been. "The Gestapo is a few houses next door! Would you like to go into hiding in Assen?" she queried.

"No thanks, Mrs. De Beer," Freddy said.

"My name is not de Beer," the woman replied. "That is my neighbor. They arrested her husband some time ago and she now lives with her family. My name is Steinfort. My husband has been called for the *Arbeitseinsatz*. How can I help you?"

Freddy explained that it was better not to stay in Assen because the Germans would certainly comb the whole town. In such a small town, the social monitoring would also be heavy and he didn't want to endanger Mrs. Steinfort. "I have a sailing friend in Heerenveen," Freddy said. "He can help us reach Amsterdam. There we will find a hiding place."

"Would you be able to advance us the money for a train ticket?" I asked.

Mrs. Steinfort shook her head. "Too dangerous! I think it's better that I first go and look at the train station to see if it's safe to travel and only then buy the tickets. You may be able to board the train for the other side of the station."

Fifteen minutes later, she was back with the news that the Germans were checking everybody's identity cards near the station. "Both the Landwacht and the police are looking for two escaped Jews," she said. "I have a better plan."

A few hours later we stood outside, dressed like tourists.

"I suggest Freddy carries my child," Mrs. Steinfort said. "Harry, you take the dog and I take the bike. We walk to the outskirts of Assen and from there you take the steam tram in the direction of Heerenveen."

Mrs. Steinfort bought our tickets and we joined the anglers on the back balcony of the steam tram.

Assen—station with steam tram

"Enjoy your holiday!" Mrs. Steinfort waved us goodbye.

It would take 47 years before I saw this angel who rescued us again.
Via a roundabout way, with the help of a Dutch television program called
"Without a trace," I would be finally able to trace her in 1990.

CHAPTER 11
A Hiding Place in Amsterdam

Around noon, we safely reached the home of Freddy's friend in Heerenveen. He and his wife, who ran a furniture store, were moved to see us. "I already figured you were part of the Resistance," Jaap Borger said after we told him our story.

How wonderful it felt to be dressed in clean clothes, even though my new trousers were too long and the shoes that were too big for my feet made me look like Charlie Chaplin. Though everything was better than the rags we had been wearing. The Borger family never knew we were Jewish. Now, they too offered to hide us in their home.

"Thank you so very much for the offer," Freddy said, "but we prefer to go to Amsterdam."

"How can we help you then?" Jaap wanted to know.

"Is it possible to take a boat to Amsterdam?" Freddy asked.

There was. Twice a day, the Lemmer boat sailed the IJsselmeer from Amsterdam to Lemmer and vice versa. As we missed the noon day boat, we planned to take the midnight boat. After a short period of rest and a good warm meal, the three of us took the steam tram to Lemmer.

"People smuggle butter and eel on this boat," Jaap knew. "That is why all passengers are thoroughly checked."

Jaap managed to get us past the military police without being seen. He warned us that during the crossing, the Germans were always on the lookout for people in hiding. We quickly hid under the tarp of a rescue boat.

Around midnight the boat left the Lemmer harbor to begin the five-hour crossing to Amsterdam. At the same hour, the Lemmer boat departed in

opposite direction. According to the time-table, the two boats would meet around 2.30 a.m. near Enkhuizerzand. The Germans commanded that boats were to sail in complete darkness made the crossing very dangerous.[1]

D-Day, the landing of the Allied troops in Normandy on June 6, 1944, spread a wave of hope through occupied Europe. When the Allied forces conquered Belgium at the beginning of September, it seemed only a matter of time before the Netherlands were liberated.

Radio Orange even broadcasted a proclamation by Queen Wilhelmina, *"Long live the Fatherland. The Netherlands rises again. The liberation had begun. Fellow countrymen much depend on your quiet, orderly and united attitude these coming days. Me and my advisors soon hope to be back on our native soil to take up our leadership role again."*

September 4, at 5 a.m. the Lemmer boat moored at the de Ruijterkade behind the Central Station in Amsterdam. We managed to get from board without being seen and began walking the quiet streets to the Transvaal neighborhood in Amsterdam East. Only later we learned that we arrived in Amsterdam on *"Dolle Dinsdag"*[2] .

1 Six months later (January 8, 1945) two Lemmer ships collided at midnight. 50 people drowned in the icy waters of the IJsselmeer.

2 *Dolle Dinsdag* (Mad Tuesday) took place in the Netherlands on 5 September 1944. After a broadcast by the Prime Minister-in-exile that alleged Breda had been liberated, many rumours spread across the occupied Netherlands that the liberation by Allied forces was at hand. On 4 September 1944 the Allies had conquered Antwerp, and it was thought that they already advanced into the Netherlands. Many Dutchmen celebrated on the streets while preparing to receive and cheer on the Allied liberators. Dutch and Orange flags and pennants were prepared, and many workers left their workplace to wait for the Allies to arrive. German occupation forces and NSB members panicked: documents were destroyed and many fled the Netherlands for Germany. The Allied advance could not continue as the Allies had overextended themselves and had to halt in the South of the Netherlands. The northern part of the Netherlands had to wait until 5 May 1945 for their liberation.

An hour later, we stood in front of the house in the Cilierstraat. When Freddy ran the bell, almost immediately the door was opened.

"Freddy?" I heard a woman call from upstairs.

"How did you know it was us, Mijntje?" Freddy was out of breath when he reached the second floor.

"Through the Resistance, we learned that the Nazi's were going to liquidate Westerbork," Mijntje said. "You are not someone who is being led like a sheep to the slaughter, Freddy. So, when the bell rang at this early hour, I just knew it had to be you."

We were introduced to the Groen[2] family, who since 1942 were hidden in Mijntjes small apartment. Of course, they made room for Freddy and I as well. Mijntje had two daughters, Marianna and Wilhelmina, called Willy. Marianna was married to Dr. Emanuel (Manie) Leisen, a widower. They lived around the corner in the Pretoriusstraat no. 57. As a result of their 'mixed' marriage, Manie[3] could continue practicing medicine.

Within a few minutes of our arrival, Freddy had a terrible asthma attack – I had never seen him suffer so badly.

"Go and fetch Manie!" Mijntje told Willy.
Thanks to the fast and professional treatment of her son-in-law, Freddy's life was spared for the second time.

Mijntje[4] demanded us to adhere to her strict house rules: nobody was allowed to leave the house and we always had to be very quiet.

On the floor below Mijntje lived a couple whose husband belonged to the Dutch SS and who had fought near Stalingrad. In times of danger, we immediately had to crawl into the double cupboard that was turned into a hiding place. Mijntje and Willy had been working hard to rescue Jewish children from the Crèche opposite the Schouwburg. People from the Resistance only knew her as "tante (aunt) Koos" or "Oma" (grandmother). Amazing to think that I lived in an apartment that played a central role in the resistance against the Germans.

---

[2] The Groen family's only son was murdered in Auschwitz.
[3] Together with Jacob Sweering, Manie falsified identity cards and documents. They were able to rescue many children and adults. Dr. Leisen was a much loved and appreciated family doctor.
4 In 1965, Mijntje refused to be honored by Yad Vashem for her assistance to Jewish people during the war. Only 20 years later did she accept the honor.

Mijntje also had many things from Jewish friends in safe keeping, like the dental equipment from one of my uncles.

"A human being is a human begin," she always said when someone asked her why she helped the Jews.

Letter to Jaap Borger, to let them know we were safe

5-9-1944

Dear Jente and Jaap,

We arrived safely and are jubilant. Any moment we expect the Americans to arrive here and all Amsterdam is excited. Can you imagine how terribly happy we are? We can hardly believe it. We thank you for being such darlings to us. The moment we are free we will drop by and return everything we borrowed from you. My headaches from everything. The boat trip went fine and I have slept a few hours. We found a good place to stay. We anxiously wait for what happens next. Again, thousand thanks and warm greetings. Be safe. Greetings from Harry and Freddy.

CHAPTER 12
Amsterdam 1944-1945

Mijntje was a sturdy, straightforward, no-nonsense woman, absolutely not sentimental, but with a heart of gold. November 1st that year I celebrated my nineteenth birthday in hiding and decided to let my mother know we were doing all right by way of sending her a postcard[1]. Unable to use Mijntje's address, I used my uncle Stam's address.

1-11-1944 translation German postcard

Dear Friends,

We hope you are doing well and that you are healthy. Since Freddy's birthday, we live in Amsterdam, which suits us much better. Our friends are very kind and look after us as if we are their children. We don't mind it one bit to have departed from our previous address. It took a long time before we could make this journey. Because today is Harry's birthday, we particularly think about you. Stay healthy.

Warm greetings from Freddy and Harry.

The Resistance provided Willy with additional food coupons for us. It wasn't easy to fill four extra mouths. Even during the Hunger winter of 1944-1945, she managed to get hold of a bag of potatoes and onions. Coals were no longer available, and wood too became scarce. We became very inventive and learned to cook with wood chips in a tin with small holes. When the water in the kettle or pan began to boil, the food was placed into a hay-box and covered with blankets. The heat did the rest.

[1] Mother kept this postcard. She survived Theresienstadt, because the Wehrmacht needed Jewish seamstresses to produce their uniforms and insignia.

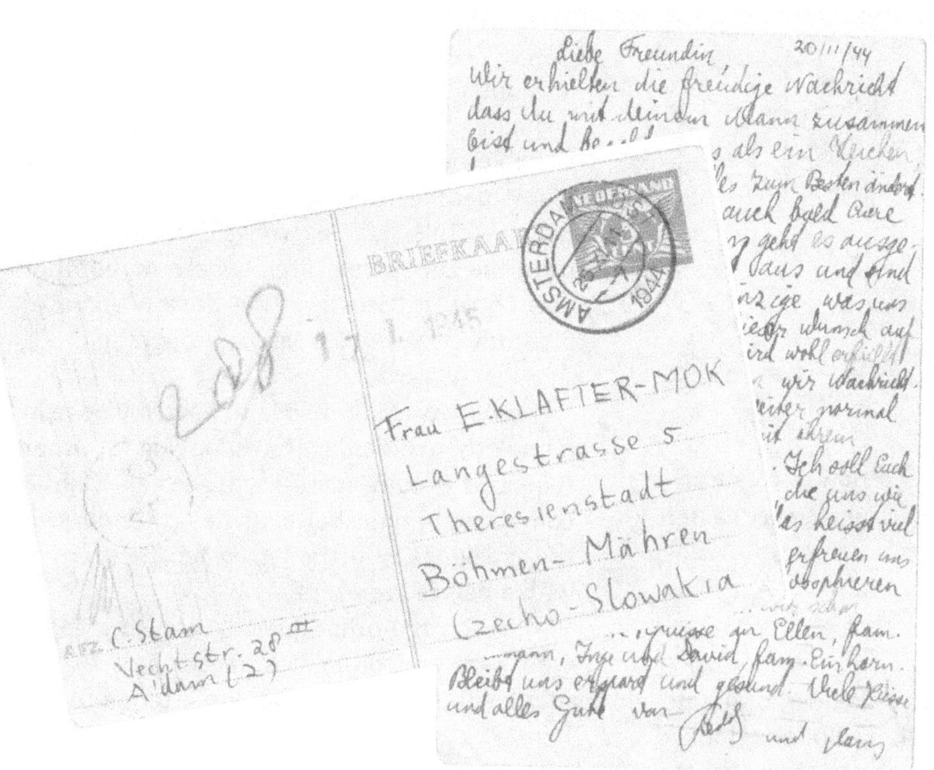

Note card dated: 26-11-1944

To Frau E. Klafter-Mok, Langestrasse 5, Theresienstadt, Bohmen-Mahren (Czechoslovakia.) From. C. Stam, Vechtstr. 28 III, Amsterdam (Z) **translation from the card that was written in German.**

"Dear friend, we received the happy news that you are now reunited with your husband and see this as a sign that everything turned out well. We hope that soon you will see your children again. We are doing fine, look well and are generally healthy. You are the only thing lacking. And may this wish for a speedy reunion will be granted soon. Annie send us a message that everything seems normal in the shop. I must send greetings from Mijntje, who looks after us like a mother. That's very significant in these difficult times. We are grateful to be alive. Fantasizing about the future has no use. That's for later. Warm greetings to Ellen, the Reichman family, Inge and David, the Ein Horn family. Keep us in your thoughts and healthy. Lots of greetings and all the best from Freddy and Harry.

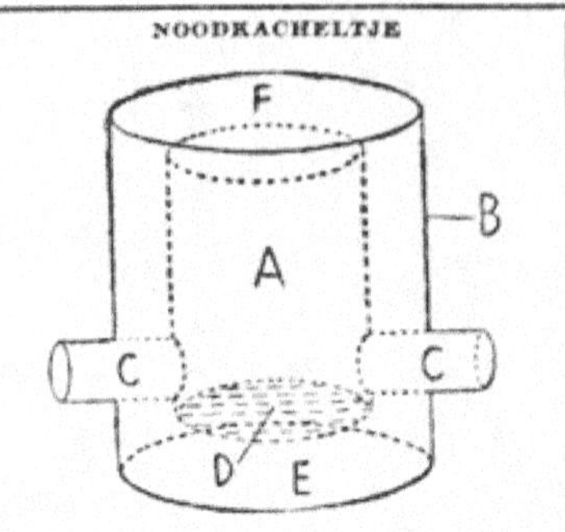

How to create an emergency heater

It wasn't easy to be stuck day and night in Mijntje's small apartment with four people in hiding. I tried to use my days as best as possible by studying. Of course, Manie knew many people, one of them was Professor Groen[2]. This leading physician originated from the Lepelstraat area, where my mother was born. Dr. Groen let me borrow some of his study books which Manie brought me.

As it was impossible to have my nose in a book the whole day, I was looking for other things to occupy myself with. When Mijntje complained about her cat's fleas, I embraced the challenge and tried to catch the vermin with a pair of tweezers.

With the other guests, I played a game with dice and draught stones, cards or we played chess, draughts and read many books. Every hour we listened to the BBC radio and looked at a map how far the Allied Forces were advancing.

During Spring in 1945, it was clear that Liberation Day was nearby, those in hiding dared to leave the house in the evening to visit the Leisen family. Manie was a cordial man; they always had friends visiting them on Shabbat and Sundays. Gradually, we began to taste normal life again.

---

[2] Dr. Groen introduced psychosomatic medication to the Netherlands. He was married to a non-Jewish actor.

Freddy and Willy had fallen in love and didn't want to wait until after the war to get married. They married in Amsterdam City Hall on April 25, 1945, under a false name[3].

A Dutch proverb says something like, "Until the horses defecate in front of the City Hall, there has been no wedding." I, therefore, took a shoebox, collected horse dung and dumped it on the street in front of the City Hall.

Picture below: Left to right: Resistance woman, myself, Daisy (daughter Marianne) Freddy and Willy, Mijntje, Marianne and Manie Leisen.

[3] The Jewish wedding took place after the war. Chief Rabbi Tal blessed the couple standing under the *Chuppah*. Before the war, he had been chief Rabbi in Utrecht; after the war, he moved to Amsterdam. I didn't like the man because he belonged to the anti-Zionist Agudah group.

CHAPTER 13
1945-1946 - The Survivors

After the War, countries counted their dead;
the Jews counted the survivors.[1]

My time in hiding lasted from September 1944 until May 1945. During those last weeks, I met a pathologist from the Antonie van Leeuwenhoek hospital. Dr. Waterman had been released from Westerbork because of his crucial scientific cancer research. Determined to study chemistry after the war, I gratefully accepted the use of Dr. Waterman's biochemistry books.

On May 4, 1945, the German troops surrendered to British field marshal Montgomery. The day before the outcome had been discussed in Hotel 'de Wereld' in Wageningen with Prins Bernhard (commander of the National Forces) and was signed on May 6. After five long years of German occupation, the Netherlands was finally liberated! Those who emerged from hiding didn't feel part of the liberation celebrations. Even though they tried, they lacked the festive mood. Many from the Jewish community experienced the liberation and the first post-war year like a big black hole, filled with pessimism and without purpose.

When the war ended, nobody knew if our parents were still alive. Until some clarity appeared in the post-war chaos, we stayed with Mijntje in Amsterdam. Freddy also didn't know yet what had happened to Father's property, except that all the factory machines had been taken to Germany, and that both perfumery shops had been pillaged.

For us to be able to inherit, Father had to be officially and lawfully declared deceased. We could only receive the inheritance after an interior ministry clerk compiled a death certificate and Father was registered in the death registry of that city. Because nobody knew anything about Father's fate, he was declared 'missing.'

---

[1] There are different counts, but the average number is that there were 30.000 Dutch Jewish survivors of a pre-war Dutch Jewish community of about 140.000 people.

The Military Authorities appointed Freddy as interim manager of NV Negum, the company Father had established. All kinds of committees were created to assist the victims of Nazi oppression. Freddy went to different authorities and slowly we began to understand what had happened to Father.[2] It was the beginning of Freddy's fierce battle with the Dutch bureaucracy, called "the little Shoah" by Jewish survivors.

When the Dutch people began rebuilding the destructed, plundered country, for the Jews the sorrow after the "Main Sorrow" began.

Two Jews meet each other on the street.
"Your parents?" one asks the other.
"Didn't come back," the other replies.
A dialogue of four words with an overpowering content.

Until Freddy found a suitable place to live in Utrecht, I stayed with Mijntje. One day, I ran into Manfred Rosenbaum who had been deported from Westerbork to Bergen-Belsen. Manfred told me that upon his return to the Netherlands he had been treated so terrible that he didn't want to stay here any longer.

"I heard there is an orange boat in the harbor leaving for Palestine," he said. "Do you want to join me?"
I liked the idea. We decided to make a run for it the next morning. At 6 a.m., Manfred and I boarded the first tram at the Berlagebrug. By feeding the machine many coins, I hoped the tram would reach its destination faster. From the Central station, we walked to the harbor, only to find a heavily guarded ship. When it became clear that it would be impossible to sneak on board unseen, I decided not to try any further and said goodbye to Manfred.

---

[2] Frits Preuss, Father's German rival, fled to Germany. Accountant van Dijk fled to Germany on *Dolle Dinsdag*. Mr. van de Riet, the *Verwalter* of the two perfumeries, was 'punished' with fourteen days house arrest, after which he could go and do as he pleased.
[3] The Hebrew word *Shoah* is mentioned twelve times in the Old Testament, meaning "destruction, elimination, darkness, doom." Today, when we mention the word, we mean the Persecution of the Jews during the Second World War – a man-made disaster; an inexplicable and senseless occurrence, a story without logic.

At the age of twenty, I did my best to study even harder while Freddy tried to rebuild the family business. Academics tried to make up for the lost years by teaching classes from early morning until late evening. Students also received crash courses.

A few months after Liberation we received the happy news that Mother was to return from Theresienstadt. Most camp survivors entered the border from the south, and daily a train left Eindhoven and Maastricht to a central collecting point – Camp Amerfoort, a former concentration camp! Even though I desperately wanted to welcome Mother, it seemed impossible because of the chaotic public transportation. Eventually, I hitchhiked to Breda on a Canadian Tank.

Canadese tank

My 50-year old mother looked like an old woman. She didn't speak much about how she had been able to survive Theresienstadt by working as a seamstress, especially not in detail. For her, the war was a closed book. The only thing she told me was an incident directly after Liberation.

"A Russian soldier gave me a piece of bread. At that moment, a man with a horse passed by. He wanted to swap my bread for his horse."

"So, what did you do?"

"Ate the bread."

Freddy managed to get back the apartment above the shop on Oudegracht 111. He and Willy lived in two rooms in the back of the house while the former *Verwalter* continued to live in the front part of the house. Mother and I were given an ex-NSB apartment in Utrecht at the Michiel de Ruiterstraat 15 bis.

Of course, Mother wanted to continue working in the shop but the relationship between Willy and Mother wasn't good. Not only did Freddy modernize the shop, but also the sales methods had changed.

Mother, who was used to the pre-War situation, could not cope with the changes, the different products and the new suppliers.

Many survivors found it difficult to pick up the rhythm of daily life. They constantly struggled with chronic fear and guilt. Mother also suffered from these, as we only found out years later.

Being totally immersed in student life, I didn't notice the stress, the tensions and problems. I had my own challenges.

University departments were spread out over the city, so I had to use my bicycle with wooden frames (rubber was still rationed) and cycle from one lecture to the other.

Oudegracht after the war

One day, while listening to a lecture in the packed auditorium in the botanical lab of professor Koningberger, a side door opened. The laboratory assistant whispered something in the ear of the professor. Scanning the crowd in front of him, the professor called, "Someone called Harry Klafter in this room? You have an urgent phone call."

My heart was beating wildly when I followed the assistant to the telephone. It was Freddy. "Someone just called with news that Papa returned from Auschwitz," he told me. "It seems Papa is somewhere near Groningen. When we pay him, the man promises to bring us to Papa."

The small flame of hope was quickly extinguished. Freddy and I were almost certain that Papa had not survived the Camps.

"This cannot be true!" I exclaimed. "I think that man is a crook. Can you deal with this? I have to return to my class."

A few months later I was at home when Mother received an official letter from the Red Cross confirming Father's death. He had been murdered in Birkenau.

Michiel de Ruiterstraat, Utrecht

Mother and I in 1946

Of course, I joined a student organization. The initiation of this aristocratic club consisted of 'serving' an older student for one week. Everyone also had to shave his hair, which I refused to do. Because I had been in Westerbork, they made an exception for me.

After classes, we usually went to the club where a waiter served Dutch gin. I didn't like being drunk and didn't smoke either. Being part of the student body meant working together, studying together, helping each other but also having fun together. Together with a group of seven students we created our own sub-club. Our motto was DDT, but I can't remember what it stood for. Our group had to organize a dinner for the rest of the students. We opted for Huize Doorn, the country house Keizer Wilhelm once received from the Dutch government. We rented the tea house, including butlers and the dinner was a great success. Of course, there were many student parties, and for a short period, I was even a member of the Triton rowing-fraternity.

After the war, I didn't see or experience any anti-Semitism and didn't think about the role of the Dutch government during the war. That black page had been turned. After all these years of living with fear, worries and imprisonment, I wanted to enjoy life for the full 100 %.

Before the war, Zionism and partaking the Jewish-Zionist life played a big part of my upbringing. In one of my letters to Johan Westdorp, I mentioned the *Chaloetsiem* that went to *Eretz* Israel.

Upon rejoining the Zionist Youth movement, I received more leadership tasks. Soon, the Zionist activities were running like before the war, but without many of my murdered friends. Many of the new youth members were preparing to leave for Palestine because they had nothing left in the Netherlands. Their families had been murdered, their possessions had been stolen, and their fellow Dutch didn't show any empathy about the horrors they had experienced. I had not yet decided what to do because the British were still in charge of Palestine. To me, it wasn't relevant going there yet. Above all, I wanted to study chemistry.

Jewish Brigade Soldiers arrived in July 1945 in Belgium and the Netherlands. They fulfilled a military, social, political and economic Jewish and Zionist function. These soldiers helped find and return Jewish children from monasteries and foster families and placed them temporarily in Jewish orphanages. Jewish schools were assisted, also by giving Hebrew lessons. The *Hachshara* schools were also actively supported by the Brigade.

The Brigade was also active in Utrecht. During a visit to our youth group, I learned about the possibility to be smuggled into Palestine. I didn't want to become a pioneer, nor did I want to work the land, but very much liked the idea of continuing my studies in Jerusalem.

One of my girlfriends, the granddaughter of Jacobus Kan, a man who had played an important financial role at the beginning of the Zionist movement, joined a group heading to Palestine. I struggled with the decision and found it hard to leave my mother behind. But when the worrisome news began to filter through that Dutch boys were to be sent to Indonesia to fight the Japanese, I really had to decide. The Dutch government might have granted me exemption from military service, but I didn't want to take that risk.

Within the Youth Group, we discussed everything with the soldiers of the Jewish Brigade. The growing tensions in Palestine, the British resistance and the Arab attacks made our Zionist zeal grow even more and we decided to go to *Eretz Israel*. Pesach 1946 was to be the last time we would celebrate the Exodus from Egypt in the Netherlands. Next year in Jerusalem!

The Pesach Hagada[4], a gift from my Jewish school, also survived the war. The youth members who were going to Palestine wrote their names inside the cover of the book.

By that time, I had been studying chemistry at the University of Utrecht for one and a half years and wasn't sure when I would be able to continue my studies in Jerusalem. My rucksack with the most necessary items was packed. It wasn't easy to say goodbye to Mother, Freddy and Willy, but they understood my desire and fully condoned my decision. With their blessing, I embarked on my personal exodus.

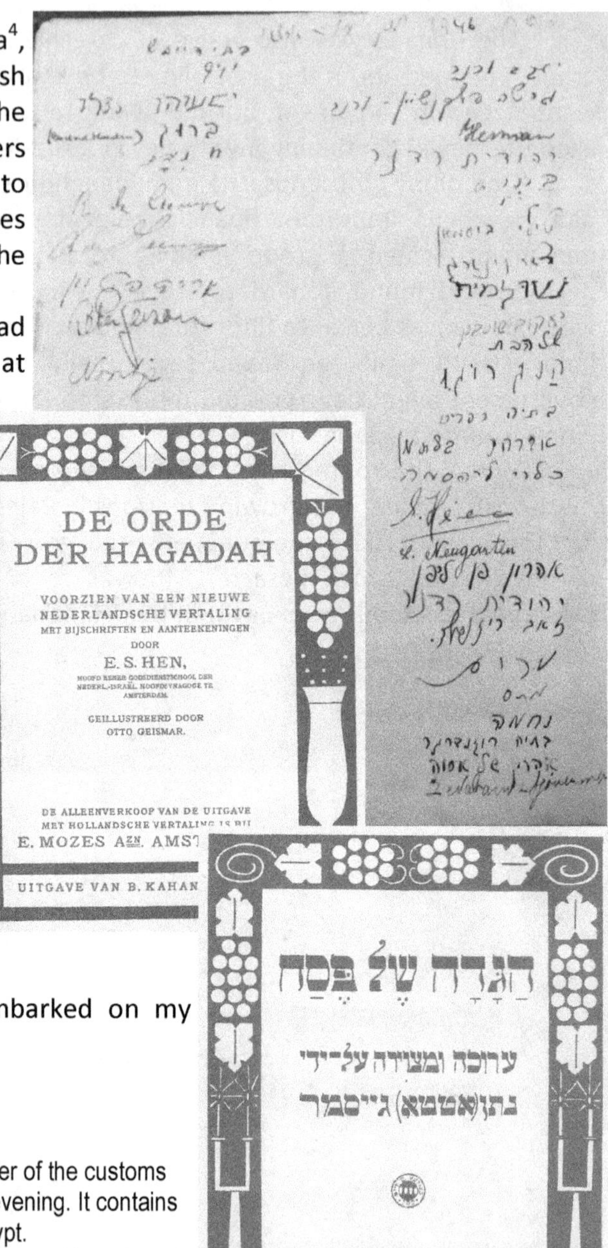

4 The Hagada -'story'- is the order of the customs used during the *Pesach*, seder evening. It contains the story of the Exodus from Egypt.
Each year, I continue to use this same Hagada and tell my children, grandchildren and great-grandchildren about my personal exodus.

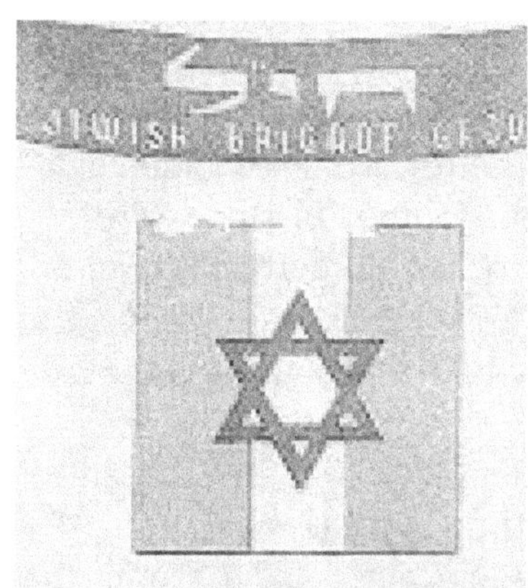

In April 1946, a lorry from the Jewish Brigade waited for us at the agreed rendezvous point. As most of the travelers were dressed in their own clothes, they had to sit in the back. Wearing the Jewish Brigade uniform, I could sit near the tailboard. Thanks to the so-called orders from the 'TTG brigade[5],' road blocks were removed and at military checkpoints barriers were lifted. Also, the Belgium border was crossed without any difficulties. No one looked inside the lorry where the Jewish youngsters were hidden. Because we were travelling as a group, nobody had official travel documents. By day and by night, the Jewish Brigade smuggled youth groups from different European countries over the borders.

5 *'Tilhas Teezee Gesheften'* (commonly known by its acronym TTG) was the name of a group of Jewish Brigade members formed immediately following World War II. Under the guise of British military activity, this group engaged in the assassination of Nazis and SS conspirators, facilitated the illegal emigration of Holocaust survivors to Israel, and smuggled weaponry for the Haganah. The three words that make up the phrase are Arabic [*"tilhastizi,* "lick my ass"] and Yiddish [*gesheften,* "business"], combined to form a modern Hebrew slang expression, meaning "You-lick-my-ass business."

Our convoy drove to a castle in the Belgium Ardennes, a meeting point for groups coming from the East. Our next stop was a camp near Paris, and the last one near Marseille. In LaCiota (Cette), organized ideological Jewish European youth groups assembled for the journey by ship to *Eretz.*
Our group got to know youth from other countries. After getting acquainted with the Polish Jews, we realized they had a different ideological background than we had. In my opinion, they had been influenced by the socialistic thoughts of Engels and Marx.

"In Palestine, we want to build settlements that are based on communistic and socialistic dogmas," one of the youngsters told me. "The kibbutz will create a new society, a new people and a new family that collectively will raise their children."
All those passionate statements were a bit too much for me and I didn't understand the connection between the singing of the "International," hoisting the red flag and Zionism.

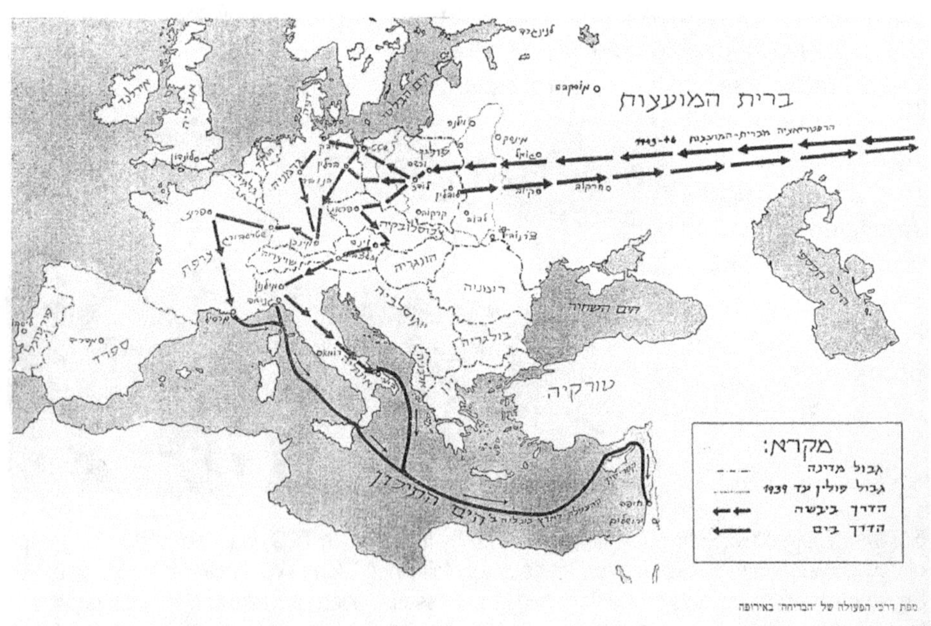

'Aliyah-Beth' routes, the so-called 'illegal' immigration to Palestine

In this letter, I describe my experiences of the past month:

25-5-1946

Dear Willy and Freddy,
Lacking the time to write you extensively, I will try to do so later when
everything has been processed somewhat. We experienced a series of
events that followed on the heel of one another. The last sensation is
that I peed against a palm tree. That didn't often happen in the past. I
hope it won't be long, but that doesn't help much. I've learned that it
doesn't do to make plans, especially when you try to divide the future
into time frames. I had hoped to quickly continue my studies, perhaps
through evening classes. However, I think I will lose some time to adjust. Our goal won't be reached soon. Last night I took a stroll over the
rocks. It was getting dark and you could see the bottom of the sea. The
water is clear and at the bottom of the sea you can see all kinds of colored stones. Sometimes you see little fish. Everything had made an
enormous impression. Seaweed grows against the rocks and the water
moves it. When you listen carefully, it is as if Neptune takes a bath.
He squeezes his sponge, fluctuates under water, and hits the water that
escapes through the holes in the rocks. The rock itself is really solidi-
fied lava, a group of pebbles that stick together. And all the stones have
a different color: deep purple, yellow, red, brown, black, green, etc. A
pity we are surrounded by people with whom we cannot communicate
because they still have the camp mentality.
In the mornings, I work in the garden, very useful work. Digging up
the earth, remove weeds and other work, also organizing things, it is
all part of my job here. We don't have a library, so you'd make me very
happy by sending books on a regular basis. Perhaps Mama can send
me some of her newspapers? That would be great. What do you hear
from America? I hope you write back soon. Also, how mama is doing. Is
she strong? I hope she will be able to follow me soon, away from that
place. Because I stayed with her for some time I miss her terribly. Not
that we spoke a lot, but because of her often very matter of fact re-
marks, Mama has a good influence on me. I admire her even more
when meeting other people who returned, especially their character after
having been away for so long. I don't think we have given Mama
many reasons for joy these past years. Write me extensively. How is
Annie? 5 Please greet that old, faithful woman! So many times, I have
said good-bye to her! Did mama already send a package?

Presently, the moment, the food is bad. This morning they gave us a slice of bread and for the rest, it's only pasta. I hope we soon will be able to eat fresh vegetables. Don't get the impression I'm suffering, it's just that I had been used to things that were too good! Also, warm greetings to Amsterdam, Mother Mijntje, Marjan, Manie and also Mrs. Friedman. Warm greetings from Harry. **הרי**

[5] For years, Annie worked in Perfumery Apollo and I liked her very much.

Waiting was difficult for me, especially when the holiday feeling and newness of the palm trees had worn off.

Finally, we were told that the ship had arrived. It was about time!

Let the Palestine-adventure begin!

La Ciota harbor in 1945

PART 2

Sh'erit ha-Pletah: ('the surviving remnant' ,(following their liberation in the spring of 1945, the Jewish refugees who survived the Holocaust called themselves by this name which was based on Ezra 9:14 and 1 Chronicles 4:43.

Aliyah Alef (to go up to Israel) was the 'legal' Jewish immigration. This was an official quota allowed by the British government for Jews to immigrate in small quantities.

Aliyah Beth, the, the illegal immigration according to British Mandate Palestine, began because of the violation of the 1939 "White Paper." *Ha'apalah* is another name for *Aliyah Beth*. Such a journey began in the refugee camp, via one or two collection points in the American Zone in Germany. From there, the *ma'apalim* (Jews who immigrated illegally to Palestine during British control in the 1930s and 1940s) travelled by truck or train or by foot to the harbors at the Mediterranean Sea.

The **Gesher Bayam** – the bridge over the sea from the *Aliyah Beth* was not less spectacular than the Exodus from Egypt. Jewish refugees reached *Eretz* Israel by the most unbelievable ways.

At the beginning of 1946, the Jewish Agency bought two Corvettes from the Canadian marine – the *HMCS Norsyd* and the *KMCS Beauharnois*. The latter was called the "*Wedgwood*," in honor of Josiah Wedgwood, a British statesman who had been an advocate for Zionism. The *Norsyd* became the "*Balboa*."

April 1st, 1946, both ships left the New York harbor for a journey to Marseille, France. June 18, the *Wedgwood* departed with more than 1,250 people on board in great haste from the harbor La Spezia, Italy. Unfortunately, not much later the British intercepted the ship, confiscated it and changed it in the Haifa Bay harbor. The people on board were imprisoned in the Atlit Camp in Palestine. The second ship, the *Norsyd/Balboa,* was to play an important role in my life.

This was the ship that brought me to *Eretz Israel* – the Promised Land.

The story of this journey has been chronicled in the book "Underground Palestine."

CHAPTER 14
The *Gesher Bayam* – THE BRIDGE OVER THE SEA

In Ciota Harbor, near Marseille, the hold of the SS Balboa was outfitted with wooden pallets, ostensibly to transport bananas. In truth, these were beds for about 1,250 *olim* – new immigrants. Four to five people had to sleep on those unpainted wooden beds. Each section had a letter from the alphabet and each bed was numbered. British agents, instructed to prevent Jews from embarking a ship bound for Palestine, suspiciously watched at the lorries delivering fresh bread. The pantry was stocked with food tins and egg powder. Thick soups were cooked in large bronze kettles – one set apart for those who kept Kosher. The covered toilets and bathroom facilities were on mid deck.

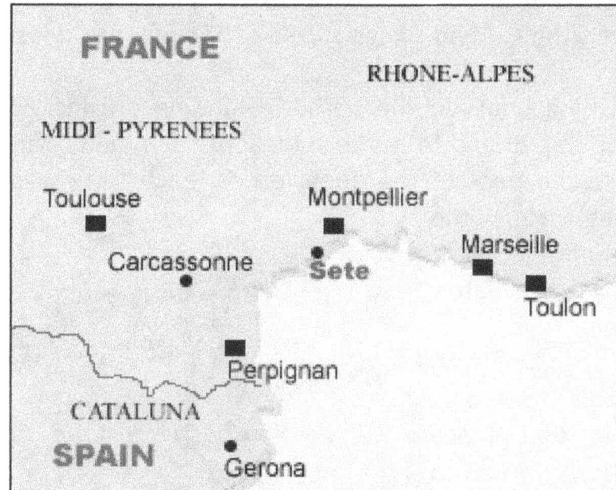

Friday, June 21, 1946, the SS *Bilboa* departed for the smaller, less conspicuous harbor of Sète, about 30 miles away.

Here, the Haganah set up training camp where *olim* learned about agriculture, different trades and Hebrew.

The new immigrants lived in simple barracks or temporary quarters in nearby fishing villages. I was amongst the lucky ones who stayed in one of the villas.

Sète harbor

[The detailed information about Harry's following adventures came from the book *Underground Palestine* by I.F. Stone. After all these years, Zvi could only recall certain highlights of this hazardous journey.]

D-day: SHABBAT, June 22, 1946

Around 8 a.m. the first ten trucks entered the freight shed in the harbor. Abba Kovner's Polish Partisans, including his wife, Vitka, were the first to board the ship. When our turn came, I took my rucksack and followed the *shomer* (guard) to the quay, shivering in the cold sea wind. A crew member handed out slips of paper with a letter and corresponding bed number. Our group of 19 walked up the high, wobbling gangway, onto the ship. The older passengers immediately went to bed, but most of us stood talking in the narrow alleyways of the ship. Those speaking Yiddish were from Poland. I had never travelled further than Antwerp or Knokke, so everything was new and interesting for me. Everything I had experienced so far made a deep impression on me.

There were many fishing boats in the harbor. Standing on deck, I noticed lorries and trucks driving to and from the ship. Some *olim* had been standing the whole night in the back of the open lorries. Each lorry was accompanied by someone from the Haganah. A group of volunteers went straight to the kitchen. Six hours later, the departure sign was given.

Later I learned that an American journalist, I.F. Stone, was the only passenger on board with an official visa for Palestine. From the deck, we waved to the Haganah workers staying behind to help other *olim*.

Our captain, Yehoshua Baharav, was assisted by a *ma'palim* commander, Betzalel Drori, a *palyamnik*. The *Palyam* was the marine branch of the Palmach, and part of the *Hagana*. The ship sailed under Panamanian flag. In Paris, the head of *Mossad le'aliyah Beth* gave this ship the most honored name he could bestow on a ship of this 'illegal' float: *SS Haganah*.

"Attention! Everybody is requested to go down into the hold," the captain announced. "We're preparing for departure. The pilot must not see any passengers."

About 6.30 p.m. the ship had reached the open sea. As there were no other ships in sight, the captain blew the whistle. "This is the signal allowing you to go on deck again," the *shomer* responsible for our group explained. Filled with wonder, I looked out over the Great Sea that would bring us to the shores of *Eretz Israel.*

With so many people from sixteen different countries, the ship resembled a floating tower of Babel. In my youth group were youngsters who had lost one or both parents during the Holocaust. In contrast to many on board who had fled their home country, our group deliberately had chosen to go to Palestine to build a Jewish homeland.

I found it hard to sleep on those low, narrow wooden pallets. Only sick people could sleep on a mattress. Due to bad ventilation, the hold

began to stink and it was never quiet: people coughed, sighed because they couldn't sleep or groaned because they were seasick. At night, the *shomrim* also kept watch and when somebody vomited, the work detail came running with a pail and rag. Youngsters wearing an armband with a red Magen David gave those suffering from sea sickness a slice of lemon or a wet compress.

A frightened passenger was reassured but a hysteric one received a slap in the face. Only very sick people were brought to the former officer mess that was turned into the sick bay. Here, the French doctor kept his instruments and medication.

After two stormy days, the sun broke through and the sea became calm. During the day, I enjoyed the beautiful Mediterranean Sea and at night the star-filled heaven. The moment the captain spotted another ship, we immediately had to go down into the hold. A work detail swept and cleared the deck. Curfew began at 11 p.m. and everybody had to be in bed.

Despite the primitive and much too small oven, the four bakers were able to bake enough bread, and the American chef managed to cook a simple meal for all on board. Only the crew, nurses and work detail could drink coffee and tea, while the rest of us had to do with water.

Most people ate their 7 a.m. breakfast on deck. From a pail, a leader and assistant ladled the portions for each group on paper plates. Besides a piece of fresh bread, everybody either received cigarettes or chocolate. For those who wished there was even powdered milk. Lunch was at noon and the hot meal at 6 p.m.

Our group spend the days with conversations and discussions or we sang Hebrew songs accompanied by an accordion. At the railing, couples stood holding hands, staring out over the water. Nearby a group *Chalutzim* were dancing the *Horah*.

DAY 4:
Suddenly it was too quiet. Something was amiss.
"What happened?" we wondered.
The steering mechanism broke down, therefore the captain ordered the engines to be stopped. The heavily rolling ship made many people seasick again. A collective sigh of relief went up when half way through the morning the engines could be heard and we continued our journey.

DAY 6:
"All passengers are requested to come to the forward deck at 4.30 p.m." we heard through the speakers. "A Haganah worker has an important announcement for you."

Amidst the packed forward deck I listened carefully to the man explaining how to behave when we were arrested and interrogated by the British.

"Whatever the British will tell you, in the eyes of the Haganah you are already citizens of Palestine," the man said. We cheered and applauded and then laughed when he warned us that it might seem that we didn't arrive in Eretz but a prison *in Eretz*. Who cared if again we ended up behind barbed wire? As long it was in our home country! Forms were handed out. *Could this mean we are nearing the end of our journey?* I wondered while joining the long line.

While waiting for my turn to receive my personal 'illegal' immigration certificate in the captain's hut, I had time to fill in the blue form. One side had English questions, the other was in Hebrew.

"Entry permit for Palestine" was written at the top. I filled in my name, the name of my parents, date of birth and place of birth but hesitating at "nationality." During the war, the Nazi's had called me stateless because Father fled from Germany to the Netherlands. "Dutch", I wrote.

The certificate declared that the representatives of the Jewish community in Palestine qualified me for repatriation in *Eretz Israel.*

To authenticate this action four authoritative Bible verses were stated:

- Ezekiel 37:25 "Then they shall dwell in the land that I have given to Jacob My servant, where your fathers dwelt; and they shall dwell there, they, their children, and their children's children, forever;"
- Isaiah 54:7 "For a mere moment I have forsaken you, but with great mercies I will gather you."
- Balfour Declaration of November 2nd, 1917
- The British Mandate for Palestine.

The signature of the quarantine officer read: "Rabbi Moishe Ben Maimon."

DAY 7 – FRIDAY

According to Jewish tradition, the Shabbat candles were lit and blessed by orthodox women one hour before sunset on Friday evening. After the evening meal, I took part in the open-air synagogue service on the transformed forward deck.

DAY 8 – SHABBAT

Also on Shabbat morning a service was held under a cloudless blue sky. The captain was given the honor to read the daily Torah portion that 'happened' to be Isaiah 66:13, 14. The passengers who understood Hebrew began to cry when they heard these words:

> ***"As one whom his mother comforts, So I will comfort you;***
> ***And you shall be comforted in Jerusalem."***

I would never forget that moment.

"Everybody is requested to pack his rucksack and personal belongings and be prepared tomorrow morning," we heard through the loudspeakers.
A wave of excitement spread over the ship. The somber worded Yiddish songs, that belonged to the *Galut* (Diaspora) were no longer heard on the ship. Until deep into the night we sang Hebrew songs about our new life in Palestine. Tomorrow morning we hoped to set foot on our land.

DAY 9 - SUNDAY, June 30

The next morning I wondered why the small wooden ship was so close to the *Hagana*.
"*Akbel*" the name read. It sailed under Turkish flag.
"All passengers are requested to leave their luggage on the front deck," we heard through the loud speakers.
"Everybody will be transferred to another ship."
Confused, we looked at each other. Thankfully, this unexpected news didn't cause panic nor hysterical reactions from our fellow passengers.
Later, I learned that Mossad decided to use the S.S. *Hagana* for another journey and therefore had to take the risk of a dangerous mid-sea transfer. The plan was to secure the Akbel, a freighter built in 1898, to the SS *Hagana* for the transfer. From where I stood on the deck I saw the two ships colliding, damaging the *Akbel*. Later, I learned from Stone's book what happened behind the scenes.

A Greek Jew sent a message in Greek to the first mate of the *Akbel*, who translated the message into Turkish for the captain who didn't speak English. A Belgium crew member translated the French answer from the Greek Jews back to English for the *SS Hagana* captain. The *Akbel* captain didn't want to do business unless he received 1,000 British gold coins. He refused paper money and to make his intentions clear, he blew the whistle three times, as a goodbye signal.

Nine armed men, Polish partisans amongst them, sailed with the life-boat to the *Akbel* and boarded the ship. While holding a pistol against the Turkish captain's head, Bezalel Drori convinced him to keep his promise, so that the passenger transfer could begin.

Thankfully, the sea was calm without high waves. After the men were transferred first, the alarmed women put on their life vests. Some had to jump from the high railing into the arms of a sailor standing in the lifeboat.

At 11.35 a.m., the doctor and the last shipment of sick women boarded the *Akbel*. Realizing this ship had not been equipped according to what the captain had promised, a work crew began creating space for the passengers. We didn't know that the ship was in a bad condition. The crew had to make several trips to bring the lunches and drinking water from the *Hagana* to the *Akbel*.

Everything had been so chaotic that there had been no time to eat breakfast. Later, we heard that our *Hagana* captain didn't want to run the risk of being intercepted by the British and wanted to withhold our luggage.

Thankfully, one of the crew members convinced him to do so because for many passengers, their luggage contained the last precious memories of their murdered families. 90 minutes later, all the rucksacks were on board, and the moment the last luggage was transferred, a warship appeared on the horizon. Grey, evil, its big cannons were pointing to the little *Akbel*. With great speed, *SS Hagana* sailed away, in their haste leaving one of the motor launches behind.

On the heavily overloaded *Akbel*, tilting about 15 % sideways, the *Hagana* leadership hoisted the Star of David flag and renamed the ship *"Biriah"* which means creation. She had been named after a Jewish settlement Biriah in the Galilee, which, despite being razed several times by the British, each time had been rebuild. Below deck was a terrible stench and great confusion.

Passengers that had fainted were moved over the heads of other passengers and carried to the doctor who sat somewhere between them. A bell sounded. The wooden ship creaked and shook when the antique engines were started for the journey to Palestine. With difficulty, the ship reached a maximum speed of seven knots.

We sighed a sigh of relief when the warship wasn't British. From the high deck, friendly French sailors waved at us but nobody gave us a hand. We later learned that the British forbade other countries to help Jewish ships on their way to Palestine.

Utterly alone on the open sea, her hull so deep in the water that we could dangle our feet in the sea while sitting on deck. The *Biriah* began her short journey that would take one day.

People were packed like sardines on the main deck, the three smaller upper decks, the front, mid and quarterdeck. In every nook and corner, you'd find people. In the wheelhouse, the harassed captain had to step over sick and exhausted laying between his feet. The precious water supply was guarded in the antique galley.

The passengers were used to walk around on the big ship. However, we quickly realized that this would be impossible on this little boat, which almost keeled over.

"The Captain forbids passengers to move around," came the announcement. When this ban was disregarded, the captain shut down the engines and refused to continue.

We had no choice but to stay put.

You could almost (literarily) walk over the heads of other passengers. The heat, hunger and thirst made the often exhausted passengers also irritated. The only toilet on board stank terribly.

At least those in the two open cargo hold between the decks could see the sky. Inside the hold, it was dark, humid and boiling hot. When fights broke out for a place near the small ladder, just to get some air, a guard was posted to keep order.

Only at 3 p.m. guards opened the food and water crates. I took out the mouthwatering Bologna sandwich from my paper lunch bag. We also received a chocolate bar and handful of raisins, not realizing that this would be our only food for the next two days. *Shomrim* distributed water from big jars. Thirstily, I wanted to empty the dirty glass. "Only a few sips!" the *shomer* warned.

In the wheel-house, the *Hagana* leadership had to decide between trying to run the British blockade or ask for help. Fearing the ship would capsize and sink, they opted to send out an SOS signal and surrender to the British. While the signal was sent through the portable radio they brought on board, a sailor hoisted the emergency flag.

About 5 p.m. an airplane circled the ship, followed by another plane, and flew off. In the evening, an aircraft dumped flares around the ship and then left the small *Biriah* alone again in that dark, ominous sea.

I had a terrible night. There was no water or food left. Due to lack of deck space, the *shomrim* made sure the men in the hold rotated every few hours. Angry fights broke out, bringing back memories of the concentration camps these people had just come from.

Nobody had the energy to think about anything other than themselves. People fought for a place to sleep, to breathe, for life itself.

During the War, a former strongman from the Russian circus had been a Kapo in Auschwitz. By virtue of his position, Rudy had been able to 'buy' many lives and save those prisoners from a certain death. This huge man became 'head of security' on board of the ship. Wearing only trousers, Rudy barked, "Into the hold!", then blew a whistle while transferring the uncooperative passengers.

DAY 10 – MONDAY, July 1st

Waking around 4.35 a.m. and saw a red sun appear above… land? Everybody was so disappointed upon learning it was Cyprus. Our *Biriah* journey began when we were only 100 miles from Palestine. The Turkish captain admitted the distance was now 180 miles. The *Hagana* leadership hoped that appearance of *R75 Virago*[1], a British torpedo boat on starboard was in response to their SOS signal.

Using a megaphone, Bezalel Drori conveyed our requests, after which six British sailors and an ensign boarded the *Biriah*. Bezalel asked the British for water and food, if they could take 100 sick people and tow the *Biriah* to Haifa harbor because of malfunctioning engines.

Through a confusing chain of translations: English, Hebrew, Russian and Turkish, the ensign compiled a message which he signaled to the *Virago* by way of flags. Via a signal lamp, the *Virago* asked if we had enough food and water on board. No we did not.

---

[1] Since the Biriah was still outside territorial waters, the British could not confiscate the ship. A British report later stated that our SOS signal had been thought of as a ruse. On board the *Biriah,* the French doctor remarked it would be a miracle if we ever reached *Eretz.*

At 7 a.m. the sailors returned to the Virago. On board of the *Akbel/ Biriah* we patiently waited for the British to bring over a cable to attach to our ship. To our utter shock and horror, the war ship sailed away. Their silence said enough. We had been left to our own devices.

There was no drinking water left on board. On deck, it was very hot and we tried to find ways to cool down.

"Let's tie our clothes together, hang them in the sea and put them on again," someone suggested. That worked well, until the knot loosened and I was left the green-white soccer shorts I was wearing. Those who wanted could get a cold shower with a bucket of sea water from one of the *shomrim.* Many were sick from the heat and thirst. Shelters were created from blankets, people crawled under the lifeboats and looked for places in the shadows.

Most passengers were too miserable to think and now the doctor himself had become ill. Everybody was short tempered and quickly angered. The water crisis caused new serious fights.

"I know there is a way to distill drinking water from seawater," I told the *Hagana leadership.* They gave me permission to enter the engine room of the old ship and give it a try. Lacking the necessary equipment, unfortunately, my efforts didn't succeed.

Thankfully, most passengers from the German DP camps and those from Zionist youth movements were young and reasonably strong.
During the night the sea became very calm. The silence before the storm. One look at the at the barometer and the captain panicked, which in turn, alarmed the *shomrim*, who chased everybody from the deck into the hold. Like a fire, the news spread that the ship would probably sink during the approaching storm. Men fought and women became hysterical.

After sending out a second SOS, around 2 am, the *R-75* appeared again. This time, Bezalel's megaphone requests were met with silence. The only answer the British captain gave him was that the *Biriah* was only 35 miles from Haifa.

"Can you please take our sick and tow our ship to Haifa?" Bezalel asked the *R-75.*
The *Biriah's captain* turned off the engines. With bated breath, everybody waited for the British response. A deafening silence was the answer.

Fifteen minutes later, our captain started the engines and at a speed of 5.5 knots our little *Biriah* sailed towards Haifa.[2]

DAY 11 - TUESDAY, July 2, 1946

At sunrise, someone on deck shouted, "It's *Eretz Israel!*"

For the first time in my life, I looked at the coast of my Jewish homeland – the Carmel range and the city of Haifa. Many passengers had tears in their eyes. How they had been longing for this moment, risking their lives by illegally crossing several borders. When someone began singing *Hatikvah,* I joined him wholeheartedly. People embraced and kissed each other. The Turkish flag was lowered and the Jewish blue and white flag hoisted together with the Union Jack.

And then, it seemed as if the whole British fleet was waiting for us. The moment the *SS Biriah* entered the territorial waters, she was accosted by the same *R-75 HMS Virago* that twice had refused to help us. This time, the British warship willingly assisted us sailing into Haifa harbor.

At 8 a.m. the *Virago* ensign entered the *Biriah* wheel-house together with an Arab policeman to officially confiscate the ship. The American flag was replaced with the British flag but at least they allowed our blue-white flag to stay there.

The long journey had come to an end.

Again, I was a prisoner, but this time in *Eretz Israel!*

The chained *Akbel in* Haifa harbor

[2] Later, Golda Meir remarked that the sea transfer had been a suicide mission and that it was a miracle that the *Biriah* had not sunk.

WHAT HAPPENED TO THE *SS HAGANA*?

Passengers of the *SS Hagana* were transferred to the *Akbel/Biriah* at the rendezvous point. The *Biriah* sailed to *Eretz Israel* while the *SS Hagana* sailed to Backa (Yugoslavia). More people than expected were waiting for them (about 2,670) and there was no time to build more beds. Two babies were born on this voyage. Near Haifa the *SS Hagana* underwent the same fate as the *SS Wedgwood* – she too was confiscated by the British. The moment the State of Israel was born in 1948, both the *SS Wedgwood* and the *SS Hagana* became part of the Israeli navy. *Wedgwood* was renamed *K-20* and the *Hagana* became the *K-18.*

WHO IS WHO?

The *SS Norsyd* became the *Balboa*, later the *Hagana*.
The *Akbel* became the *Biriah*.

A FEW FACTS

The *Norsyd/Balboa* had 1,086 passengers; 53 came from the Netherlands. Harry Klafter was number 877 on the passenger list. The youngest girl, 10 years old, came from Poland; the oldest woman, 78 years, came together with her family from Russia. The biggest group olim came from Poland, amongst them were many partisans.

Abba Kovner's partisans in the Vilna Ghetto, during the war.

Represented countries:

Austria, Belgium, Germany, Netherlands, Hungary, Latvia, Poland, Czechoslovakia, France, Rumania, Russia, Turkey, Egypt (1) and the American crew. Amongst the passengers was only one non-Jewish girl, from France.

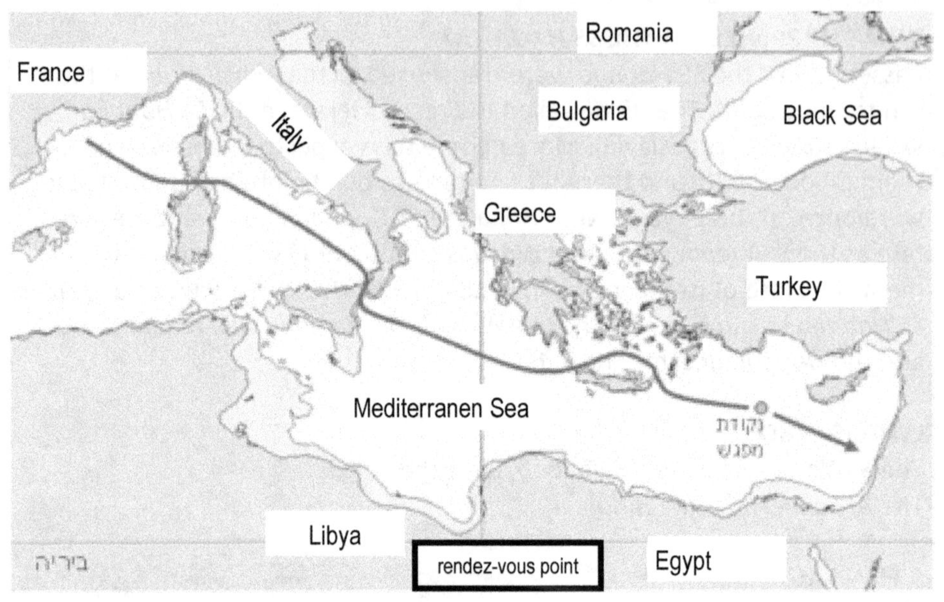

The 11-long day voyage:

Day 1:	La Ciota (Marseille) – *Norsyd/Balboa* – only the crew
Day 2:	Sète harbor, departure in the afternoon, June 22, with 1,068 passengers.
Day 3:	Street of Benifacio
Day 4:	Street of Messina
Day 5:	Kristi, Koufonision – rendezvous point
Day 6:	Transfer passengers from the *Norsyd/Balboa* to the *Akbel/ Biriah* , June 30
Day 7:	Encounter with the *R-75 Virago*
Day 8:	Encounter other ship, July 1st.
Day 9:	*Akbel* passes Limasol on Cyprus
Day 10:	*Akbel* is 35 miles (65 kilometer) from Haifa
Day 11:	July 2nd, on 7.50 am. The *Akbel* sails with a speed of 5 ½ knots direction Haifa. Confiscated by the British at 8.00 a.m.

CHAPTER 15
Welcome in *Eretz Israel!*

"Everybody has to go to Atlit," somebody said. "However, the British are faced with a problem, for after their Black Saturday/Shabbat actions the Camp is full."

"What's going to happen now?"

"I have no idea. Guess we have to wait and see."

The 24 sick passengers were brought to shore by a British patrol boat.

Around 10 a.m. we finally received drinking water but it was only at noon that everybody's thirst was quenched.

Our little ship was moored next to eight other 'illegal' ships, the *Wedgwood* among them. The harbor was completely fenced off.

"They want to keep us two weeks on board of this ship!" someone yelled.

"What? What for? Why can't we get off?" Everybody began talking at once.

"Attention everybody!" someone spoke through a megaphone. "According to the British, two of our sick passengers have the plague. All of us are quarantined for two weeks."

Around me people were mumbling, groaning helplessly or softly cursing the British.

"Part of the passengers will be transferred to the *Wedgwood* and the rest will go to the *Max Nordau*[1]."

Our Dutch group ended up on the *Wedgwood*. It was great being able to walk the clean, wiped decks of this huge ship. Gratefully, I filled my rumbling stomach with food brought on board by Haifa's Jewish community: a bottle of *leben* (kind of yoghurt), a large bunch of grapes, two rolls, one heaped spoonful of white cheese, two tomatoes and a red pepper.

After all these hardships, everything tasted wonderfully. The sleeping quarters in the hold were similar to those on *the Hagana,* but because the ship's engines were shut off, there was no electricity and therefore, no ventilation nor lights. Sleeping proved impossible in that boiling hot hold.

---

[1] *SS Max Nordau – one* month earlier, this ship brought about 1,000 Rumanian Jews to *Eretz.*

Confiscated *Aliyah Beth* boats chained by the British in Haifa Harbor.
Left the SS *Nordau*, right SS *Wedgwood*

Added to this came the terrible stench from latrines that could not be flushed. The moment it became light, I ran upstairs, on deck, and wasn't the only one. Everybody had red eyes from exhaustion and was at the end of their tether. Due to lack of water in the washrooms, a long line waited for the galley. It took many hours before everybody filled their water bottle under the slowly dripping tap. The alternative was getting a water bottle from the canteen, but there too was a long line.

I felt imprisoned in my new home country. In Westerbork, it had been the Nazis, and now the British forced me to live with stench, dirt and in misery. I.F. Stone, the American journalist who had been traveling with us on this voyage, figured he had seen enough. The only passenger with a valid visa, he was allowed to leave the ship.

After what seemed like an eternity, the quarantine of the *Biriah* passengers was lifted. Still, we were not free to go as pleased – being prisoners of the British government, we still had to go to Atlit camp.
Representatives of different Jewish organizations awaited the *Biriah* passengers. Mr. Araten, a representative of the Dutch *Irgun Olei Holland,* tried to assist our Dutch group.

" Harry Klafter, how can I help you?"

I didn't need long to think about that.

"I would like to have the book "*Organic chemistry*" from Holleman please."

Surprised, Mr. Araten exclaimed: "You arrive here almost naked and all you want is a chemistry book?"

I was too embarrassed to ask for clothes. "We are being sent to Atlit, that British camp," I reasoned. "So I must have something to do."

Mr. Araten promised to do his best.

Our group boarded one of the Egged busses waiting on the quay and soon I was on my may to the British prison camp Atlit, about 13 miles south of Haifa.

© Egged

141

CHAPTER 16
Atlit 1946

Built by the British in the 1930's, during 1930-1948 the Atlit camp was used as a detention camp for 'illegal' immigrants. Some stayed as long as 23 months in this former military camp. When more and more immigrants managed to enter Palestine, the British decided to deport them to Cyprus.

The passengers from our ship were the last 'lucky' ones to be sent to Atlit.

After an enjoyable short bus ride from Haifa to Atlit, I swallowed hard when I noticed the high barbed wire fences, the soldiers in the watchtowers and the brown painted wooden barracks. The last thing I wanted was to be reminded of Westerbork. This time a British soldier forced me to walk the narrow path to the registration barrack.

"They say there are more than 100 barracks in this camp," somebody said. "They have a separate men and women camp."

For many of the boat passengers, the selection procedures of the extermination camps were still fresh in their minds.

Not surprisingly, people panicked when the men were sent to one side and women to the other. After being sprayed with DDT, we were ordered to undress to take a shower.

Even more, people panicked. It took a lot of effort to assure the traumatized survivors that there would be really water coming out of the faucets and not gas. The very hot temperatures used to 'sterilize' the passenger's clothes destroyed the last mementoes people had left in their pockets.

Carrying my blanket and pillow, I walked to my barracks in the men's camp. The windows had screens, but inside it was boiling hot. 32 wooden planks stood in two rows with less than a meter between my 'bed' and my neighbor's, on the rafters hung bags with personal belongings.

Like in Westerbork, the barracks leader explained the rules to me,

"Roll call at 6 pm. You stand next to your bed to be counted by a Tommy. When someone is missing, this means he escaped and then all hell will break lose."

"Do people manage to escape from here?" I wanted to know.

"Occasionally, with outside help," the man said. "If you're caught, you'll end up in jail."

I decided not to try to escape this time.

Due to the summer heat, most men only wore shorts and an undershirt. Married men often stood near the fence dividing the men- and women camp so they could catch a glimpse of their wife and children.

The dining room was filled to the brim. Thanks to the assistance of several Jewish organizations, at least there was enough food, clothing, toys and books in the camp.

During the daily visiting hour, a guard supervised family members who came to visit the new immigrants. Standing between the rows of barbed wire, they were only allowed to talk with the prisoners.

Between 3 p.m. and 6 p.m. the men could enter the women camp, so I used this opportunity to visit the girls from our Utrecht youth group.

"You men have it much easier!" one of the girls complained. "While on kitchen duty, we have to peel potatoes and clean onions for hours on end."

"And in this heat, we must work on the guarded vegetable plot," another added. "That's where they grow cucumbers and onions."

Soon I was used to the camp rhythm. The washrooms had warm water, there was soap and I even had a toothbrush and a clean new towel. Within the men's camp, I could walk around freely and choose between different activities. People could learn Hebrew, twice a week and there was sport and gymnastics. This way, the *Haganah* recruited their youngsters. In a corner of the camp, there was always a group dancing the *Hora*, and Hebrew songs were sung throughout the day. Every free moment I used to study my "Holleman" book.

The European *Olim* had to get used to the heat of *Eretz* which made us tired and sluggish. The main topic of conversation was when we would be released from the Camp. Each morning at 8 a.m. in the dining room, the names were announced of those who were set free. There were cheers, excitement and tears of joy. Of course, everybody wanted to know who was on the list.

After breakfast the camp doctor checked the lucky person and if everything was o.k. he or she could go to the barracks to pack their belongings. The moment the bus with the freed immigrants drove off, camp life resumed to normal. I couldn't help it, but this situation always brought back memories of Westerbork where most deportees were murdered in the Nazi gas chambers. However, those who left Atlit began a new life in *Eretz.*
Being a new arrival, it would take a while before my turn came to be freed.

A few days after arrival in the Camp, every *oleh* caught the so-called "Pappataci illness." For three days, I too was in bed with a high fever, terrible headaches and shivers. There was no medicine for this disease and only when complications arose the patient was admitted to the camp clinic of Dr. Orbach. A few days later, I was on my feet again; still weak but on the mend.

Each free moment was used to continue with my studies. A few weeks after arrival in the camp, my name appeared on the list. Dr. Orbach listened to my heart and lungs, looked in my throat and ears and declared me healthy. Jubilant, I ran to the barracks and quickly threw my meagre belongings in my rucksack. Mr. Josephstahl had tried to convince me to join the others at kibbutz Gal-Ed, but that didn't appeal to me. I didn't want to work the land or milk cows, but wanted to study.

In the registration barracks, I received my release certificate. People who were not being picked up by family members were taken by the Camp-bus to the Egged bus station in Haifa.

Entering the Central bus station, I took a deep breath. My new life in *Eretz Israel* had truly begun!

CHAPTER 17
Tel Aviv

"Things that happened in Eretz Israel, the struggle against the British, the establishment of the State, the War of Independence and all the other wars, the birth of the children and the struggle for existence, fully occupied us. We had enough to deal with the daily challenges and joys. We didn't have to get rid of the past. It took care of itself." **Mirjam Bolle**

When Shalom (Fosh) Zussman, a Jewish Brigade soldier and friend of my brother Freddy heard I was going to Palestine, he gave me his parent's address in Tel Aviv. From Haifa, the Jewish bus cooperative Egged had a regular bus service to Tel Aviv and Jerusalem. I barely sat down in my seat when somebody asked, "Where are you from?"

"What is your destination?" another passenger wanted to know.

The people on this bus not only asked all kinds of personal questions or gave me unsolicited advice, many invited me to come to their house and even stay with them.

I had the feeling they were sincere.

"Thanks, but I already have an address: Sderot Rothschild."

This prompted another discussion: what would be the best way to get there.

As we travelled, our jovial bus driver told us many interesting things about the cities we passed.

Central Busstation Tel Aviv. Photo: Egged

Dutch busses always had a sign posted that read, "Talking to the driver is prohibited!" The Egged bus didn't have those, just the opposite: everybody talked to everyone, including the driver. Every hour he turned up the volume of the radio so the passengers could also listen to the news broadcast. Regularly, the bus stopped to let people get off or allow new passengers to board, even when there was no official bus stop. Nobody seemed to mind that in doing so we were far behind schedule. By the time stepped off the bus in Tel Aviv, it felt like I had been given a big new family.

Thanks to the directions of the passengers, not much later I stood in front of the big house of the Zussman family on Sderot Rothschild.
The couple, both dentist, welcomed me like a son. I even had my own room[1].

"You are always welcome!" they ensured me. "During the holidays, the Jewish Festivals, whenever you want. We'll be your host family."

I had to get used to the daily rhythm in Palestine because here, life began much earlier than in the Netherlands. At 6 a.m. everybody was up and running.
"Don't drink the tap water," Mrs. Zussman warned. "It will give you diarrhea, *shilshul* in Hebrew. Drink only boiled water or tea. We usually drink tea around 10.30 a.m."
I also had to be careful eating unwashed fruit or milk, but it was safe to drink Tnuva's pasteurized milk.

While my hosts went to work, I sauntered through the streets of Tel Aviv. The modern and cosmopolitan city also looked somewhat eastern.
On both sides of the tree-lined street were elegant shops and terraced restaurants. There was a carnival atmosphere: a lot of noise, people laughing, children screaming, neon signs and bright colors.
The beach was beautiful and it felt wonderful to wade barefoot in the warm sea water.
Despite all these new impressions and knowing that I now was truly in *Eretz Israel,* I felt lonely without my family. I decided to write a letter to my mother and brother. One of the many that would follow.

---

[1] This was the fourth open door!

It was a fact: nothing was easy, fast or simple in *Eretz* and the bureaucracy was terrible. Through the *Histadrut haStudentim* in Jerusalem, I found a room in an old house on Rehov Jaffo, near the central bus station. I only had a bed, no cupboard or even a table to study and had to share the room with five other students.

Via a winding, narrow road through the Arab Sheikh Jarrah neighborhood bus 9 brought me to the Hebrew University on Mt. Scopus. At the University Campus, which also housed the Hadassah hospital, you had a beautiful view over the area. On a clear day, you could see the Dead Sea from the amphitheater. On the other side of the hill was the Old City of Jerusalem and behind it the 'new city' – the modern Jerusalem.

Compared to Tel Aviv, this was a provincial backwater. It was beautiful to see how the setting sun gave the buildings a golden glow.
I couldn't wait to begin my studies biochemistry and bacteriology, but had to wait until after the Jewish holidays.

[1] Moshe Baram was the *Shaliah* of the *Sochnut*. Before the war, this active Zionist sometimes visited our house. When his father was hospitalized in the Utrecht eye hospital Mother brought him a kosher meal every day.

Excerpt letter 7-10-1946 to Willy and Freddy.

"My feet are cold while writing this letter.... Wearing slippers while standing at the Wailing Wall, where I stood among a tight mass of gently rocking people. Quite a difference with the Oude Gracht 111 above the shop. Not only it's further away and a floor higher, the Kotel is like first floor, but the atmosphere is so different. After the ceremony, one of the "Wailers" dared to blow the Shofar, which has been forbidden since 1920 because it may drive the Arabs crazy. Every year, someone tries to smuggle a shofar to the Kotel. The next morning you read in the papers that an Englishman has been shot dead and you feel like it's the 'wild west' because then you see tanks with their tough crew racing around town. When you continue reading you can either laugh or cry or shrug." Despite all the troubles people don't want to leave, but stay. Then the radio announces that 11 new points have been established in the Negev during one night and you conclude: how is it possible?... I often think of home and throughout the day I often look at Mama's new picture standing on my little table.... I finally received your letter and hope you won't let me wait so long until the next one arrives. I almost sent you a postcard with "I'm still alive". The Baram family is very nice to me. He is going to participate in the Basel Congress and plans to visit you.

[Harry writes about Freddy's extensive update on the business and his plan to open a shop in Paris.]

"One in France, one in the States – the world will become too small for the Klafter family!...

"Especially in the beginning it's not easy and one has to learn from his mistakes. Often, when I order something, I get the opposite of what I wanted. I'm struggling with my nerves, which makes it difficult to study on a regular basis. The lectures begin in November and before that I have to catch up with my homework. At the moment four people give me lessons. One of the teachers is from Russia. After hearing my Hebrew stuttering she offered to teach me Hebrew and Tenach, for free. Mirjam de Leeuw-Gerzon and I are taught by her son and I also follow two Histadrut lessons per week.

Chemistry I learn from English study books because you can hardly find any good Hebrew books in that area. It's not easy reading English technical texts with its small nuances and different expressions, which are essential to be understood correctly. Because of this I don't make a lot of progress, not as much as I would like and often need to consult a dictionary. I'm relieved to read that your relationship with mama is improved. I understand the difficulties this brings and believe that Mama struggles tremendously.

Probably rather late, I often berate myself for leaving her, even though I debated this in the past. One day I hope to bring Mama here, but it doesn't look like it will be soon. I hope the political situation will bring more security. This continuous insecurity forces many people to withdraw to their families, also in the kibbutzim.... As always, it's the basis of the whole society.... When is Papa's Yahrzeit? Last night I met a girl who has been with Papa – Margaret Goldberg. Mama knows her. She was not able to tell me anything new except that papa seemed strong and even found time for humor.... The country is small and my circle of acquaintances is growing fast. Even though this pleases me tremendously, I want to stay in the shadows and dedicate myself as much to my studies as possible. It will be very tough. When I'm finished, around my 23rd birthday, I will have enough time to enjoy myself. This thought consoles me. I then will have a profession which in all circumstances is important. Of course, I have plans but don't know what will happen to them after two years. Anyway, having a plan is already an improvement because many survivors have the tendency to live one day at the time. They lack the courage to make long term plans....

Freddy, I remember that we drew dolls for Willy's birthday and you bought a bottle of perfume. You wondered if you didn't spent too much money on that. Willy has done so much for us, or did you already have other feelings for her, that you gave her that perfume? You'll have different things to eat, the family comes, Mijntje bakes cakes, Freddy gives a certain kind of flowers (I'm acting as if I'm there with you). Oh, I will be so embarrassed when this isn't your birthday! Anyway, please add a cake crumb to the next envelope. "Shalom (Fosh) went to Switzerland. The last evening, he took me to an oriental restaurant where I ate TWO meals! I almost rolled home. During the meal, we blew pepper in each other's faces (not an oriental habit). Time for me to go to bed. Good night and many greetings from Harry. Tonight, I will definitely dream of pepper and *shofarim* and barbed wire and perfume, etc. Harry.

P.s. On Yom haKippur I ate Chremslach (chremzlekh) The Ost-Jews eat this in honor of the 39 beatings the Shamash gives them to chase away sins. (That was worthwhile to share with you.)

In consequence of the fact that I had no definite address in Jerusalem, packages were sent to the Zussman address in Tel Aviv. One day, I received an official card telling me in British lingo that a package that arrived was addressed to me, which within one week had to be picked up from the post office in Tel Aviv between 8.00 a.m. and 1 p.m. I had to be so kind to open this package to be inspected. Further, the note stated that the Jerusalem post office was closed on Sunday, in Tel Aviv closed on Saturday and on her Majesty's birthday. It was forbidden to mail weapons, glue or checks. The note was signed: your obedient servant.

Everybody entering a public building was frisked. The 'obedient servant' happened to be an Arab who commanded me to sign in two languages: Hebrew and English. Before I could receive the package I also had to show my passport. "Open it!" the postal clerk ordered.
How thankful I was the package didn't contain food, otherwise I had been forced to pay import tax!

Letter to Freddy (Willy was in America) 25-10-1946

"Dear Freddy, I'm very happy with your letter. Was in Tel Aviv at the Zussman family. Received everything. Two packages containing books. I'm glad to be finally able to read a general book that is not connected to politics... Spoke with Mr. Rosenschweig - when need is highest, boot is nighest, for the time being I now have enough. University studies begin in 1 ½ week and before that time I hope to find a new room in a new student flat, together with another man. It's on the outskirts of the city, but the good thing is, is that it's clean and quiet. I will also have a cupboard to store my things and hopefully also a table..."
"Each time I receive mail I feel like I'm a little at home. Home still has the sound of a certain security to me, a different security Palestine can give me. It's not easy when you don't speak the language well; imagine a situation when you want to interact with other people than those who speak German or Dutch. And visiting people isn't everything. They often invite me to dinner and then ask, "Please come back again, soon." I detest that because it always makes me feel like beggar that only visits people for a meal.
Having some money now gives me an independent feeling. It's not pleasant, needing a lot of help, even though the people love to do so. Streets are full of election posters that are being held today. I don't like the way they use public-

ity. On a large wall, there is a competition between the 'gluers' who pastes his poster at the highest spot and after each step somebody pushes a piece of paper in your hand… Propaganda… They should forbid using these methods at a time that, according to me, is the most heavy that we ever have gone through. Everyone should ponder about his vote before he casts it…. This is the first time in my life that I must vote and it's a big responsibility. My vote won't have a lot of influence, but besides long thought and knowledge of facts I must take a certain position…

"The program of the *Shomer haTsairis* ethnically the best; *AchdutAvodah's* program is the best for the Jewish people; *Mapaiis* the only possible one: perhaps partition where we might only lose Arab areas like Hebron and Jaffa. About the future of Palestine, I'm rather pessimistic because I don't see a possibility for us to live in a Palestine with a majority of Arabs, supported by Arab countries; I don't think we will manage to coach the Arabs socialistically and they suddenly want to create a government with us…

… "*Achdut avodah* wants to give the mandate to the UNO … the whole of Palestine as a Jewish state in cooperation with the Arabs is a nice plan but I don't trust the UNO's Mandate – they will not permit a free Aliyah. … A mandate that must be shared with about 50 heads of state… That's why I feel it necessary to vote for Mapai; even though I don't like the socialist program, and I find the solution as the best of three bad ones. How a possible partition will look like is another issue we can talk about – you cannot say no to everything… The fact we lack leaders is the greatest 'sof', but our greatest strength is that, despite everything, they keep on building. "I'm now sorry I didn't give all my pocket money to the JNF when I was young. The *Galut* Jews should begin a mass protest and call on their governments to put pressure on the British.

"With all possible means the Aliyah should be forced otherwise we can hang ourselves… Only now I see how weak the Dutch Zionist Federation's propaganda has been. [Harry calls on his brother to speak up for the Jewish Homeland and to consider moving to Palestine and not stay in the *Galut*. The least he could do was come visit the country for a holiday.] The *Sochnut* should declare itself an official government…. In the meantime, I'm going to enjoy myself with my chemistry formulas. Freddy, I soon hope to hear from you. Many greetings, of course also to mana, from your brother, Harry.

Despite the fact that I missed my family terribly, I was determined to stay in Palestine and begin my studies at the Hebrew university. The Sabra students all knew each other from high school. I wasn't part of the Yishuv yet and because my Hebrew was still basic, I often felt like an outsider.

Letter to Freddy 29.10.1946

"Dear Freddy, another letter from you – you don't know how happy that makes me! [Freddy wrote about their big plans for the factory and Harry admits he is a bit jealous about the perseverance of his big brother, who more and more began to resemble their father.]
"I bought a book for you about the future of the industry in Eretz with tables and reports about the export and import and different branches of companies, how they developed, what their markets are, if raw materials are or are not available, the import of it, etc. In a word, exactly what you asked for in your letter. For some time now I collect economic news items that I will send you in batches. The book will be mailed today, but will take a month before you'll receive it, but it's up-to date, from 1946. I hope you'll enjoy it. In my enthusiasm, I completely forgot to thank you for that idea about the violin. When I get it, I should take lessons, but will find a way. I'm anxiously waiting to hear how much I will have to pay for the university. I handed in a request for exemption but have not heard anything about it. The elections are over and I think they are a big *sof*. Compared to the other parties, the revisionist received many seats: 12. Mapai 28, Mizrahi 10, Shomer Hatsair: 3; HachadutAvodah – off shoot of Mapai: 9; Aliya Chadasha: 6. This new party mainly consists of German Jews. I wonder if the revisionist will opt for the opposition.
I think that the 100.000 people who didn't vote bear a great responsibility... I don't think a lot will change politically. Many people think there has been chosen what they want or is wanted, that the future has been decided. Did I write you that I lived in the house of Mirjam de Leeuw for one week? She was on holiday, and I stayed there together with a Dutch correspondent. He often writes for *Het Volk* or *Vrije Volk* or *Vrij Nederland [Dutch Newspapers]*. We talked a lot in the evenings. He has been everywhere and told me many interesting stories about his meetings with several heads of state. Also about how he writes articles and different influence factors. He loves the Jews and is amazed by what is happening here in *Eretz*.
I don't have a lot to write now, but will do so in my next letter to Mama. I'm waiting for her letter. This was just an extra letter between 12 and one.

Finally, lectures began at the Hebrew University. My chemistry study would take between four and five years. Upon leaving Utrecht, I was already a third-year chemistry student, but because of my weak Hebrew skills, there was much I had to catch up with. I decided to do the very best I could and show my family in the Netherlands that I had a lot of potential.

British soldier
guarding the *Kotel*

CHAPTER 18
Jerusalem 1947

Hepatitis is a liver infection which was common in the unhygienic Middle East. I too was infected, either from eating contaminated food or drinking unboiled water, and had to be hospitalized in Hadassah Mount Scopus.

Letter to **Willy and Freddy d.d. 6-1-1947**

"Dear reunited couple – welcome home! Sorry, I meant Utrecht of course. Such a joy this must have been. I heard all about if from Mama, all the preparations, including poultry and streamers. I still bivouac in Hadassah, today enter my sixth week and my guess is that it will need a 7th as well. My liver is still enlarged and tender. My bloodwork is still not right. Today, my diet has been augmented with an egg, after it had been taken away several times. By now all the nurses know I'm fond of eggs – my egg-complex seems to be an ongoing thing. There's not much happening here and I spend my days with all kinds of little things. When I get out of bed I walk to the end of the brand-new corridor. They continue building new floors on existing departments, and gradually are extending the building. At the end of the corridor is a large balcony with deck chairs from which you have the most beautiful view you can imagine. It is similar to the view from the university's amphitheater.... You can see the mountain ranges stretching to the north, and the deep valley of the Jordan River. When you look carefully you can recognize the different mountain ranges, their bumpy, rolling surface is covered with grey, spongy stones that looks like soup froth (remember Mijntjes huge pots?). I love the area. Looking at the landscape you suddenly understand that the word 'ruler' originated from here. That would never have happened in the flat Netherlands. From Jerusalem, you look out over large tracts of land which made the king living here feel like a ruler. North of the Dead Sea you see Jericho and with a little fantasy you can see the Jews enter, a small army pushing through the mountains. In North-Eastern direction, you see a yellow-white mass of stone against the backdrop of brown mountains. Those are Arab villages. Below the hospital is an Arab village built on a hill. Small paths crisscross the valleys. Early in the morning the Arab women riding their donkey, with pitchers on their heads, go to the well to draw water. Sitting here for a while you can see what's happening in the little village below. Children playing, men smoking and the women doing laundry. The clothesline with its many colors against the greyness of the village is my favorite. A little further you can see the ancient, now neglected terraces. The Jewish people have to fight a heavy struggle to receive the right to bring it's withered earth back to life. Jehoshua (Joshua) passed Jericho with his wagons on this road.... Now it needs to be reconquered.

A strange world and the relentless Jews are a rare species here. Even more

Mt. Scopus University with the Judean Mountains in the background

strange is a congress like the one held in Basel. Reading the newspapers discourages me, but the moment I look outside, to the continuing rebuilding, I know: "But still!" So much reality, through so much work and idealism, it cannot stop. Every day I see the landscape in front of me. Early in the morning I watch the sunrise. That is so beautiful. It is already light but you cannot see the sun because it's still hidden behind the mountains of Trans-Jordan. Because of that mountain range it is as if *Eretz* is in a picture frame. The painting in that frame is not finished yet. Many hands continue to paint it in many colors.

The design however is still too much fenced off with barbed wire. *Eretz'* neighbors are regrouping themselves. (Turkey contracted Egypt, which lusted after the Italian colonies like Eritrea and Sudan. Turkey tried to become an industrial superpower and influence the Balkans. I'm fantasizing about an industrial Palestine with lots of cultural activity.)

"Yes, not being able to do anything for five weeks gives you enough time to loaf around. [The Palestinian Jews were invited to join a pan-Asian conference in British India. Harry was pleased that people considered them.]

"On this ward is an Arab patient, nice fellow. We talk about all kinds of things, except politics.

He told me that I must come and visit him when I'm discharged. He is an art teacher and it's interesting to learn about the Arab customs. There are so many different ways to say "Good morning" in Arabic. It is a rich language. While drinking a cup of coffee with someone there are different expressions they use: while pouring, how you say thanks, how you invite someone. They are extremely hospitable and each Arab will invite you for a meal. At the moment, I don't have an appetite. The riots increased and you can hear the explosions. How this will end, I have no idea.

[Harry writes about the new man in Mother's life and he is sorry not to be able to personally get acquainted with him. He asks about the factory, if they have new machines and how much personnel now works for Freddy. He asks his brother to send him the French and English dictionary.] "… especially English, because I mainly use English study books and often come across words I do not know. I'm optimistic and therefore you can send the next letter to Ruth Hameren, and not to Hadassah. In the meantime, I'm lacking behind more and more, which makes me nervous… I'm now going to eat and then a siesta. Warm greetings and I hope to receive good news from you soon, particularly from Willy - write extensively about your trip. Two hands from Harry. P.s. warm greeting to the Reichman family. How is David? What kind of work does he do?

After being discharged from the hospital, I tried to catch up with my lost study time. Gradually, I began to feel more at home in the eastern society with her colorful mix of cultures. Because even in summer German Jews kept wearing their jackets they were nicknamed *"Jekkeem"* (from *jacke*). The mainly poor Jews from Eastern Europe (Ost-Juden) kept their specific customs. The beautiful dark-eyed Yemenite Jews spoke Hebrew differently. They were precise, religious and intelligent people. Jews born in Palestine were called *"Sabras."* Like the cactus fruit, they were prickly on the outside but soft and sweet in the inside. Sabras were rough, easy going, direct, friendly, without mercy and very good improvisors.

I tried to live as frugally as possible from the money my mother sent me. I didn't go out at night and most of the time, I ate at the *Histadroet Hastudentiem* cafeteria. Despite Mother's financial help, I still had to get a loan to be able to live. On a regular basis, students organized a 'kumsitz,' with or without a bonfire. It was a time for passionate discussions that went on until late at night.

Besides studying, thankfully there was some time for recreation. Fosh (Shalom) Zussman invited me on a hike (tiyul) with Mordechai Gicherman (later Gichon). Nature treks, a national sport I fell in love with ,was an ideal way for getting to know the country. Noortje Kan and I travelled the land while sleeping in kibbutzim.

During Pesach, I took an Arab bus to celebrate the Samaritan Pessach feast in Sichem (Nablus). It was an unforgettable experience, but when my friends learned about my trip, they told me I was crazy. "A Jew cannot do that! Way too dangerous!"

'Jekkeem'

As nationwide riots increased at an alarming rate, British soldiers regularly checked busses and cars. Since everybody was a suspect, I often had to show my passport. Jewish settlements were raided by the British and often curfew was initiated. The newspapers often reported about weapons being confiscated in Jewish settlements while the Arabs openly wore their rifles.

On the eve of *Rosh Hashanah*, the streets were crowded. Many people bought flowers at one of the many flower stalls that suddenly appeared on street corners. Busses were filled to overflowing and everyone greeted each other with, *"Shana Tova!"* During those high holidays, I missed my family more than ever but thankfully, I could choose from several invitations.

> **"A tree may be alone in the field, a man alone in the world,**
> **but no Jew is alone on his holy days."**
> **Abba Kovner, ex-partisan**

Presently, Jerusalem was a barbed wire city patrolled by nervous British soldiers who were prone to shoot. Pressured by the Arabs, the British government forbade further Jewish immigration and the Jewish national rights were declared null and void. Jews were even not allowed to defend themselves against Arab attacks. British soldiers passively watched Jewish people die during a riot, without lifting a finger to help.

On a regular basis 'exercises' were held in Jerusalem. The sound of the air raid sirens made the population even more nervous because the 'all clear sign' often followed only half an hour later. All kinds of 'incidents' took place but nobody knew what had happened until you read about it in the newspapers.

Despite the tensions and riots, I prepared myself for the new academic year. On October 29, 1947, the academic new year was opened in the auditorium of the Hebrew University on Mt. Scopus. The speech by the university president was followed by another one from the principal. After singing Hatikvah, everybody left the building. There was no official registration and somebody advised me to follow a few lectures and then ask the professor to sign a card.

Filled with hope, I began my studies on October 30. Among others, I attended lectures from the brothers Ephraim and Aharon Katzir.

Everybody talked about the November 29, UN resolution. The British, fed up with their Mandate of Palestine, handed over the problem of the Jewish and Arab claims for their own state to the UN.

Top: Together with fellow student

Right: my friend Noortje Kan

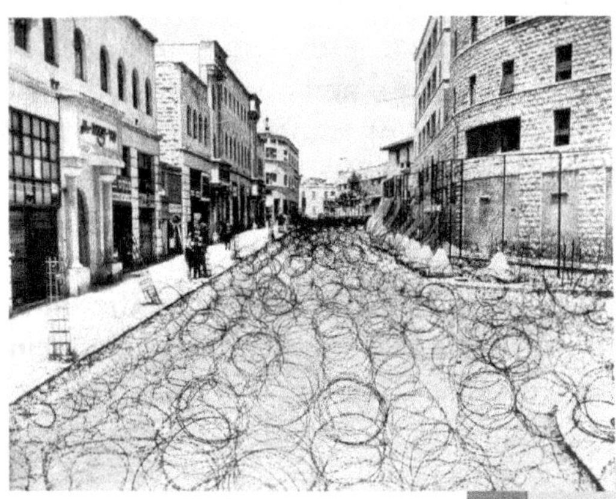

Jerusalem: Barbed wire and
patrolling British soldiers

The UNSCOP suggested a two-state solution: an Arab and a Jewish state with a special status for Jerusalem. For the 600.000 Palestinian Jews, this partition plan would mean their long promised national home and the fulfillment of their 2,000-year-old dream. It would also provide a haven for the remnant of the European Jews who had survived the Nazi concentration camps.

At 11 p.m. on Shabbat, November 29, everyone listened to the live radio broadcast of the UN vote at Lake Success. 33 countries were in support, 13 against and 10 abstentions. The Jewish state was a fact!

Soon, the streets were filled with masses of people dancing the Hora. In Jerusalem, the *Sochnut's* courtyard was crowded. The Jewish flag was hanging from the building and Golda Myerson (later Meir) appeared on the balcony. Too overwhelmed, the only thing she could say was, *"Mazal tov!"* and then burst into tears.

Sunday, November 30, was a beautiful day for the people to continue their celebrations. Pathé[1] men filmed British tanks driving through the streets loaded with Jewish celebrants and people singing, dancing and waving flags.

That afternoon, David Ben-Gurion stood on the balcony overlooking the people that filled the *Sochnut* courtyard. After raising his hand, everybody fell quiet.

"Ashrenushezachinulayomhazeh– Blessed are we, having the privilege to witness this day," he began his speech that ended with: **"Tcheehamedinahaivrit! Long live the Jewish state! (Which didn't have a name yet.)"**

1 In the early 1900s, Pathé became the world's largest film equipment and production company, as well as a major producer of phonograph records. In 1908, Pathé invented the newsreel that was shown in cinemas prior to a feature film.

There were few dry eyes when the *Hatikva* was sung. Touching the blue-white flag hanging from the balcony Ben Gurion raised his voice and said,

"WE ARE A FREE PEOPLE!"

Jerusalem celebrated. Bars and shops handed out free drinks. Everywhere where you saw blue-white flags and Herzl's picture appeared in shop windows. Herzl's words continued to inspire the Zionists:

"If you will it, it's no dream."

Seething with anger, the Arabs declared a three-day strike. While Arab shops, markets and businesses were closed, Muslims flocked to the mosques where imam's fed their flock with inflaming speeches. The next day at 3 p.m. another mass gathering took place at the *Sochnut*. Having heard about the Arab ambushes on the Haifa-Jerusalem road, the mood was much more somber now.

The British divided Jerusalem into three zones: A, B and C. To enter the military zone dividing the Arab and Jewish area, one would need a special pass. The King David hotel and the YMCA were included in the military zone. Most British families lived in the protected German Colony.

As bus 9 passed through the dangerous Arab part of the city to Mt. Scopus, I was unable to attend evening classes. Jewish vehicles were constantly harassed because the winding, uphill road made them an easy target for an ambush. The American Hadassah women raised funds for armored busses to transport the hospital workers and students. In truth, the 'armored' vehicle was a regular bus sandwiched between two thick steel plates to protect against snipers.

Due to British initiated censorship, I could no longer openly write about everything, unless I found somebody who could deliver the letter personally.

Officially, lectures were to resume after the Chanukah holidays, but I wondered if this would be possible. Most students, instructors, professors and administrative staff were too busy with 'other' things. Neither did I have much time to study because I was also involved in the Haganah that secretly trained local and foreign students.

Those who didn't speak Hebrew received a stencil with English instructions. I realized being a Zionist in the Netherlands was quite different from being a Zionist in *Eretz*. Here, they didn't need nice sounding words – they expected deeds. My first task as a recruit was *'shmirah'* – watch duty.

"You must observe Beit Albright," the man in charge told me. The building was in no-man's-land, opposite the *Sochnut* building.

We worked in three shifts: from 5 – 9 p.m.; 9 p.m. – 1 a.m. and 1 a.m. – 5 a.m.

During my training, I learned to take apart a pistol in the dark. In all student hostels, also Pension Reich, one student was always on guard duty in case of an Arab attack.

Since the British didn't frisk women, we were often accompanied by a girl when sent on a mission. Preferably sturdy girls, who were better 'equipped' to hide weapons, were asked for these 'outings.' When a British soldier caught a Jew with a weapon, this often meant a death sentence, while Arabs freely walked around showing their weapons.

One day I had to accompany a *Haganah* girl through the Mahane Yehudah market. The highlight of that day's mission was removing the pistol from her blouse.

The sound of shooting and explosions became a part of daily life in Jerusalem. We became nervous when suddenly everything fell quiet.
Arab snipers made travelling between cities too dangerous, therefore many teachers and professors no longer could come to the university.

By mid-December, the student body was divided into two groups. Faculties lectured a group of students for two weeks, after which it was the turn for those who had been 'free' for two weeks. Thanks to this solution we were able to continue our studies and at the same time actively pursue our other 'activities.'

I now lived in Pension Reich in Beit Hakerem, in the middle of a sensitive, open area. Due to the riots, Egged busses seldom were able to reach Mt. Scopus. Hardly anybody studied. The post office was closed for days on end, except for telegrams. Arabs attacked Postal trains and all mail addressed to Jews was destroyed. I wondered how long it would be before I received a letter from home.

The euphoria of the past month evaporated like the morning mist.
It was clear to me that we were not going to receive our state on a silver platter. If the need arose that we had to fight for it, I was determined to do my share.

My fellow chemistry students. During the Independance War, everyone ended up serving in different HEMED units

Haganah training for men and women

CHAPTER 19
Mandate Palestine 1947

KAPAP- *Krav Panim el Panim*

Our Haganah instructor taught us KAPAP — fighting with sticks — and then sent us to Shlomzion ha Malka street, near the Mamila neighborhood and the Arab cemetery.

We were to stop a group of armed Arabs who set fire to the Rex cinema. Under the watchful eyes of British soldiers, who kept their safe distance in their armored trucks, my friends and I tried to keep the enemy at bay. It was quite an experience and I was grateful to make it safely back to Hovevey Zion street in the Talbiye neighborhood.

I now shared a basement apartment with three Dutch students: Hugo de Groot, Rudie Reijsel and Phil Oppenheimer. The fifth guy was the son of a member of parliament and the boyfriend of Ben-Gurion's daughter.

Jerusalem's houses were very cold in the winter, and after a few days of intermittent rain, it felt even more cold and humid inside. Outside, the icy wind took your breath away. Kerosene (*neft*) heaters were not enough to warm the room and when the reservoir was empty I had to stand in line for two hours to buy new kerosene. Because the electricity was cut on a regular basis, I had to study by candlelight. Milk, eggs and fresh vegetables had become very scarce.

When Mt. Scopus became impassible for the armored busses, there was talk about halting university studies. I didn't mind because by then, I was too busy with one or other *tafkid* — mission that increasingly became more dangerous. American students who didn't want to become involved in the conflict returned home. In the eyes of the Palestinian Jews, there was only one type of Zionist: somebody who wanted to come here to help build a Jewish homeland.

I felt completely at home in Israel and didn't even think of returning to the Netherlands. I was excited to hear that our student group was to be sent to Gush Etzion, an area about 13 miles south of Bethlehem. Surrounded by Arab villages, four Jewish kibbutzim created the so-called Gush Etzion 'bloc'. Since the beginning of the riots, they had been attacked often. Due to the road used by Arab troops and the Jordanian Legion to transport weapons and goods to Jerusalem, this area was very important strategically and economically.

The Palmach sent Danny Mas with a group of students to help the kibbutzim. I had seen **Kfar Etzion's** ' Lonely Oak' from Pension Reich. This four-year-old settlement had a modern dining room, a children's house, showers and toilets, a recreation hall and a library. They kept bees, built furniture and had a modern poultry farm. This beautiful Jewish village with about 220 people was surrounded by hostile Arabs who would not stop before they either had killed all the Jews or driven them out.

Massuot Yitschak was surrounded by high hills and deep wadis. The houses of the two-year-old settlement with its 123-people had front gardens that were connected with each other by narrow paths. During the summer holidays, the residents lived in tents and rented out their homes to people from big cities.

Ein Tsurim was only one-year-old. 55 people lived there, and the dining room doubled as synagogue. They had a leather factory, a cow shed and poultry farm. In the hills, hand dug v-shaped channels collected rainwater in a concrete reservoir. Throughout the year, the inhabitants had to make do with the filtered water, until the next rainy season.

Kibbutz **Revadim** had been established only four months before by the secular *haShomerha Tsair* group. The living quarters of the 80 inhabitants consisted of two very basic huts. The only permanent feature was the barbed wire fence defining the borders of the kibbutz, the concrete water tower and the sandbag barricades.

The defense of these four Jewish settlements with a total of 480 residents was to be strengthened by the presence of about 220 Haganah soldiers. I was one of them.

End December 1947, I travelled to Kibbutz Ramat Rachel and presented myself to the student unit of the Michmash Battalion. A Haganah officer divided us into four taxis. Each car received one weapon and via Bethlehem, we drove to Gush Etzion. I had never been in this area and enjoyed the ride. The next day our duties began: eight hours at a defensive key position with was a reinforced, well-armed place; then we trained for another 3-4 hours. It was terribly cold having to sleep in a tent and hardly any of us wore suitable clothes. As we didn't have a choice we tried to think about happy things. As the Arab blockades cut off the kibbutzim from the outside world, we made fun whenever we could.

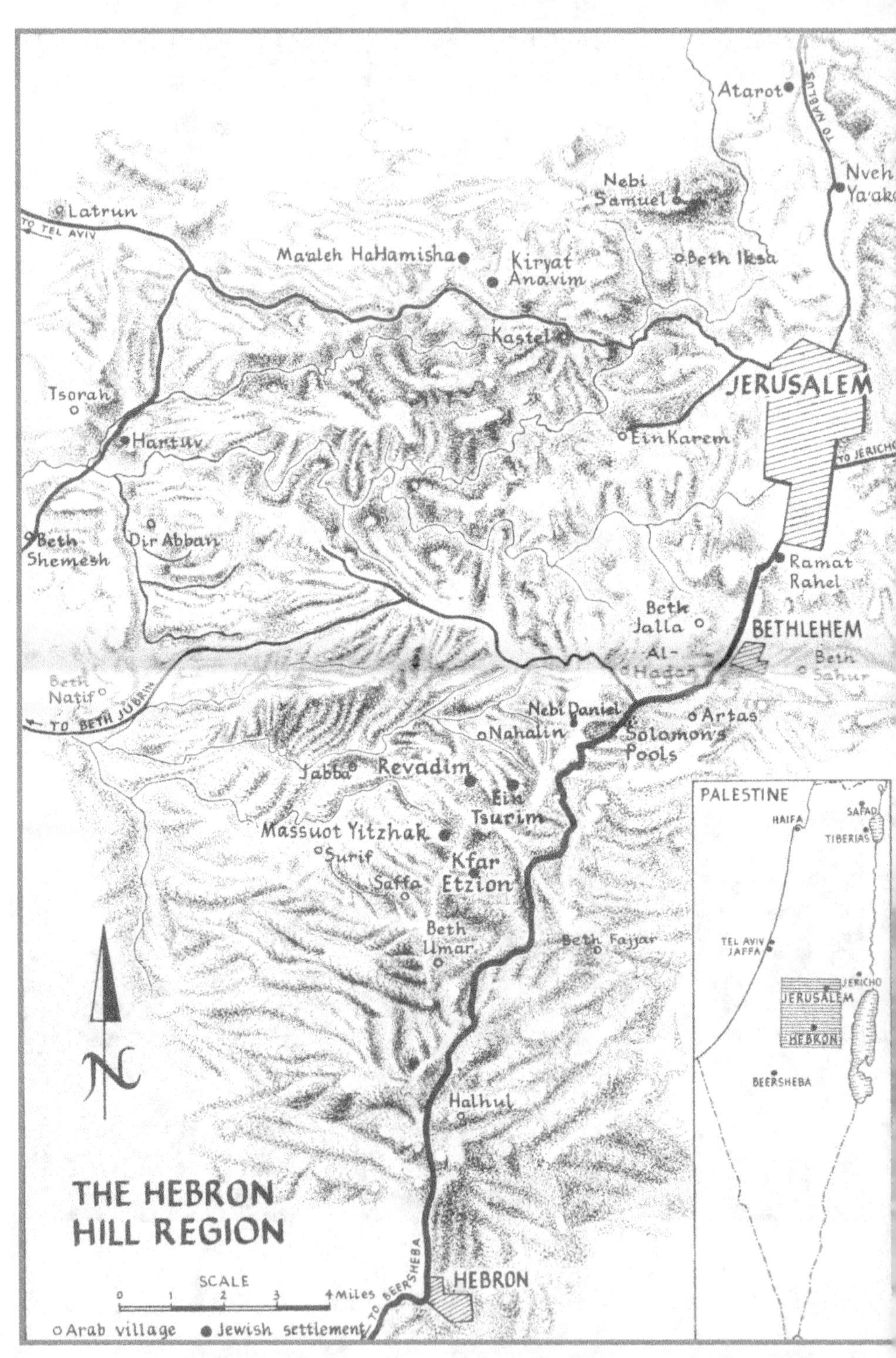

Atarot
TO NABLUS
Nveh Ya'akov
Nebi Samuel
Latrun
TO TEL AVIV
Ma'aleh HaHamisha
Kiryat Anavim
Beth Iksa
Kastel
JERUSALEM
Tsorah
Ein Karem
TO JERICHO
Hartuv
Beth Shemesh
Dir Abban
Ramat Rahel
Beth Jalla
BETHLEHEM
Al-Hadar
Beth Sahur
Beth Natif
TO BETH JUBRIN
Nebi Daniel
Artas
Nahalin
Solomon's Pools
Jabba
Revadim
Ein Tsurim
PALESTINE
HAIFA
SAFAD
TIBERIAS
Massuot Yitzhak
Surif
Kfar Etzion
Saffa
Beth Umar
Beth Fajjar
TEL AVIV JAFFA
JERICHO
JERUSALEM
HEBRON
THE HEBRON HILL REGION
BEERSHEBA
Halhul
N
TO BEERSHEBA
SCALE
0   1   2   3   4 Miles
HEBRON
o Arab village   ● Jewish settlement

From mid-December, we constantly had to watch the Jerusalem-Hebron road. We left in groups of three and as we got closer to the road, we hid behind a stone wall. When a Jewish convoy approached we took our positions at a ruined house. If there was no convoy to protect I was kept busy with routine training: taking a machine gun apart and putting it together again, first aid, and signaling.

Danny Mas, responsible for the defense of the Bloc, regularly visited us for a pep-talk. The special bond and camaraderie amongst us was an unforgettable experience. Even though I had been practicing a lot with my Canadian weapon, because bullets were scarce, I had never once shot for real. The first time I pulled the trigger, the weapon bounced against my shoulder. My friends laughed when they notice my painful expression.

Winter truly began on December 28 with an icy, stormy wind. A heavy mist enveloped the area like an impenetrable curtain and the heavy mud stuck to our shoes and boots. The falling temperatures that turned the rain into snow made our expeditions even more unpleasant. Because of the snow-covered roads and pathways, we lost our way in enemy territory. How relieved we were when our beloved *mefaked* Danny Mas localized us and brought us safely back to the base.

Danny Mas

January 4, 1948 a convoy delivered fuel, food and concrete to the kibbutzim. A group of students from the field battalion joined the next convoy to help strengthen the Etzion Bloc.

I knew *MemKav* Sigi Samson from Westerbork. He took our group with Benny Jeter, Judah Kot and Yehoshua Marks to a training exercise at Chirbet Zechariah, south of Revadim. In 164 BC, there was heavy fighting between the Maccabees and the Greeks in this area. Judah's brother died when a mortally wounded elephant fell on top of him.

171

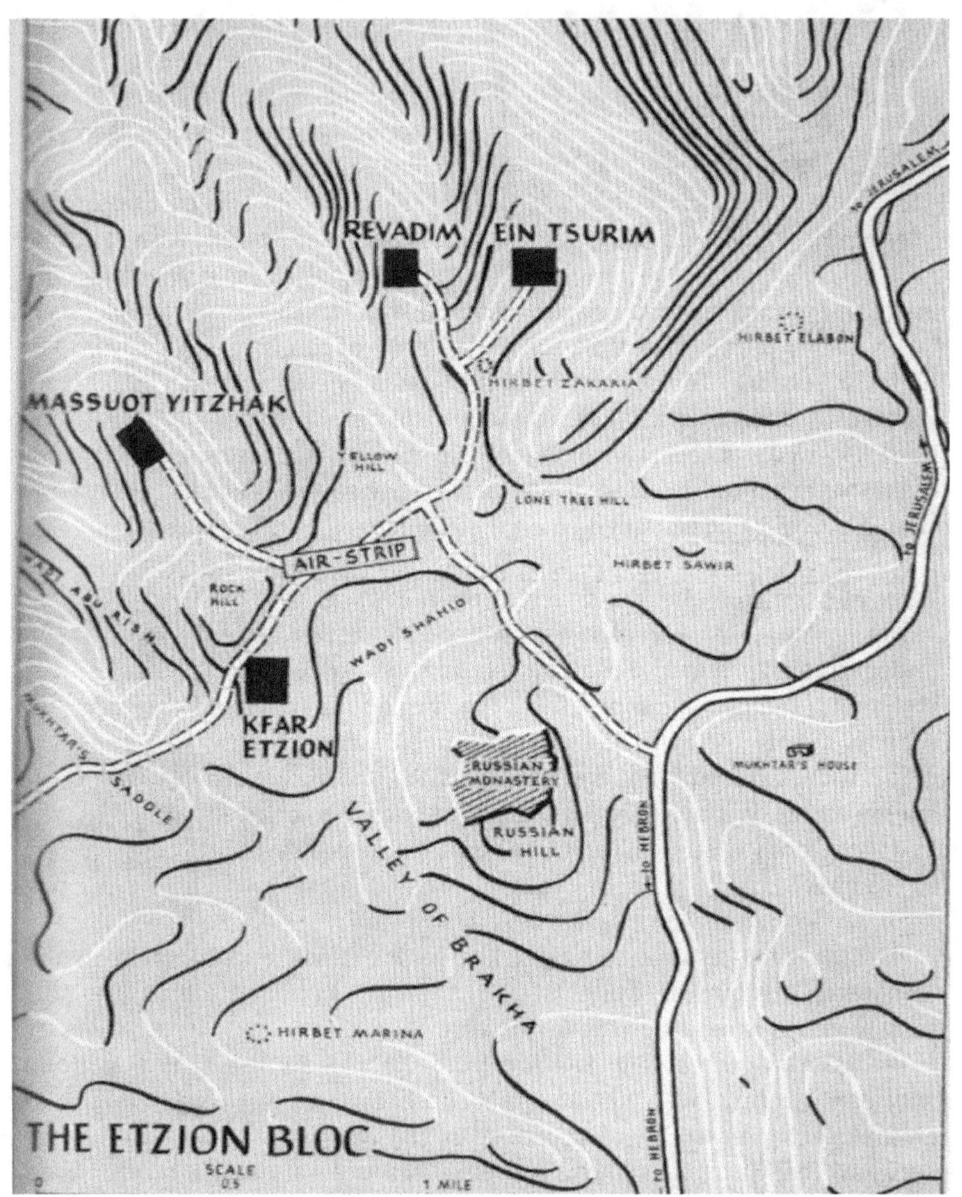

REVADIM
EIN TSURIM
HIRBET ZLABON
HIRBET ZAKARIA
MASSUOT YITZHAK
YELLOW HILL
LONE TREE HILL
TO JERUSALEM
TO JERUSALEM
HIRBET SAWIR
AIR-STRIP
TEL ABU EISH
ROCK HILL
WADI SHAHID
MUKHTAR'S HOUSE
KFAR ETZION
RUSSIAN MONASTERY
RUSSIAN HILL
MUKHTAR'S SADDLE
TO HEBRON
VALLEY OF BRAKHA
HIRBET MARINA
THE ETZION BLOC
SCALE
0.5
1 MILE
0
TO HEBRON

After the Arab residents had fled on December 12, 1947, the Haganah took over Chirbet Zechariah. The village consisted of twelve dilapidated huts, a few stables and an area for sheep. A few high trees stood near the mosque in the center. From this vantage point, we had a good view of the road leading to the village and see a possible advancing enemy. Behind the village, the road split in two: to the right was Ein Tsurim, and left below was Revadim. During the Arab attack the Bren became overheated.

"Everybody on your knees!" Sigi ordered, "and urinate on the weapon!"

Everybody called Eliezer Shafrir 'the Sten' because he did nothing but

Chirbet Zechariah

talk about his beloved weapon. He drove everybody nuts with his stories about what kind of problem his gun had given him and the solution he had found for it.

January 5, 1948, the mothers and children from the Etzion Bloc were evacuated by the British. They found shelter in a rented place of the Ratisbonne monastery in Jerusalem.

De Schwarzlose

Everybody was sad when Danny Mas was recalled to Jerusalem on January 8. He was replaced by Uzi Narkiss, the new Haganah commander for the Gush Etzion Bloc.

Our unit didn't have many weapons. Besides the Bren, kibbutz Ein Zurim had an old Austrian machine gun dubbed the "*Schwartslose*." The weapon malfunctioned more often than it worked.

January 12, we learned that a big concentration of non-local Arabs had been spotted. Near Surif, two Syrian officers, led by Abdul Kader el-Husseini, established a big training camp for about 1,000 men.

Also, two Arab gangs had been spotted in the village of Beit Sachur. January 13, another convoy from Jerusalem was ambushed by the Arabs, killing two Haganah soldiers. The situation for the Bloc's settlements became increasingly grim.

On January 14, my unit was still stationed at Chirbet Zacharia. From the roof, I had a good view of the surrounding area. News that the Arabs were preparing to attack was confirmed by our reconnaissance unit who kept an eye on the main road. The area teemed with Arabs who were clearly scouting the area. From behind the agricultural terraces surrounding Chirbet Zacharia the Arabs began shooting at our unit as it returned to base.

Around noon, the Arabs stormed the hill while shouting, "*Allahu Akbar, itbach el Yahud!-* God is great, butcher the Jews (ritually)!"

"Now the war has truly started," a friend exclaimed.

"This is no war," I shouted, "but a pogrom!" and quickly got down from the roof. The moment I reached the ground something hit my elbow. When blood appeared on my shirt I pressed the painful spot. There were a few more wounded.

"Harry, are you able to get to Revadim to ask for help?" Sigi asked.

"On my way!" While the bullets whizzed past my head I ran into the valley and raised the alarm in Kibbutz Revadim.

Around 2 p.m. reinforcements were on their way with munition and food. The unexpected counterattack killed many Arabs and the rest fled. That day, the Jewish defenders had experienced a few miracles, but they wondered how long they would be able to keep up this defense. Here they were, a small island amidst a stormy sea full of hostile Arabs.

Three soldiers were killed that day: Yehoshua Marks (from our unit), a former Jewish Brigade soldier and two of my student friends. In the Kfar Etzion clinic the local doctor looked at my bullet wound. The Arabs had used their favorite bullet: a dumdum. The cut bullet head explodes and causes massive injuries.

"This young man has to be transported to Jerusalem as quickly as possible to be operated on," the doctor said.

Accompanied by British soldiers, the transport of wounded soldiers and citizens was brought to Hadassah Mt. Scopus. There, Professor Joseph Ehrlich and professor Josef skillfully operated on my elbow. Waking up from the anesthesia, I learned that another miracle had taken place: if the bullet had been a millimeter to the side, it would have injured the ulna nerve. Then, I never would have been able to become a surgeon!

While recovering from the operation, I heard the terrible news that a few days after our victory, 35 soldiers, including Danny Mas, had been slaughtered and mutilated by the Arabs.

The moment I was declared fit for duty, I returned to my unit in the Bloc. At the beginning of February, the land blockade was still in place, but now, thanks to the air transports, a life-line with the *Yishuv* had been established. Not only did the small Piper planes bring weapons, munition and medical help but also newspapers and letters. Newspapers were always opened with trepidation because very often the reader learned about the death of a friend by looking at the obituaries.

My unit stayed in Gush Etzion until March 1948, after which our soldiers were transferred to different units and fronts. I was sent to join CHEMED, the scientific corps established by David Bergman and Shlomo Avigur. Specific units like physics, biology and chemistry, were divided into department *Alef, Beth, Gimel* and *Dalet*. This unit created weapons and explosives, amongst other things. I was sent to the biological department, and until this very day, I am not allowed to talk about my missions. As I was sent from one Palmach brigade to another, as a *Katsin Miftsa'im* (Operation Officer), I experienced the most fantastic adventures. The longest time I spent with the *Chativatha Negev*, the Negev Brigade. Since our isolated units were stationed far from the big cities, only much later did we learn that the State of Israel had been born!
The official end of the British Mandate of Palestine would be on May 15, 1948 - a Shabbat.
This was the reason that David Ben Gurion declared the state a day earlier: on May 14.

"The whole world was certain that within ten days, at best two weeks, not a living soul would have been left in Israel," Ben Gurion wrote in his diary.

When Egypt, Syria, Iraq, Lebanon, Jordan and Saudi Arabia invaded, the newborn state seemed to be truly destined for destruction. Thanks to their British friends and assistance from several superpowers, the Arabs had a lot of weapons. They thought they could easily wipe the young state from the map.
Israel, on the other hand, had no artillery, tanks or fighter planes, only primitive and too few weapons. However, their enemy had not considered the secret Jewish weapon: *Ein brerah!* The Jewish people had no other choice, no alternative. We just had to win this war.

CHAPTER 20

"In Israel, in order to be a realist you must believe in miracles.
David Ben-Gurion

The leaders of the Yishuv, particularly Ben Gurion, knew that the Haganah soldiers were not a homogenous army. Their guerilla tactics were not a match for the well-trained Arab armies. Israel didn't have pilots, navy captains or officers who knew how to use foot-soldiers, weapons and planes to either attack or defend. Machalniks, an abbreviation of *Mitnadvim michuts leAretz*- also called the '*meshugaim*'- crazy ones- *mi chuts learetz*, were volunteers from abroad who wanted to use their WWII experience to help Israel. Beside these volunteers, specific officers were discretely recruited. The first and only for-eign colonel willing to stick out his neck for the Jewish people was David (Mickey) Marcus. In 1945, this decorated Westpoint Colonel had seen the Hell of Dachau with his own eyes and knew that a Jewish state had to be established.

While visiting different army units he boosted the moral of the exhausted Jewish soldiers. His multi-faceted personality always left a deep impression. He had sparkling, penetrating eyes, a loud voice and a great sense of humor. Mickey knew how to rub shoulders with kings and peasants. People loved him, respected him and were willing to learn from him. Because he did the work of five people, it was hard to keep up with him.

[Many details in this chapter were gleaned from the book: *Cast a Giant Shadow*, by Ted Berkman, as Zvi could not remember many details of this time period.]

Since the Palmach originally was a people's militia without ranks, there was no need to salute. Later the Palmach and the Haganah became *Tzahal* (IDF) Almost every soldier had a nickname and Brigades were often called after their leader, e.g. the "Carmeli Brigade" or after the area they were stationed, like the "Negev Brigade." After finishing the intensive and strenuous follow-up training, the soldier became an officer to a group of fellow soldiers. After more advanced training they could rise to become leader of a larger group. Because of their motto: "Follow me!" many officers were killed as they were always the first to enter the battlefield. After a Peloton came, a Squad and the biggest formation was called a Brigade, made up of several battalions and independent units, (like the Negev Brigade). A front (North, Central, South, etc.) was the biggest command.

Mickey Marcus alias Stone

Ben Gurion asked Mickey to be the advisor for the Negev offensive.

When an Egyptian column moved via the coastal road in the direction of Tel Aviv, and another in the direction of Beersheba, the time had come to stop them.

The vast Negev desert was home to twenty isolated Jewish settlements. Beside the British built main road, there were only dirt tracks and small footpaths crisscrossing the fields.

Israel Carmi oversaw the new unit consisting of two jeep companies with 15 vehicles each. These "Negev Beasts" (*Hayot Hanegev*) were outfit with modern machine guns. Three jeeps were a peloton, nine a company. The Palmach Negev Brigade (*Hativat Hanegev*) was to play a key role in the liberation of the Negev. In total, Carmi commanded about 700 soldiers, divided into different groups. He was to accompany the second company south while Mickey Marcus, in his capacity as an official 'advisor', led the first company.

I was ordered to report to a unit which assembled at Givat Brenner. After darkness, the sign to depart was given. Mickey jumped next to his driver in the lead jeep and motioned me to come sit in the back, next to the radio. With dimmed head lights, we travelled in a long line southwards, making sure to avoid Arab villages. An intercepted radio message described the jeeps as a 'light Russian-made tank'. They probably had gotten that idea from the sleeping bags that were roped to the hoods of the jeeps. During that cold night, the slow-moving convoy of jeeps, half-tracks and armored vehicles constantly came to a halt for all kinds of reasons. By sunrise, we had reached our company kibbutz Negba.

About 220 residents lived in this dry, dusty entrance to the Negev. The moment the sun broke through, the cold night was forgotten. It now was boiling hot, my tongue stuck to my palate and I didn't succeed getting rid of horseflies attacking us in droves. The camouflaged Jeeps spread out over the kibbutz and the exhausted soldiers fell asleep under a hastily assembled blanket-roof. The following night we would deeply penetrate enemy territory.

Soldiers standing guard in the trenches crisscrossing the kibbutz suddenly spotted two dots in the bright blue sky. The moment the buzz became louder, everybody dove for cover. Frozen, I just stood there, staring at the Egyptian spitfires that seemed to come straight at me. One bomb slammed in a barren hill but the second destroyed a shed. The pilots began preparing for the next round. The roar of the engines and the ping of the bullets from the machine gun were deafening. People followed suit when Mickey grabbed his machine gun and began shooting at the airplanes. The surprised Egyptian pilots broke away quickly. Besides the wounded, many soldiers were badly shaken. This air raid experience also left me in shock. Micky

Trenches in Negba

spoke to us, encouraged us and even made jokes. Our appreciation for him grew more and more.

With Egyptians patrolling the area, we could only travel by night. After sunset, the line of vehicles began moving again, this time to Dorot. This kibbutz, surrounded by deep wadis and rolling hills consisted only of primitive wooden huts.

The headquarter of the Negev Brigade was situated in kibbutz Nir Am, about 6 miles north-east of the Gaza Strip. The settlement had a hospital and functioned as the storehouse for the southern settlements.

Nahum Sarig, head of the Negev-Brigade, set up his temporary headquarters in kibbutz Dorot after the Egyptians bombed Nir Am. Mickey encouraged Sarig's disillusioned soldiers and the additional soldiers from Carmi's unit also strengthened their morale.

"I suggest teaching the Egyptians a lesson," Mickey said. "Tonight, we pay a visit to the Egyptian army post in Beit Hanun."

Under cover of darkness, our unit approached the Egyptians while constantly shooting at them followed by hand grenades. Knowing that Muslims are very superstitious we screamed like evil banshees. Our unit was already gone before the enemy realized what happened. We didn't do a lot of material damage that night, but even more was the panic we had sown. The intercepted Egyptian radio message described the action of the nine jeeps, two half-tracks and six armored vehicles like, "A Russian armed column the size of a division." This action changed our morale completely.

The next day, while I was getting dressed in the room I shared with Mickey, I heard the buzz of engines. Three Egyptian spitfires began emptying their machine guns on our kibbutz. With bullets whizzing around me, I dove through the window, straight into the trench. They bombed a

shed and the command hut. Mickey's rucksack was full of bullet holes and I swallowed hard when I noticed my bullet ridden belt lying on the bed I had been sitting a few minutes before.

"When you hear the bullet, it didn't hit you," one of the soldiers joked.

Noticing that this Egyptian attack had plummeted our morale below zero, Mickey put on his bullet-ridden *kovatembel*.

"Walking like this in Tel Aviv, people will think I'm a hero," he joked. He took a knife and cut off the ruined shirt sleeves. "Nice work of those *Grippos*. I now have a summer shirt." Because his khaki trousers on the clothes line were also bullet ridden he cut them off as well. "Well... now my summer costume is complete!" Everybody began to laugh. "What did those bombs really hit, despite all that wasted petrol and bullets?" he asked the young soldiers. "A few wooden planks!"

The seasoned solider knew exactly how to raise our spirits. Filled with courage we began to prepare for the next action. When Ben Gurion recalled Mickey to Tel Aviv, Chaim 'Kidoni' (Bar-Lev) became the operational officer but Sarig continued to be the commander.

Bar-Lev

Nobody knows why, perhaps the Egyptians were under the impression that a superior Jewish force was waiting for them, but they halted on June 2 and dug in at a bridge near Isdud. Later, this bridge was called the "*Gesher ad chalom*" -the 'until here' bridge.

June 11, the first ceasefire, brokered by count Folke Bernadotte began. The IDF used this breathing space to reorganize, give soldiers the necessary basic and follow-up training and to import big quantities of weapons and war material. Those that fought with Mickey Marcus, were shocked when we heard that he had been killed by 'friendly fire.' The 47-year -old Machalnik was the first IDF officer who received the rank of *Aluf.*[1]

July 8, fighting resumed when the Egyptians attacked kibbutz Negba and Be'erot Yitschak. Despite being outnumbered by the enemy, the courageous defenders managed to keep going until assistance arrived and the attackers were driven off. One day I was sent on a mission with two jeeps behind Egyptian lines, east of Beersheba. While driving on a narrow road between two mountains, we encountered an Arab man.

"We must shoot him, otherwise he'll betray us," one of our soldiers said.

"Is that really necessary?" I protested.
After discussing the situation, we decided to spare the life of the Arab. Bound hand and feet we put the man in a cave, after which we resumed our journey through the gorge. Everything seemed to be going well until suddenly we were attacked. The Arab probably managed to free himself and immediately alerted the nearby Egyptian soldiers.

1 *Aluf* (lit. "champion"). In other countries, officers would have the rank of general, air marshal, or admiral.

There were four of us in a jeep, so we quickly dove for cover and began shooting at the airplanes. Our jeep kept rolling and stopped when it hit a mine. One of the tires was torn to shreds but to our great relief we could change the wheel and return safely to our base.

Top: Dakota; below: Piper Cup

As I was constantly sent away for short missions involving different units, there was no time to make friends. Most of the time, I travelled as a *'trampist'* (hitchhiker) in an airplane. This could be a WW II Dakota cargo plane but most of the time, it was a two-passenger Piper Cub.

Because of the plane's balance, I had to come forward during take-off but squat in the tale for the rest of the flight. We departed from the airstrip between Dorot and Ruchama and flew to Sde Dov, near Tel Aviv.

The Israeli air force began with a squadron of nine pilots, all Machalniks. Approaching Sde Dov, I could see the runway, cleared from the sand that each night blew over it. Planes were parked on both sides of the landing strip, adding to the danger of each landing and takeoff.

The control tower, located in a big wooden crate, doubled as office and weapon storage. The pilot received permission to land either through flag signals or colored fireworks.

Sde Dov control tower

A flight to and fro the Negev took about three hours. Not only did the little planes bring newspapers, mail and light equipment to the settlements, they also did reconnaissance flights and evacuated the wounded. I greatly respected these foreign volunteers who had earned their stripes during WWII.

Beit haArava kibboets 1948

During the War of Independence, Israel had used two water planes – the Grumman G-44 Widgeon, also called the Gosling. From Sde Dov airport, the small five passenger plane flew towards the east, where the pilot landed on the Dead Sea. I was brought to land in a rubber dinghy and received further instructions in Kibbutz Beit HaArava. The sound of the jackals in the fields surrounding the kibbutz made the night even more frightening because it sounded like Arab war cries to our tense ears.

I took part in a special mission near Jericho, deep into enemy territory. I was never sent on a mission alone, but always as part of a group of Palmachniks. After the successful mission, I was picked up again by a Piper cub and brought back to Sde Dov. It was a tense but exciting time.

Sometimes, I managed to spend a few days with my guest family in Tel Aviv. They spoiled me with good meals, a warm bed and clean clothes. Because I stayed for long periods in one place, it was difficult to stay in touch with my family in Utrecht. Obviously, my mother was very worried, as you can read in the following letter from September 22, 1948, on the next page.

"My sweet boy, I don't have to tell you what I think about not receiving a letter from you since 21/8. The most terrible thoughts come to mind and I can't describe what you do to me – it is almost unbearable. It seems you are not in Tel Aviv, otherwise I would have received mail and you surely would have received my letters. There is no news except that Freddy will fly to the States next week. Friday, they open a new Apollo branch in Baarn under the leadership of Annie. For the rest, no news to share in my weekly chat. I debated sending you a telegram, but keep postponing it because I think, oh, the mail will be here soon. Only to be constantly dis-appointed… About the murder of Bernadotte, the Jews were shocked but amongst all people are extremists and a murder cannot be condoned. Doesn't matter who, even if it would be our enemy, at least, that is what I think. No one has the right to take the life of another. In the meantime, we have to wait what the committee will say and what will happen next. The Arabs, I heard today on the radio refused Bernadotte's suggestions. Wait and drink tea, like I do with the letters that don't arrive. I fervently hope nothing happened to you. For the holidays, I wish you, also in name of my husband[2], all the best and may everything will be fulfilled in the New Year. Many warm greetings and kisses, your loving mother."

[2] Mother remarried an older widower, Mr.Krochmal.

In August, a primitive airbase was established near kibbutz Ruchama in the Negev. Since the planes had to fly over an area that was still occupied by the Egyptians, they could only fly during the night. Each night, the pilots flew eight times to and fro, delivering war material and about 2,000 passengers, many new soldiers amongst them. Finally, the Negev brigade veterans could visit their family after eight months! The second ceasefire between July 18 and October 15 was regularly broken by both parties.

When the Egyptians stopped a Jewish convoy, used as bait, the Israelis launched operation *"Yoav"* to open the entrance to the Negev and evict the Egyptians from the country. Before the UN security council demanded a new ceasefire, Yigal Allon grabbed his chance and conquered the Negev Desert.

"We thought you were not able to attack us," the Egyptian major said when he was arrested in Beersheba. "Our intelligence told us you had been beaten and fled towards Tel Aviv."

When travelling by jeep I was always grateful for being allowed to sit in one of the first staff cars. The rest of the convoy was eating clouds of dust and sand.

Because of the chronic lack of jeeps, the guys from the Negev Beasts just 'borrowed' a

Jeep and truck from the "Negev Beasts"

few from Tel Aviv and quickly painted them in the army colors. They treated their jeep like a horse. Because they depended on it, it was looked after very well. To them, it became a family member about whom they spoke with great fondness. The boys lived, slept, ate and fought from or nearby their jeep. The vehicle transported their food, water, weapons, ammunition and sleeping gear – everything they needed.

Army food mainly consisted of tinned Canadian kosher corned beef, crackers and marmalade. To give the one-sided army menu a bit more taste and color, one of the soldiers always made sure he carried a sack of onions.

On a regular basis, soldiers were sent on a reconnaissance mission and night patrol in enemy territory to check out the enemies' defenses. At the same time, they visited isolated Israeli posts. One of these routes was from Ma'aleh Akravim to Ein Husub; another via the Red Wadi to Sedom.

A large part of northern Israel was in the hands of the Syrian, Lebanese, Iraqi and other Arab soldiers who were led by general Kaukji. During the British Mandate, many of these fighters had entered the country illegally. *Chativat* 7 was led by *Machalnik* Ben Dunkelman who was ordered to wipe clean the north till the internationally acknowledged border with Lebanon.

The "Seventh Brigade" had no tanks but did have a Druze unit. 'Operation Hiram 'began on October 28, 1948, with the reconquering of the ancient city of Safed. For me, this was the beginning of a very intensive period of short, one-time actions that took place both on Syrian and Lebanese soil.

One of the missions began in kibbutz Ein Gev on the shore of the Sea of Galilee. Founded in 1937 on a narrow piece of land between the lake and the foot of the Golan, you could only reach the kibbutz by boat from Tiberias.

Ben Dunkelman

Fearing a possible German invasion, in 1941, the British built a defense line along the Golan Heights. After the British left, the village Taufik (Fiq) became a Syrian army base. The elevated village looked out over the Sea of Galilee and the Hermon mountain range. From the former British bunkers, called "pillboxes," Syrian soldiers were constantly shooting at Israeli settlements down below.

Instructed what to do, I prepared myself for a dangerous mission. Together with a group of Palmach scouts, we stole into the pitch-dark night. A shepherd who knew the area well, led us through the fields towards the steep hills, in the direction of the Syrian village. At one point, I looked up and my heart stopped when I noticed the Syrian soldier. As it was a cold night, the soldier had wrapped himself in a blanket. The sudden squall that made the blanket flutter warned of the impending danger. Standing on higher ground, this enemy soldier could have killed our group with one hand grenade. I managed to quietly warn the others about the impending danger and we quickly retracted our steps. After safely reaching the kibbutz it took a while before my heart was beating normally again.

The *Chiezbatron* was the entertainment troupe of the Palmach who with Shaike Ofir visited the soldiers to encourage and spur them on.
Everybody enjoyed their plays, sketches and songs.

One of the most favorite songs was: "*Hey, hajeep! Hey, hajeep!*"
The picture was taken near kibbutz Revivim, 24 hours before the 9th battalion began with "Operation Yoav". The public consisted of different units, the jeep unit among them, the French commando and the half-tracks.

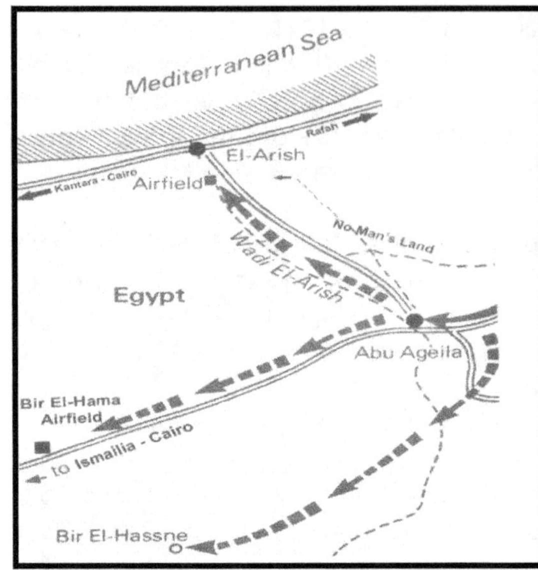

Operation *Chorev*, also called "Operation *Ayien* "lasted from December 19 1948 till January 7, 1949. Its objective was to banish the Egyptians from the Negev and the Gaza strip.

The army leadership decided to use an old Roman road which had been discovered by Palmach scouts. Heavy winter rains caused delays and gave us a lot of trouble because the wadis overflowed and mud clogged the caterpillar tracks of the vehicles. After three days of heavy fighting and several setbacks, the Negev Brigade reached the border with Egypt and pushed as far as Abu Ageila.

Egyptian Spitfires were flying to and fro and shot at everything that moved. I found myself in the middle of it all and quickly hid under the Abu Ageila bridge. This important Egyptian army base was located about twenty miles from the Israeli border.

I'm between Bibi, our intelligence officer and the driver

After heavy fighting, the Negev Brigade got the upper hand. They confiscated fifteen trucks, several pieces of heavy artillery and took about 300 Egyptian soldiers prisoner. Furthermore, they found big quantities of cigarettes, good Egyptian officer's food, ammunition, petrol and lots more. Everybody was exhausted, but seeing the bounty changed the mood into a jubilant one.

December 29, Abu Ageila became an Israeli army base. The lived UN security council demanded that Israel and Egypt arrange a ceasefire. I had my own trophy: Abu Ageila's flag which I proudly showed to everyone.
For years I kept that flag but eventually donated it to the Palmach museum.

Our troops could have easily captured El Arish as well, but Ben Gurion wanted us the leave the Sinai desert within 24 hours.

I was ordered to report to kibbutz Gvulot for a special mission. The settlement's name spoke about the lack of borders, *'gvulot,'* because it was situated in the middle of the vast Negev desert. Because of her location near the Egyptian border, not far from the Gaza strip, this kibbutz was a suitable base for the 8th brigade. Sitting amongst a group of soldiers, I listened to the instructions from our officer. "By foot will take too much time, therefore we took horses," he said. "Is there someone who cannot ride on horseback?" I was the only one of the group. The officer discussed the strategy of the mission and told me to follow him to an open field.

"We're going to practice here." The officer helped me on the horse. "Look, if you do this, you go left, and this way you turn right." He pulled the reins to show how and then it was my turn. After managing the horse to walk in the right direction, I received the following task, "Now walk around in a big circle."

The next day, we departed with ten people, each on a horse, in the direction of the Gaza Strip. I lagged behind on a horse that was blind in one eye. Due to the rain, the wadis were filled with water and everywhere small rivers crossed the usually dry and barren landscape. When we had to cross one of those little streams, the horses refused to step into the water. My horse didn't see the problem and without hesitation crossed to the other side. Promptly the other horses followed suit. Our unit executed the mission successfully and we returned safely in Gvulot.

Again, it was *Chanukah*. Again, I celebrated the Feast of Light in unique surroundings; this time under a cloudless sky dotted with millions of stars. For us, Jewish soldiers, who were now fighting for our own homeland, the songs we sang at the top of our voices had an even deeper meaning.

December 11, 1948: when it appeared that the Israelis not only were winning but also had penetrated deeply into enemy territory, UN resolution 194 called for a ceasefire. It would become a recurrent pattern during Israel's future wars.

Operation Uvda, from March 7-10, 1949 liberated the Negev, including the most southern point, Um Rashrash (Eilat).
Even though it consisted only of a few clay huts that were surrounded by sand, it was now Israeli territory. Avram Adan (Bren) from the Golani brigade won the race to Eilat from the Negev brigade.

Raising their handmade ink flag the jubilant soldiers sang the *Hatikva*. Later, the singing of the national anthem was seen as the ceremonial end of the War of Independence.

Eilat in 1948

Hatikvah—the HOPE

Kol od balevav penima	As long as within our hearts
Nefesj jehoedi homi'ja	The Jewish soul sings,
Oelefa'aatee mizrach kadima	As long as forward to the East
Ajien le Tsi'jon tsofi'ja	To Zion, looks the eye –
Od lo avda tikvatenoe	Our hope is not yet lost,
Ha tikwa bat shnot alpayim:	It is two thousand years old,
Lehijot am chofsjie be'artseenoe	To be a free people in our land
Erets Tsi'jon ve Jeroesjalajiem	The land of Zion and Jerusalem.

Between February and June 1949, the newly formed Israeli government was busy nego-
tiating; eventually, three separate ceasefires were signed with Egypt, Syria, Lebanon
and Jordan. Because of the War of Independence, Israel received 50% more territory
than was suggested by the UN partition plan. The Gaza strip became Egyptian and Jordan annexed the West bank of the Jordan River. Forced to look after about 726,000
Palestinian Arab refugees, the Arab world decided to put them in camps instead of absorbing their Arab brethren. Until this very day, Israel's enemies use these refugees as
pawns in a chess game.

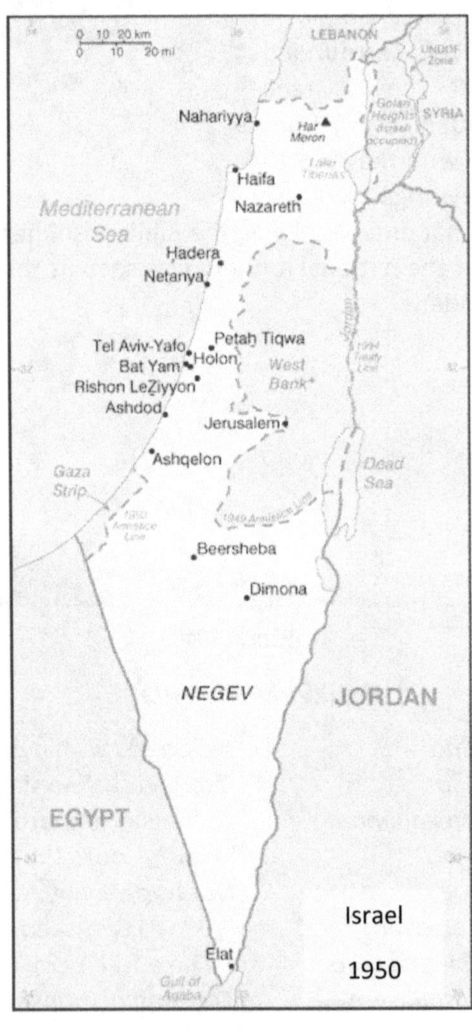

CHAPTER 21
1949-1950

During the Independence War, I became friends with a female biology student who had many friends that were active in the Haganah.

Hefzi's parents had arrived in British Mandate Palestine around 1922, during the Third Aliya. They changed their family name from Grünberg to Giladi. Hefzi's parents came from Odessa, Ukraine and her mother had been taught by famous poets like Bialik and Chernokovski. She was a Hebrew teacher, and no Russian was spoken in their home. Hefzi was born in Givatayim, Palestine. Her father worked as a carpenter in Tel Aviv, a city that was still being built during that time. Daily, he rode a donkey named *Ahasverosh* to work and because the animal knew the way, father Giladi could read a book while travelling. The family moved to Jerusalem, where Hefzi studied zoology until the outbreak of the war. When their 11-month rental contract ended, the family moved back to Tel Aviv.

The Giladi family. Hefzi's older brother was killed at Latrun in 1948

The moment the State of Israel was born, its 600,000 Jewish citizens had been forced to fight for their lives. One percent of the Jewish population, about 6,000 people, died during this Independence War. Everybody lost a family member or knew somebody that mourned a loved one. Hefzi's family also paid a high price: her brother Benyamin died during the struggle for the Latrun fortress. Before joining the CHEMED, Hefzi had been recruited by the Haganah to guard convoys on their way to Mt. Scopus. She was armed with a pistol and a hand grenade. During the war, Hefzi lost many of her high school buddies. I knew several from them from the Etzion Bloc and some of the *Lamed Heh* group that had been butchered by the Arabs.

There was no time process for this grief because previous events were so quickly replaced by new ones that I later found it difficult to remember specific situations.

Tel Aviv, November12, 1949

Dear Willy, Freddy and Frits,

This week, we received your letter and were very disappointed to read that you won't be coming. Tomorrow, Hefzi and I will travel to Haifa to welcome Mama. For me it will be the first time to meet her new husband and for Hefzi to meet her in-laws. (sounds great!)
Because Freddy had asked if we could postpone our wedding date, we had thought you would be able to come. The day before yesterday I did the oral part of my exams and even though I didn't receive the test results yet, neither from the written nor oral, I'm certain that I passed. It was such a relief, just before the wedding. The injections that were given me these last three weeks have weakened me very much. These were against the amoebas I picked up during the war. The whole family is excited getting to know the new *mishpoche*. The *Chuppah* will take place on the 22nd, because by then the exhumations in Etzion and Latrun have taken place and the *Lawayah* (funeral) will take place this week. Also from Hefzi's brother. It was rather unexpected and even though it already happened two years ago, it gave quite an upheaval. The *Yishuv* experienced the latest miracle: the 20,000 Jews from *Teman* (Yemen) have been flown in. It was called "Operation Magic Carpet". For them, if felt as if Messiah had come. From the desert, where they still lived like 2,000 years ago, by plane, something they had never seen, to the 20th century. All in one day! After the 10 to 12-year-old blind children amongst them

were operated on in Hadassah hospital they were able to see for the first time in their lives! They are very good people: diligent, they are willing to take on everything, have good brains and not many demands. They are also wise. Many of them already live in the abandoned Arab villages in the *Galil* (Galilee) and work there. Presently, women in the big cities collect clothes for them because they arrived from the *Galut* almost naked.

From Freddy's description, I understand he is very busy, but I'm very sorry this prevents you from being here. Also, a pity you didn't write me when you were going to the States, for then I could have asked for several things that wouldn't have taken you a lot of time. I don't know if January will be a suitable month to come here because it is winter. I don't know how long Mama will stay here but after she leaves we can house you in our second room....

I also wrote to Mijntje. I don't have David's address, neither that of uncle Jacob. Can you please convey our warm greetings to them and tell them about the *Chupah*?

In one of my earlier letters I asked you, Freddy, about the sale of the stocks but you didn't answer me. Another request: I want to introduce you to my in-laws but don't have a picture of you and Frits. I don't know him well, so can you also send a picture of him? Warm greetings, and see you later in the next letter.

Warm greetings to Annie and her mother. Don't forget!!! Write to my new address; Weisel street 18, Tel Aviv.

Harry veHefzibah   חפציבה והרי

With the War over, Hefzi and I could finally make wedding plans. However, my bride-to-be was not willing to take on the name 'Klafter'.

"Do you know what that means in corrupted Hebrew?" she said. "Somebody who always has to say something about everything."

During that time, it was common for new immigrants to choose a Hebrew name.

My first name wasn't a problem, for according to Jewish custom, I received a Hebrew name at my *Brit Milah* (circumcision). I was named after my grandfather: Zvi. Finding a suitable family name was not easy, until one day we passed a train station and read its name: "Eyal". So now you know how Harry Klafter became Zvi Eyal.

During the war's many ceasefires, both Hefzi and I were able to continue our studies within the CHEMED framework and write our theses. I was coached by the same teachers from the closed Hebrew University in Jerusalem. Before our wedding, another Chemed soldier and I shared the apartment of a 'Habima' actor in the Dov Hoss street.

The young state of Israel now faced a new challenge: absorbing thousands of new immigrants. They came from all corners of the earth: from devastated Europa to the Arab countries. The growing anti-Semitism forced many Jews to flee and leave all their belongings behind. Only one country was willing to receive them: Israel!

> *"Israel has the biggest arms of the world,*
> *embracing and welcoming each homeless Jew."*
> **Ruth Gruber**

Because there were not enough homes, the Yemenite, Iraqi and Moroccan Jews were housed in tent camps - *Ma'abarot*. In 1950, one tenth of Israel's population either lived in tents, huts or army camps.

An austerity – *Tzenah* - plan was needed to cope with this challenge. Most products were rationed and only available with food coupons. It was the only way to provide everybody in Israel with necessities. Minister Dov Yosef was given the ungrateful task to fulfil this plan.

The monthly ration of meat consisted more of bones than meat. People received a few eggs per week. Officially, everybody was supposed to receive one glass of milk, but due to shortages, it was only given to children. To buy clothes, shoes or textile you needed coupons. The only food available without a coupon was bread – there was no limit to the amount of loaves you could buy.

With all this scarcity, we had to be very inventive to prepare for our wedding. The *Chupah* took place in a WIZO restaurant and a family member took the wedding pictures. I was grateful that my mother and her second husband were present at the wedding and also Michael Feldman, Hefzi's fellow zoology student and our fellow CHEMED soldier.

Front row left to right: Hefzi's parents, Mr. Krochmal and my mother

Tel Aviv, January 3, 1950

Dear Freddy and Willy,

Your letter surprised and made us happy at the same time. By now, our parents will have returned and told you all about their impressions. We didn't receive news yet of their safe arrival. I must say that from letters one cannot pick up much and being rather displeased, I have given Mama a piece of my mind. That is why I didn't expect you to write such a letter, hence my surprise. If that is the case, even better! I think your plan is a good one but think it's better not to take Willy, or at least only for a few weeks or a month. You can prepare everything for your trip but Willy has to acclimatize and for women, it's usually more difficult in the beginning. Willingness is most important. You know everything is very expensive here. We earn about 100 pounds per month and can manage with that, but you cannot do excessive things.

The satisfaction of being able to live in your own country and the feeling to be part of building it up, having its own atmosphere, sharing sorrow and joys, that is the background of the life for which you must make sacrifices. That which has not been reached by effort won't give you lasting joy, and only that, for which sacrifices have been made, can become a part of life's content. You have to separate two things: either build a factory here or find a job. A job allowing you to expand your capacities will expect things from you, and I don't think you can begin something with the pre-conceived idea of leaving it again. Perhaps combinations are possible. Besides the relationships you yourself have established, I surely will be able to introduce you to different trade groups and bring you into contact with people who can bring you up to date about everything related to business. These are people with positions. My father- in- law also will be able to give you whatever helpful information you'll need. Because he came here 36 years ago, during the 3rd Aliyah, he now has many connections. I also know trade union leaders, people with business knowledge who can run a factory. The industry is growing and there are few trained workers. I don't think it will be difficult.

A pity you won't be able to come because of the room which we have to rent out. We expected you to come in January. I wrote earlier that you would save a lot of time by bringing your own car, even for the short time you'll be staying. The connections are bad and busses always filled to overflowing. Now about our plans:

Until October this year we are bound to the army; then we take our last exams and receive our diplomas… After that, there are several possibilities.

First: if I decide to continue studying, then we both will get our doctorates.
We can do that in *Eretz* or abroad. If we chose to go abroad then it will be either America or Holland. In case we decide to stay connected to the Army they
may sent us out. The down side of that is that we have to commit to several
years, and we don't feel like it at the moment. This means we'll have to be self
-supporting. In Amerika, this will be a lot of money – we'll need two years-
and in Holland this will be easier. The best way in choosing a scientific career
is to choose the best city, because this automatically will decide the rest. The
wide ranged specialty makes it impossible to change. On the other hand, when
you wrote about factories I thought about the possibility of going more into
your direction. We can better talk about it when you are here. Now I have another request: beginning next week I will start working at the Weizman institute and will daily lose 3 hours travelling to and fro by bus. I arrive home
so tired that I'm unable to continue studying at night. By car, the journey is
only 20 minutes and we would have an easier connection to Jerusalem, where
our parents live. In short: we could use a car, a small one, 10 or 20 HP, either a
Fiat or Citroen or something like that. I have no idea if this would have to
come from Holland or France, so I don't know if my question is feasible. I
would like to buy it with the money I have in the Netherlands. Here, it is too
expensive and very difficult to get a license or buy one... because new jeeps are
imported from America, we are not able to buy them. That is why I first want
to know if it's even possible, and then we'll hear if the time is right. In the
meantime, I received a letter from Mama and I am happy she arrived safe and
sound. This week, they opened an office at the trade department that gives
information to all foreign entrepreneurs who want to start a business here.
 "In closing, I want to share this quote, "In communion with others the human
personality can reach its fullest potential. The highest administration of pow-
ers and capacities only flourishes when work has become an integral part of
the community...."
Warm greetings,

       Harry veHefzibah.

Out of practical and economical reasons we moved in with Hefzi's parents in the Weisel street in Tel Aviv. In 1950, I received my masters in biochemistry and microbiology. My thesis was about freeze-drying bacteria. As I wrote in my letter to Freddy, we decided to leave CHEMED in October that year.

Hefzi had finished her studies before me. She now worked in a laboratory of the Hebrew University in Jerusalem. Because of our plans to continue our studies in the Netherlands, Professor Kluiver in Delft wrote me a letter of introduction. Hefzi and I began preparing for our journey to the Netherlands.

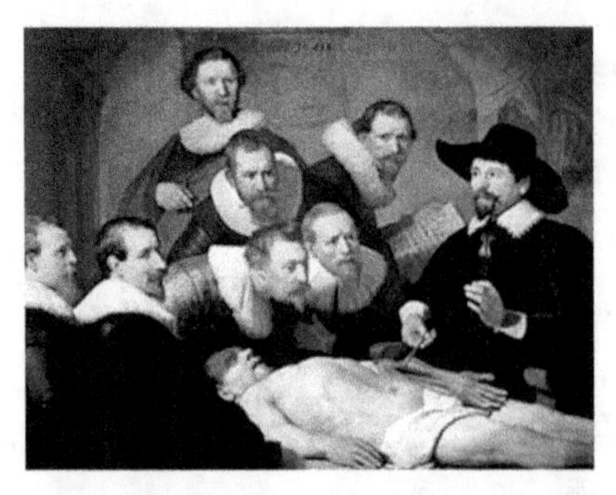

Our CHEMED friends gave us an original wedding present – a variation of the "Anatomical lesson" from NicolaesTulp. I'm in a machine which I used to do my research during that time.

Left: the original painting

CHAPTER 22
Netherlands 1950

During the boat ride from Haifa to Marseille, I had lots of time to think about the continuation of my chemistry studies. Chaim Weizman and Dries Querido were still my big examples, but deep in my heart, I knew that I lacked the talent to continue in this field of expertise. On the other hand, I loved to interact with people and preferred to become a doctor. Sharing my ideas and longings with Hefzi, to my surprise, she took it very well.

"When we get to Utrecht, you should immediately inquire about the possibilities," she encouraged me.

From Marseille, we travelled by train to the Netherlands. Hefzi had never been abroad and she feasted her eyes on everything she saw.

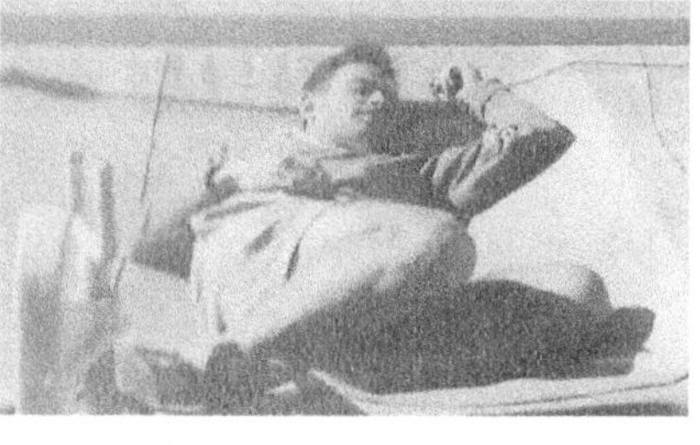

Upon arrival at Utrecht Central Station, I realized we didn't have money for a taxi. Not allowed to export money from Israel we had not been able to buy dollars. After explaining the situation to the taxi driver, the man drove us to the De Ruyterstraat. Mother paid the fare and we were overjoyed to see each other again.

The next day, I immediately made inquiries and was thrilled to hear that it was possible to continue studying for doctor. Because we arrived in Utrecht during the summer holidays, I could get a crash course botany and zoology and within a month could do my propedeuse. (A diploma obtained after completion of a first year's (preparatory) study at some European universities.)

Thanks to my Masters of Science in chemistry, I could start the second year and noticed I was one of the oldest students. After passing my Bachelor's neurology and gynecology exams and my preliminary Master's examination, I felt like a fish in the water.

My mother didn't have room for us to stay so Hefzi and I rented a room on the third floor of a house belonging to two sisters and a brother, all bachelors. As the simple room had no running water, we used a jug to wash ourselves. One day, the alcoholic brother died in his sleep. One of the sisters immediately called me, but the only thing I could do was pronounce him dead.

For Hefzi, those first weeks in the Netherlands were one surprise after another. In Israel, she had never worn lipstick, which was normal in the Netherlands. After a few weeks, the newness had worn off and she felt rested enough to get to work. However, her Dutch was not sufficient to continue studying in Utrecht. Through my studies, I came into contact with Peter van Nieuwkoop, the director of UNESCO's international center for embryology. Hefzi immediately felt at home there, even more so because he looked like a sabra, including sloppy clothes. By working together with people from different countries, a.o. from India and Indonesia, Hefzi was introduced to experimental embryology and at the same time learned to speak Dutch. Hefzi's promotion was according to a strict protocol: she had to defend ten hypotheses in front of a senate holding court in the stately, historical auditorium of the University of Utrecht. There were Paranymphs[1] and the professors wore robes of office.

Wearing a rented tux with top hat and Hefzi a Yemenite dress, we were taken by horse drawn carriage to the Pays Bas-restaurant. In the most luxurious eatery of Utrecht, we gave a dinner in honor of the official guests. It was such a strange thought: Zvi, the medicine student was now married to a Doctor!

I tried to spend my free time as best as possible. During the holidays, I took a train to Rotterdam to enhance my anatomy knowledge in the dissection room of the pathological institute. That is how I got involved with surgery. In the Utrecht 'Oog en Al' hospital, the surgeon permitted me to help him during surgeries. This physician, who also worked in the Catholic St. Antonius hospital, let me hold the retractors. These forceps keep the wound open so the surgeon can work better.

The doctor cursed terribly and each time the doctor said something irreverent, the nurse standing behind him quickly crossed herself.

Despite the intensive studies, Hefzi and I took time for a holiday. Together with a group of 15 students, we hitch-hiked to Norway, where we even swam into the Fjords. Another time, we hitch-hiked to Paris. Together with the Hubrecht-lab colleges, we cycled to the Achterhoek.

After all the hardships that we endured the years before, the time in Holland was a period of enjoyment.

1 In the Netherlands, Paranymphs (*paranimfen*) can be present at the doctoral thesis defense. This ritual originates from the ancient concept where obtaining a doctorate was seen as a de facto marriage to the university. Furthermore, the Paranymphs would also act as a backup for the doctoral candidate to ask for advice when answering questions. Today, their role is symbolic and seen as a position of honor similar to a best man or woman at a wedding.

When we were certain that Hefzi was pregnant, we immediately knew which doctor would have to deliver our child: Tus. I knew him from the time I played in the Groen family's furniture store. Tus, a much-loved family doctor in Utrecht, had many Jewish patients, including my mother.

Because of the small living space, we decided to move to a bigger room in the Buys Ballotstraat. Each night we heard the freight trains in the nearby shunting yard.

When the contractions began after an uneventful pregnancy, we cycled to the Emma clinic.

"Dr. Hardy is not in," the nurse informed us. "He had to accompany a group of pilgrims to Lourdes."

"When will he be back?" I wanted to know.

"Today. They have to change trains in Maastricht," the nurse informed us.

Later we learned what happened: the head nurse of the maternity ward made a phone call to the Maastricht train station. The moment the train from Lourdes entered the station, this announcement was heard, "Dr. Tus Hardy! You are requested to travel to Utrecht immediately. Hefzi is ready to deliver her baby!"

Tus arrived in time to assist Hefzi with the delivery of our daughter, Tali.

In those years, it was customary after giving birth that a woman stayed in bed for fourteen days. Once allowed to go outside, Hefzi showed off our beautiful daughter. The general consensus was not to spoil a baby too much and just let it cry. Thus, our daughter spent many nights in the kitchen where she could cry as much as she wanted. We found another room with a repatriated Indonesian couple. The rent also included breakfast, and when Hefzi had to go to the lab, the lady of the house offered to look after Tali and take her to the park. Since we didn't have a study allowance, my mother paid a big part of our living expenses while Hefzi's parents paid our rent. After Hefzi's promotion, there was not much she could do in the Netherlands. Before returning home, we first enjoyed a short holiday in the Alps. It gave my family the opportunity to enjoy our Tali, because nobody knew how long it would be before we would see each other again.

CHAPTER 23
Israel 1953—1963

It wasn't easy to adjust after our return to Israel in September 1953. We first moved in with my in-law's apartment in Tel Aviv. When father Giladi's newly built family home in Jerusalem was finished, I was happy to move back to my beloved city.

Experimental embryology was not a known science in Israel, therefore Hefzi received permission to open this department in Jerusalem. In Israel, someone was appointed according to qualifications and it didn't matter if you were a man or woman.

As the Jordanians did not allow the Jewish enclave on Mt. Scopus to be used, the Hebrew university's faculties and laboratories had to be spread out over forty different buildings throughout the city. The newly built campus on Givat Ram was opened only in 1958.

Where presently the Jerusalem Theater and Science Museum are located, in those days was fallow area. The only building there was a monastery that had been used by the British government as a military courthouse. Opposite was a shed with mice and other laboratory animals, part of Hefzi's zoological laboratory where she also lectured. A perfect place for us because we lived just around the corner, on Harlap 39. The first floor of the apartment building was rented out; Hefzi's parents lived on the second floor, our family with three children - Tali, Avner and Benjamin (Bibi) occupied the third floor and Hefzi's sister lived on the top floor.

Hefzi taking Tali for a walk

When the children came home from school, there was always somebody to welcome them. Because of the close proximity to Hefzi's laboratory, she always came home to have lunch with the children.

The kindergarten was in the old monastery, and somehow Avner always found a way to escape. When the unsuspecting Hefzi entered the shed with laboratory animals, she often found her little son there. The whole faculty knew about the little tyke. When Avner was a bit older, they often allowed him to join them on expeditions to catch laboratory animals.

Each morning, I walked past the animal shed on the hill, on my way to lectures in the Terra Santa building. Unfortunately, my Dutch study years were not acknowledged in Israel and I was degraded to the fourth year of medicine study. That is the reason I only graduated in 1956.

To have some additional income, I administered penicillin or streptomycin injections for *Kupat Cholim (*Israeli sick fund).

On my bicycle, I rode to the patient's address. In the Mea Shearim neighborhood, street names often were nonexistent, so I always asked where the patient lived. Thanks to these scouting expeditions I got to know the city very well.

Terra Sancta College

After the Hadassah hospital on Mt. Scopus had become inaccessible during the Independence war, director Dr. Chaim Yassky asked the leadership of the Anglican mission hospital (CMJ) in the Prophet street if Hadassah could use their building. In March 1948, the hospital was 'loaned' to the Jewish community and given the name Hadassah *Alef*.

During the Arab pogrom on a convoy of doctors, nurses and hospital workers, the beloved Dr. Yassky was also murdered. After that black day, April 13,

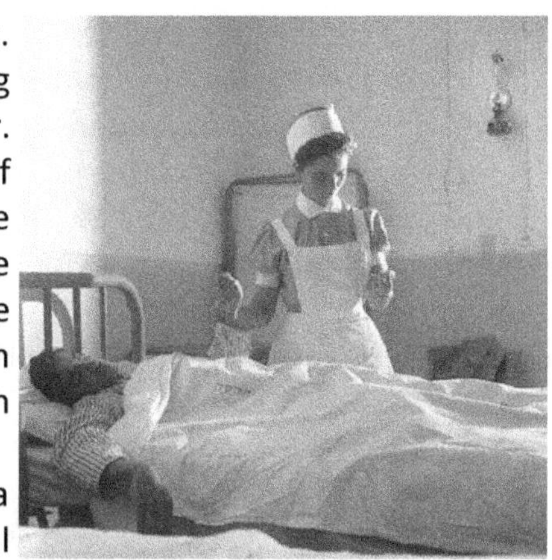
Hadassah Dalet

1948, most of the patients on Mt. Scopus were transferred to Hadassah Alef. Even the private quarters of CMJ's Canon Jones were 'confiscated': his bathroom became the delivery room and the prayer room now housed an expensive cobalt machine to radiate cancer patients. His little kitchen became the first Israeli isotope laboratory, while
x-rays were developed in the damp cellar.

The gynecology and maternity wards were part of Hadassah *Alef* as well. During the Independence War, also Hadassah *Beet* (B) was created. Tuberculosis patients were treated in Hadassah 'C', while 'D', the internal ward, was in a dilapidated building that once had been the harem of the Turkish governor. Later it had become a boarding school for girls, *Beit ha Degel*— House of the Flag. Department 'E' was in the old German-Lutheran hospital, called "Ziv", which later became the maternity ward of the *Bikur Cholim* hospital. During my studies, surgical patients were nursed there. The dermatology department was in the abandoned Arab leprosy (Hansen) hospital. Hadassah had the use of about 452 beds. The highest occupancy was 298.4%!

Most of the professors teaching at the medical training institute studied in Europe. Due to the Second World War, the European medical world was lacking behind, while America heavily invested in medical training and research. Before WWII, American medical students received their training in Germany or Vienna, now the opposite happened. The Hadassah management choose to give medical training according to the American model. The curriculum, however, stayed the same as that of Europe: a study of six years, including the pre-medical sciences.

Beit haDegel's wooden lecture hall was boiling hot in summer and freezing cold in winter. One of the well-known doctors studying here was Shmuel Nissan. Part of my lectures were giving in a group of buildings that now is City Hall. The Connet House (previous British institute) contained the zoology, anatomy and pathology laboratories. Zoology looked out over the Old City, the French Hospital and the Notre Dame building.

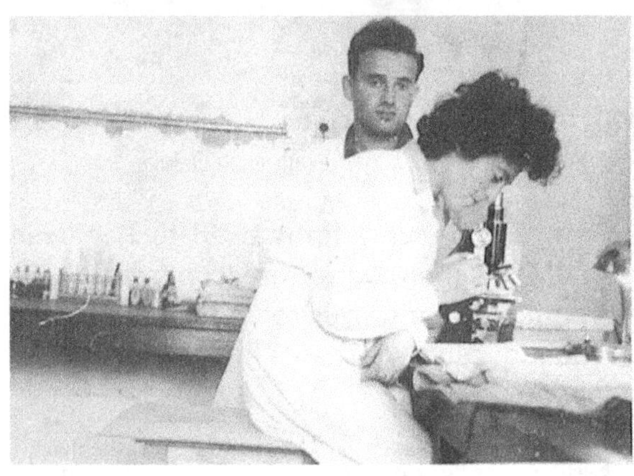

My last study year consisted of practical internship at different hospital wards. My first delivery was on the maternity ward in Hadassah *Alef,* and my father-in-law died in *Beit haDegel.* These life and death experiences helped blossom my medical feelings.

How well I remember my first patient: a young girl suffering from leukemia. I still can see the faces of her family when she passed away. Her father was a police officer and they had a Spanish surname.

During my internship, my father-in-law suffered a massive heart attack. He was nursed in a double room for very ill patients. There were two internal medicine wards: *Pnimiet Alef* and *Beth.* Father Giladi was on *Alef* where the internists treated their patients in a conservative matter. Powerless, I watched my father-in-law struggling for breath, unable to do anything to lighten his suffering. Since I was only a student, I asked the cardiologist at *Pnimiet Beet* if there was hope for my father-in-law. The specialist shook his head. I became the liaison of the family waiting in the corridor and my father-in-law. Lacking experience and not being allowed to do anything, I stayed with my dying father-in-law until the very end.

During my gynecology internship, I had to attend five deliveries and was amazed that the mothers trusted me completely, even though I was only a student who hardly knew anything.

During my internship on the internal ward in *Beit haDegel,* I encountered a consulting surgeon who was also a department head.

Being used to the Dutch surgeons, who were seen and treated as half-gods, I was amazed at this aristocratic, genial American Doctor: Nathan Saltz. Compared to the Sabra's he always dressed properly, and wore a necktie with a pin. This surgeon didn't treat me like a subordinate but like an equal. I never forgot that meeting, which made a deep impression on me.

In 1956, the moment finally arrived that I was sworn in as a Hebrew doctor. The Hebrew version of the Hippocratic oath consists of the traditional part, but Greek gods do not play a role in the obligation an Israeli doctor has for his patient and profession.

Already during my studies, the desire began to grow to become a surgeon. However, before I could continue my studies I first had to get experience as a general practitioner. For one year, I worked in a
ma'abara, an absorption camp for new immigrants near Beit Shemesh. Israel's first development town was established in 1950, and about 13 miles from Jerusalem. The residents of the nearby Hartuf came from Bulgaria, Iran, Iraq, Rumania, Morocco and Kurdistan.

Four doctors were responsible for the group of settlements and *ma'abarot* that could only be reached by jeep. I always enjoyed those rides through the hills. In spring, they were full of flowers and I often spotted gazelles, once in a while even porcupines.

The clinic and our office were in Beit Shemesh. While on duty I slept in the clinic's small room with only a bed and a shower. During one of my night shifts, somebody knocked on the door. When I opened, there was a group of people with a young woman. The rigid patient must have been about seventeen years old.

Hartuf cement factory

"Doctor! She doesn't eat anymore and also refuses to drink," the frantic mother said.

Recognizing symptoms of hysteria, I pushed the fully dressed girl under the cold shower. She was healed immediately! One of the unusual patients I treated there was a goat with inflamed udders. The owner figured I would know how to treat that problem.

"Can you give me a note stating I am sick and unable to work?" a laborer asked me one day. Realizing the man was as healthy as could be, I responded, "Sorry, but I refuse to do that."

"What?" the man exclaimed. "Well, you Israeli doctors are very different from where I came from. They would have given me such a note immediately!"

On the other hand, some patients saw me as some kind of god.

"Doctor! You have to come immediately!" The agitated family insisted. "A woman is having a baby but the child isn't coming!"

"Why didn't she go to the hospital to have her baby?" I wanted to know.

"She refused. She wanted her own midwife to do the delivery. You HAVE to come immediately!"

Taking the jeep, I quickly drove to the woman in need, who was surrounded by family members. I had no idea what I could do in this situation, but to give them the impression that I knew what I was doing, I began by palpating her belly. To the surprise of everyone, mine included, the baby was born spontaneously! Promptly, they called me the miracle doctor!

Emigration to Israel had caused the family structure to become unglued for many population groups and therefore the source of many illnesses in the *ma'abarot* were emotional and social. The immigrants struggled with all the changes in their living conditions. Added to that, Jews from Arab countries were physically in a bad condition.

My colleagues and I faced enormous challenges and were sometimes accused of discrimination.

In 1957, I began my six-year training to become a surgeon. During this time, I had to do internships on different wards like neurosurgery, urology and one month of anesthesia. Studying in an academic hospital meant I also had to give lectures and do research. I would only receive my tenure after obtaining a university degree.

During my first internship at Neurosurgery, I wondered how the treatment of the psycho-pharmaceutical chlorpromazine influenced pregnant patients. Could this medication influence the nerve system and brains of the unborn baby? I asked Hefzi, who at that time researched the embryonic nerve system. Both Hefzi and I published our findings.

During my anesthesia internship in Beersheba, for a few weeks, I worked alongside a Dutch pediatrician. The children ward existed of two barracks: one for diarrhea patients and the other was for children with pneumonia. Since it was summer and most children were dehydrated, day and night I was busy inserting IV's. As it is very difficult to insert a needle into the vein of a very sick child, most of the infusions were administered to their heads. To prevent them from removing the needle, we usually fixated it with tape and plaster. During those chaotic weeks, I also had to administer anesthesia on the maternity ward. With fear and trembling, I held the mask with laughing gas to the face of the woman. There was nobody to advise me or tell me what I should or shouldn't do. I carried the full responsibility.

Dr. Groen I knew from my time in hiding in Amsterdam. Dr. Groen and his college, dr. Bastiaans, became the founding fathers of the psycho-pharmacy. After Dr. Groen had become a department head, he offered me to come and study under him. For a time I struggled with this dilemma. What should I do? Take Dr. Groen's appealing offer or choose surgery?

During a night shift in the Ziv hospital, I shared my dilemma with two older friends who were assistant surgeons.

"I don't think there will be work for you when you finally finish your surgeon training," Rumanian born Wishnitzer told me. "It's only a small country and all the positions on the wards are already filled, especially with all these doctors and surgeons amongst the new immigrants."
I knew he was right. It wasn't a happy thought.

"Sorry, but I disagree," also Romanian born Pfau responded. "Zvi, you have to do what you love, and don't think about what could happen in the future. You have to do what your heart tells you to do!"

It suddenly became crystal clear: I wanted to become a surgeon!

And Dr. Pfau? Later he became head of the urological department.

It was such a special experience being able to assist Professor Jozef during an operation. This New Zealand born surgeon had saved my arm after I had been wounded in Gush Etzion. During the First World War, he fought in Gallipoli, then emigrated to Mandate Palestine and was now a highly-qualified surgeon in Hadassah.

Despite being a brilliant surgeon, remembering names wasn't his strongest point. He often called me, "Dr. Ayal" or "Dr. El Al" but never "Eyal." It seemed to be 'normal' amongst surgeons, for later I too had trouble remembering the names of my patients.

Even though the newly built Hadassah hospital in Ein Kerem was finished in 1961, it took nine months before the last patient was transferred. In 1962, the 'borrowed' buildings were returned to the CMJ. Thanks to their help, the Hadassah hospital had been able to keep functioning those fourteen years.

The Eichman process was held in Jerusalem in April 1961, the month in which the State of Israel turned 13. The *Mossad* had kidnapped Adolf Eichman in Argentina and brought him to Israel for sentencing. His court case revealed the horrors of the Holocaust and only now sabras began to understand what the camp survivors had been going through.

CHAPTER 24
Minnesota 1963-1964

Our children weren't too happy that both their parents were pursuing academic careers. Thankfully, the fact that we lived in a 'family' house gave them a reasonably normal youth. Once a week after school, the children went to the home of Hannah Yakhin, a Dutch artist who lived opposite the Mahane Yehudah market. Our second child, Avner, always found it hard to sit still. He preferred to play outside or with the animals in his mother's laboratory. He must have been about seven years old when we were driving the car one day when he yelled, "Stop!"

I hit the brakes. "What happened? What's the matter?" I demanded to know.

"I saw a lizard, Papa," Avner's face beamed.

One day, our animal lover took a big black, non-poisonous snake home. It escaped and found a haven between the box springs of the heavy armchair. It was quite a challenge to remove the snake from there. The first thing Hefzi often said to me when I came home after a long day, "Do you know what your son did today?"

Somehow, Avner always reminded me of Dik Trom (a book series about a mischievous oversized Dutch boy – 'Chubby Drums' in English). Avner was an extraordinary child; indeed he was!

In 1963, our whole family, including an Israeli au-pair, flew to the United States for a sabbatical. In Minnesota, our children attended an American school and learned to speak English in record time. Due to my status as a 'senior lecturer,' I had been granted this sabbatical. For me, it was a golden chance to do research at the Minnesota university, during that time the 'Mecca' of surgery.

Thanks to the letters of recommendation from both Professor Wangensteen and professor Saltz, I even received a study allowance. Professor Owen H. Wangensteen was a pioneer in the development of modern surgery. Many surgeons studying under him became academic department heads. While I did my research under Wangensteen, Hefzi researched a new embryology branch at a different department. The knowledge she gleaned there was later further developed in Israel.

Bibi, Tali and a friend

Most of Wangensteen's surgeons were Ph.D students, but that didn't appeal to me. The ideas from the research laboratory were honed and improved in the Mayo Clinic. In the lab, I worked together with Charles Mayo, one of the heirs of the private clinic. It was quite an experience to be invited to the estate of his parents – for me is strange and luxurious world.

"Our son is a good guy but we don't approve that his surgical carrier isn't his highest priority," Charles' parents confided in me. I knew he rather worked on his car collection and to enjoy life.

Gastric freezing was used to treat certain intestinal problems. Reading many published articles on the subject left me with a lot of question. I noticed that most treatments were given to patients from Minnesota, many of Scandinavian descent. These people trusted their physician completely and did exactly what they were told.

"Thank you very much," the patient even said after I inserted the drain and began pumping the minus 104 Fahrenheit fluid nitrogen into his stomach. It must have been a very unpleasant experience.

Not used to mince my words, I asked during one of the group meetings, "I question the conclusions of these experiments."

"I think Dr. Eyal doesn't like gastric freezing," Wangensteen responded.

Sensing the warning in his words, I decided to hold my tongue.

Colleagues in training tried to warn me, "Listen, Eyal! Whatever you do, Wangensteen is the one who can make or break your career."

"If you want to reach the top, you better keep your mouth shut," another colleague advised. "All academic positions run via Wangensteen."
Not planning to find work in the USA, I thankfully didn't need Wangensteen's influence. Realizing that I could only share my doubts with a neutral party, I began looking for academics that were not connected with the Minnesota University.

"Can you bring me into contact with someone who does research in clinical surgery?" I asked Charles Mayo.

"Why's that?"
Charles I could trust, so I shared my findings and question marks. "You could be right, you know," he affirmed. During this time, my Hadassah friend Joe Borman was in Los Angeles specializing in open-heart-surgery.

"Can you arrange an appointment with Martin Grossman for me?" I asked him.

Martin Grossman was editor of the prestigious gastroenterology magazine. Making the appointment was one thing, getting to Los Angeles was another story. I heard about car rental agencies that needed a driver to bring a car to a certain city – the so-called 'drive-away' cars.

Around midnight I said good-bye to a group of people who had come to Minnesota for a Hadassah fundraising event, and began the long journey to San Francisco. After delivering the car I continued my journey to Los Angeles.

"Here, take my car," Joe offered. It was an old vehicle and the rubber padding of the gas pedal fell off constantly. Overwhelmed by the ten lanes on the highway, I had no idea which exit to take. Exactly the moment I drove onto a junction, the rubber fell off the gas pedal. Desperately I tried to put it back as quick as possible. Then I heard the police siren.
The angry policeman wanted to confiscate my driver's license but because I was a foreigner, he let me go with only a warning.

To my great relief, I arrived at Martin Grossman in one piece. He confirmed my conclusions about gastric freezing. Relieved, I began the long journey back to Minneapolis.

Without a doubt, Wangensteen was a surgeon who did much for the development of surgery in America. However, I was determined to stick to my vision. Suddenly, I saw the whole academic world in a new light.

It reminded me of a similar situation in Westerbork and in Andersen's fairy tale, "The Emperor's new clothes". In the case of gastric freezing, everybody tried to appease Wangensteen. Facts that not had been tested in a scientifically responsible way should not be accepted without question. An experiment in an animal lab resulted in the interpretation of the scientist. Such an observation had to be backed up with statistical figures and critical thought. Personal shortcomings, prejudice and pet topics had to be cross examined. Political correctness was disastrous for scientific research.

Not being dependent on the American system, I decided to spill my beans. During the next meeting, I informed Wangensteen that I no longer wanted to do research under him. I had learned a lot during this period and even found a therapy that could prevent the development of a gastric ulcer. Years later, I asked someone about the gastric freezing research. He told me that the fiasco had been covered up.

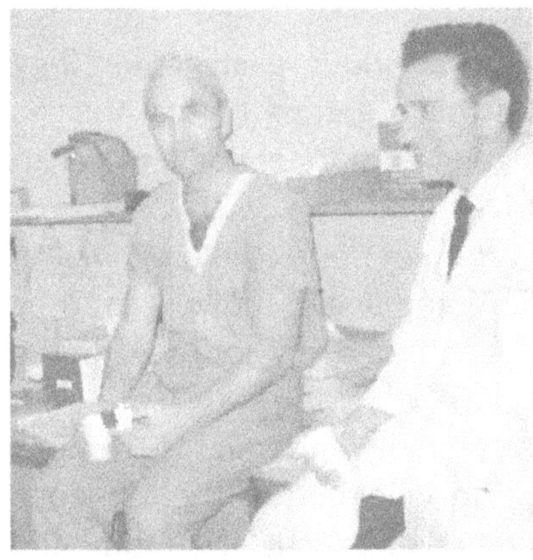

Richard Lillehei

Each of the three Lillehei brothers had their own research laboratory. Richard Lillehei worked on shock treatment, organ preservation, open heart surgeries and kidney transplantations. Since this subject greatly appealed to me, I decided to work in his laboratory. During that time, they used under-cooling to preserve harvested organs before a transplantation and were searched for a solution to extent the sustainability and prevent organ rejection after a transplantation.

Due to its many attributes, I suggested they test chlorpromazine. Hefzi and I had planned to stay only one year in the USA, but the present interesting discoveries could not be left. We decided that Hefzi and the children would return home to Israel and I would extend my research with another year.

> **The high road to servanthood is walked with integrity, empathy and understanding. People don't care how much we know, until they realize how much we care.**

CHAPTER 25
Israel 1965 – 1967

In 1965, I was back in Jerusalem and began working in the new Hadassah Ein Kerem hospital on Surgery *Alef* on the third floor. Professor Nathan Saltz was head of this department. I continued with the research I began in Minnesota and published an article about treatment with rheomacrodex.

My colleague and friend Wishnitzer also studied this subject, but in Boston. "Let's compare our methods and findings," he suggested.

Olesh Gilon, with whom I had served in the same unit in 1948, now worked as an internist in the Tel Hashomer hospital and was also the head of IDF's medical services.

"How do you treat wounded soldiers that are in shock?" I asked him. From what he told me I realized we were behind in our knowledge of the pathophysiological results of traumatic shock. As a result, our wounded soldiers were not given the correct treatment.

When Olesh heard about my Minnesota research, he promptly invited me to share my finding with the heads of the medical army departments. The many lectures I gave about modern shock treatment brought big changes within the medical corps. Despite their blood loss, most of our wounded soldiers now stayed alive because they received the correct intravenous solutions.

Again, our little country had to prepare for another war. Immediately extra infusion solutions were ordered from Switzerland. These were stored in glass lemonade bottles, ready for use.

Because a surgeon could only be attached to a medical army corps if he was an officer, I had to attend the basic course for non-combatants.

In my new function as medical army officer and surgeon I now was responsible for the mobile field hospital that followed the troops.

1 Rheomacrodex (Dextran '40') is an intravenous liquid that contains both NaCl (natriumchloride) as well as glucose. It is administered after a major blood loss (volume re-plenishment), as artificial blood during operations and to prevent thrombosis after operations.

"The Egyptians could run to Egypt, the Syrians into Syria. The only place we could run was into the sea, and before we did that we might as well fight."
Golda Meir

Olesh Gilon and Zvi

"To be or not to be is not a question of compromise.
Either you be or you don't be."
Golda Meir

SIX DAY WAR

The moment that Egypt, Jordan, Syria and Iraq signed a military treaty with each other, everybody knew another war was on the horizon. When Egypt closed the Suez Canal to Israeli ships and sent the UN troops stationed in the Gaza Strip away, war seemed inevitable. On May 26, Egyptian President Nasser declared, "It will be a total war, it's main goal the destruction of Israel. We are sure that we will win...."
King Hussein also signed a military treaty with his previous enemy, Nasser. A wave of excitement spread over the Arab world; in mosques, the mullahs whipped the masses to a frenzy with "*Yihad*! – holy war." Again, little Israel was alone. Our lives were threatened. Again. All the reservists were mobilized and a unity government formed under leadership of Prime Minister Levi Eshkol and Moshe Dayan as minister of Defense.
The Israeli population didn't harbor any illusions about the alternative: we had to win this war! Thus, instead of packing for the summer holidays, each Jewish home had a weekend bag ready in case the air raid sirens sounded and mothers and their children had to make a run for the air raid shelters. Hotels emptied from tourists were converted into first -aid stations. The two-and-a-half million Jews felt a common responsible for the survival of the Jewish State.

The large tents didn't have air condition and in the operating theater it was boiling hot, but we didn't have a choice. During the three 'quiet' weeks I visited several army units to make sure they were stocked with sufficient intravenous solutions.

The war began on June 5, 1967 when the IAF, the Israeli Air Force, attacked the airports of Egypt, Jordan, Iraq and Syria. The surprise attacks gave Israel a tremendous head start.

In the operation 'theater' tent

My anesthesiologist (right) was a maxillary surgeon in daily life

Three armored divisions totaling 70,000 camouflaged soldiers and 700 tanks waited at the Egyptian border. The most northern divisions, consisting of three brigades, was under the command of Major General Israel Tal. Each division had its own field hospital; I was responsible for the Tal division, the "*Ugda*".

Tal's troops took the shortest route through the Sinai to the Suez Canal and despite heavy losses, managed to capture Rafah and Khan Yunis. After the first Israeli breakthrough, wounded soldiers began arriving at the field hospital. Because there was no room in the tents to nurse the wounded soldiers, they were transported as soon as possible by helicopter to a big hospital. I only performed the most necessary operations and treated life-threatening injuries, e.g. by amputating an arm.

Because many tanks were involved in the combat there were many burn victims. In these wounded soldiers, it was very difficult to insert a metal intravenous needle – the thin disposable needles were not invented yet.

In total, Jerusalem's Hadassah hospital admitted more than 900 wounded people: Israeli soldiers, prisoners of war and Arab speaking patients. Professor Saltz had instructed his personal how to categorize the wounded according to a special protocol – triage[2].

---

[2] Triage is the assignment of degrees of urgency to wounds or illnesses, to decide the order of treatment of a large number of patients or casualties. In war time, triage is being done by a general surgeon or a trauma expert.

The surgical staff worked more than fourteen days non-stop to tread the wounded that were being brought in by helicopter. Because half of the medical staff had been called up as reservists, there was not enough medical personnel.

Thankfully, volunteers began to lend a helping hand. High school students transported patients from the ward to the operating theater and vice versa. Not only local doctors offered their services, but also specialists from abroad arrived and helped to operate. Many American volunteers arrived, Jews and non-Jews and a lot of students. Thanks to the help of almost 2,000 volunteers the hospital was able to keep functioning during this difficult time. The civilized world that sympathized with the Jewish people, created a feeling of brotherhood.

The Six Day War transformed the historical picture of the Jewish people, Zionism and the Jewish State. Thanks to the victory we could return to Mt. Scopus with the Hebrew University and the Hadassah hospital. The biggest miracle however was that Jerusalem had been reunited!

"Wouldn't it be fantastic to buy a house in the *Rova*?" I asked Hefzi. She didn't mind living in the rebuild Jewish Quarter of the Old City of Jerusalem.

June 6 and 7, Ariel Sharon, Tal and a third brigade raced west. Tal's units stopped at different points on the Suez Canal.

A big part of the Egyptian troops had been cut off from their units. In the oppressive heat, the Egyptians foot soldiers had to walk 124 miles in the direction of the Canal. Thousands of them died because of lack of water. Because many soldiers had surrendered to the Israelis, their own food supplies and water also ran out quickly. The army leadership decided to keep the Egyptian officers as prisoners of war and free the rest. Those officers could later be exchanged for Jewish POW's. By June 8, the whole Sinai was in Jewish hands. June 10, the last offensive on the Golan Heights was completed. A day later the cease fire was signed. Israel now had the Gaza strip, the Sinai, the West Bank of the Jordan, including East Jerusalem, and the Golan Heights. The political importance of the Six Day War was tremendous, because little Israel had shown how to defend herself against an a superior enemy. The country was celebrating!

Joyful dancing at the Kotel,
June 1967

Finally, the Jewish people were able to pray again at the Kotel,
June 16, 1967

Mandelbaum Gate in 1964, then
the entrance gate to Jordanian
occupied East Jerusalem. In 1967,
after 19 long years, Jerusalem was
finally reunited.

Chapter 26
Israel 1967-1973

As secretary of the Israeli Association of Surgeons (IAS), I joined a group of colleagues for a medical congress in Moscow. Only because the international organizers demanded the attendance of Israelis, we were amongst the first Israelis allowed to visit Brezhnev's Russia. The ministry of Foreign affairs had asked us to take many tefillin (phylacteries), prayer books and Hebrew Bibles in our suitcases. We were tense, for if the Russian custom officers would find out, they would bar us from entering the country. Thankfully, we managed to smuggle everything into the country. The first days were spent on tourist attractions, like visiting the ship in Leningrad's harbor, where in 1917 the revolution had started.

From left to right: Prof. Ehrlich, medical school Haifa; Raffi Reis, head surgeon Beilinson hospital; Prof. Moses, head vasculair surgery Beilinson; Prof. Sefadia, head urology Beilinson; Morris Levi, open heart surgeon Beilinson, also studied in Minneapolis; myself; Prof. Joseph Borman, open heart surgeon Hadassah hospital.

The KGB kept an eye on us and I was grateful that I managed to arrange a secret meeting with a woman whose husband was in prison because he taught Hebrew. Later, I had to laugh about my naivety, thinking that the KGB didn't know about that meeting in the Leningrad park. Jo's cousin lived in an old patrician home that housed several families. The cousin and her family lived in one large room that with curtains was divided into four units. There was only one cooking plate and everyone in the house had to use the same toilet. The extreme poverty I saw there was such a contrast with the very rich Bolshoi Theater where we watched a ballet performance.

Several delegations of surgeons were welcomed at the Kremlin by the minister of Health and we were offered caviar and vodka. Each and everyone was suspect and we were warned that all hotel floors had a KGB man or woman keeping an eye on the tourists.

During the congress, Joseph (Jo) Borman and I walked around the Red Square near the Kremlin, purposely displaying our El Al bags. It didn't take long before someone circumvent approached us and whispered, "Are you Jews from Israel?"

We quickly made an appointment and that same evening we told the assembled *Refuseniks* about Israel.

I will never forget my visit to Moscow's main Synagogue where I received the big honor of being called up to read the Thora portion. At the top of my voice, I spoke the *bracha.*

A Russian-Jewish surgeon I met at the congress told me that the Russian authorities prevented him from emigrating to Israel. Since I still used my Dutch passport, I went to the Dutch Embassy and made some inquiries. The consul was willing to meet this doctor. "Meet me at this restaurant."

He wrote down the name of a big hotel on a piece of paper. At the appointment time, my Russian colleague and I entered the restaurant, only to leave it a few minutes later in the company of the Consul.

Moscow Great Synagogue

Babi Yar

Because we had to be sure that our conversation would not be overheard by the KGB, we talked while walking on the shore of the Neva River. Eventually, the Russian surgeon was able to emigrate to Israel.

The American-Jewish surgeons didn't have a problem obtaining a Russian entry visa. In Kiev, they pressured the KGB to give us permission to visit Babi Yar. Back then there was no memorial site yet, but we did receive permission to remember the Jews who had been murdered there during the Second World War. However, the American request to visit the Kiev synagogue was denied. I joined a group on a train ride to Susdal, an old Russian city where all the buildings were made of wood. My visit to Russia had been an unforgettable experience.

After selling the family business in 1965, my brother and Willy, now called Esther, moved to Israel. During the Six-Day war, they had been in contact with a group of Dutch volunteers who had flown to Israel to help. With Koos and Net Wieberdink, a surgeon and nurse from the Antonie van Leeuwenhoek (AVL) Cancer hospital in Amsterdam, we developed friendship for life. They stayed in Israel until they no longer were needed and when Koos and Net came to say good-bye, I had to promise to visit them while in the Netherlands. Koos' friendship with a surgeon in the AVL, Sally van Coevorden, opened the door for me to attend many cancer operations. The knowledge I gained during that time was later used on my own patients. Professor van Slooten was a surgical 'artist' and 'master' at the AVL and I was very impressed by his operating methods.

Professor Saltz was also chairman of the Hadassah surgical departments resident's program. Once a week, there was a clinical conference where surgeons discussed the treatment of certain patients. Once a month, we also discussed surgical patients who had died. Emotions ran high during these meetings.

Terry Davidson was a British immigrant who had studied anesthesia. While I did my research in Minnesota, Terry worked at Stanford University. Back in Israel, we talked about our experiences.

"When I administer anesthesia to children, they always fight against it," Terry told me. "I wonder if I can intubate non-anaesthetized patients when administering scoline. (A muscle relaxant.)

"I'm willing to be your guinea pig," I offered.

So, one day, Terry inserted an IV line in my vein, hooked me up to the monitor, injected the medication and intubated me. Terry used a hand pump to keep me breathing and I stayed awake during the whole procedure. It worked, for I could only move my big toe. While the specialists were debating my case, I fervently hoped Terry would not forget to keep pumping the oxygen bag.

I survived the experiment and both Terry and I publicized our successful trial.

During the 60s, an American surgeon received his diploma after his final exams. In Israel, most surgeons only received a paper from the head of the surgical department stating how long he had worked there. Those who trained in Hadassah or Tel Hashomer had received a well-rounded training. However, a surgeon from a small or backwater hospital missing the experience could not be given a job in a bigger hospital. With only this piece of paper as proof, it was difficult during the job interview to know if he had enough qualifications.   Professor Saltz agreed that my faculty should find a solution to remedy this problem. My suggestion to take surgical exams was rejected by the IMA (Israel Medical Organization). Professor Saltz headed a new commission that would enhance the quality of the surgical studies by taking voluntary examinations. One committee put together the exam that consisted of an oral part and multiple choice questions. We noticed that the first candidates were mainly surgeons who had done their training at Hadassah hospital.

My efforts and perseverance were eventually rewarded: the Ministry of Health accepted the new incentive. Encouraged, I submitted another suggestion: setting up a regional residential surgical program where a Hadassah student would also intern at Bikur Cholim hospital and vice versa. Unfortunately, this program was rejected both by the IMA and ISA because it was too expensive.

It wasn't always easy to combine my job with fatherhood.

Avner, our middle son, always had been fond of animals. Since education had never been high on his priority list, it was quite a challenge to find a suitable school for our teenager. One day, I received a phone call from the First Aid department. "Professor Eyal, you are urgently requested to come down; your son is here."

I immediately understood this had to be Avner. "What happened? Is he wounded?"

"No, Avner is all right, but he brought an owl with a broken leg."

After racing down the stairs to the first aid department, Avner told me the whole story. "I found this barn owl, Papa, and during the day, the bird sits on my shoulder and at night, I put him in my cupboard. My group leader at

Tali, Benjamin and Avner

Seder meal (Pesach) in
our home

Avner with one of his many owls.

the boarding school wanted to get rid of the owl. I told him this was not going to happen and we got into a fight. As I ducked, he hit the owl. When I saw that the bird had broken its leg, I just lost it. And now I'm expelled from school."

For the umptieth time, I thought.

Avner was still mad. "Papa, did you know that the orthopedic surgeon refused to plaster my owl's broken leg? You do it!"

There was no way around it – I had to help the wounded animal. And so it happened that for the next few weeks we had an unusual guest in our home: a barn owl with a plastered leg.

MACHON JONATHAN – the Jonathan Institute

Between 1967 and 1973 Israel struggled with many enemy infiltrations resulting in many terror attacks in Jerusalem. Day and night, the Hadassah hospital had to be ready to treat the terror victims. There was no respite for Israel's population, especially because it seemed the politicians didn't understand the consequences of these terror attacks. From 1977-1978 I was asked to partake in a public commission, the so-called Jonathan Institute, which was established to fight against international terrorism. Profession Ben Zvi Netanyahu was the founder, assisted by his son Benjamin (Bibi). Through their work, I learned to understand how international terrorism was used as a political weapon. The enemy infiltration not only endangered Israel, but the whole Western world. Not being able to understand the scope and deeper meaning of this phenomena, to me, is a lack of understanding of what happened before WWII. The same factors of denial, self-deception and self-misleading, not learning from history – all this allows our enemies to use their hostile narrative.

Family and friends of the Netanyahu's established the Jonathan Institute to research the problem of international terror and share their findings. It was in honor of Jonathan (Yoni) Netanyahu, who was killed during the rescue operation of the Entebbe hostage crisis in Uganda. When Benjamin (Bibi) entered politics, *Machon Jonathan* ceased to exist.

Israel's victory of the 6-day war had stuck like a fish bone in the throat of the Arab world. After the Khartoum meeting, Israel's enemies began preparing for the next war. In May 1973, the IDF was fully alerted when Egyptian troops advanced to the Suez Canal. The alarm was revoked when it became clear the Egyptian army wasn't preparing for war. After the two month summer holiday, Israeli schools opened as usual on September 1st. Everybody looked forward to the Jewish holidays: *Rosh Hashanah* (Jewish New Year), *Yom Kippur* (Day of Atonement) and *Sukkot* (Feast of Tabernacles). The civilian population was not aware of the dangers, but the army leadership kept a sharp eye on the Egyptian and Syrian borders. To prevent international repercussions, the government chose to wait instead of attacking first. In times of war, Israel's standing army of 80,000 soldiers war was supplemented with 300,000 reservists. The country's leaders decided not to announce a full mobilization, because this would paralyze civil life. Reservists usually received a written call-up, stating when and where they had to report for duty. By way of radio, newspapers, posters, letters and telegrams, reservists could be mobilized between 48 and 72 hours.

CHAPTER 27
Yom Kippur War

In the eyes of the Jewish, *Yom Kippur* 1973 was considered a double holy day because it fell on a Shabbat. That year, the Day of Atonement also coincided with the tenth day of Ramadan. Not only did Muslims celebrate Mohammed's first victory in his Yihad, holy war, but also commemorated the battle of Badr. In the year 624 BCE, the citizens of Mecca had been forced to become Muslims or die.

The most holy day of the Jewish year began in the evening of October 6. Public life came to a standstill: busses stopped running, there were no cars on the road and both the airport and harbors were closed. There we no broadcasts on Israeli radio and TV.

Yom Kippur at the Kotel

Preparations of the Arab attack had been top secret. Officers had only been briefed the week before, while soldiers were told a few hours before the attack. The Egyptian army staff named the attack on Israel "Operation Badr"; the invasion was synchronized by way of a telegram to the Syrian defense minister. The telegram contained one word: "Badr".

Israel's enemies were certain this attack would be a military victory for the Arab world and a religious victory for Islam.

That Saturday morning, while Jews congregated in their synagogues, imams reminded their listeners in the mosque that, "Allah promises you victory... He will fulfill his promises and exterminate the unbelievers... Feel our whip. Hell fire awaits the unbelievers... If you were looking for judgment, that judgment has come..." (From the Koran, 'The Spoils of the Battle for Badr.')

The moment the Egyptian Army entered Sinai, the Syrians moved to the Golan Heights. Despite the strong opposition of a few Israeli army units the Syrians quickly advanced. And then, for unknown reasons, they halted five miles of the Sea of Galilee.

Israel's enemies had expected that at least it would take a day before our reservists were mobilized. They didn't expect the first soldiers to be at the front already a few hours later. Despite the reinforcements, the enemy still had twice as many soldiers.

At 2 p.m. the Israeli radio confirmed that Israel had been attacked both in the south and the north. Still wearing their prayer shawls, men ran

Israeli soldiers on their way to the front

from the synagogues to their home to don their uniforms. Soon, the previously empty streets were filled with hundreds of private vehicles picking up soldiers. Volunteers offered to drive reservists to collecting points, and if necessary, even all the way to the southern front. Israel and the world held their breath. Would the Jew haters this time manage to wipe the little country from the map?

During the Six Day war, I had been responsible for the Negev field hospital. As the Sinai now was Israeli territory, the army erected a new field hospital near Revadim where Hadassah surgeons performed live-saving operations. The soldiers were then flown to Tel Hashomer hospital, near Tel Aviv, the Haifa Rambam hospital or Hadassah Ein Kerem hospital.

All Hadassah's wards had been turned into surgical departments. Chronic patients who could be discharged were sent home. Day and night, helicopters brought in wounded soldiers.

Triage[1] took place in the entrance hall of the hospital. During the day, Professor Saltz oversaw the incoming patients, while I took care of the nights.

Because back then the traumatology specialism did not exist yet, only a general surgeon could do triage. Often, twenty soldiers were brought in at the same time. On the severity of their wounds, I decided which operating theater the patient went and which surgical team was to assist.

---

[1] Triage is the assignment of degrees of urgency to wounds or illnesses, to decide the order of treatment of a large number of patients or casualties. In war time, triage is being done by a general surgeon or a trauma expert.

In case of head trauma, the surgeon was assisted by a dentist, an oral surgeon, orthopedic surgeon, eye specialist, etc. Within a few days, the hospital was full. Besides treating our wounded soldiers, we also performed 'regular' emergency operations like appendectomies and gall bladders and admit heart attack patients. I often had to do corrective surgery on soldiers who received emergency treatment at the field hospital, or those with multiple

wounds who had to be treated at a later stage. We worked day and night and all medical personnel was under enormous pressure.

> *"This country, small as it is and surrounded by enemies,*
> *has decided to live. If we must pay a price in order to do so, we will.*
> *We are not a People that can give in."*
> **Golda Meir**

When war broke out, defending the Golan Heights became top priority. It was a miracle that the IDF had been able to keep standing against an enemy that was assisted by countries like Algeria, Iraq, Kuwait, Libya, Morocco, Saudi-Arabia, Sudan and Tunisia. At first, Israel was totally alone.

American president Nixon refused to give us satellite information. Eventually, he caved it to Golda Meir's urgent request to open an air bridge to counterbalance the Russian planes that were landing every ten minutes. Still, we only received 10% of what the Russians shipped to Egypt and Syria.

Worse was the deliberate delay of relief shipments. As a painful example of Jewish self-hatred, Kissinger explained this sabotage as, "Let those Jews bleed a little!" Only when it became clear that Israel was winning, did the first American shipment arrive – on the tenth day of the war!

While Egyptian tanks and troops kept streaming into the Sinai, special El Al flights brought hundreds of new immigrants and returning Israelis to Israel. After the Israeli army managed to penetrate Syria about 24 miles of Damascus, the Syrian capital came in reach of our artillery fire.

At first, Jewish civilians were happy with the victories, but their joy quickly turned to deep mourning when it became known how many dead and wounded there were. During the 1948 Independence War, almost everybody had lost friends, brothers, husbands, uncles and fathers. Did we again have to pay such a high price? Even though names of fallen soldiers were not yet released, before an IDF officer personally brought the terrible news, families often had already heard via the grapevine.

During this intensive struggle of life and death, at the fronts and in the operating theaters, I received news that Itamar, my son-in-law who was a Phantom pilot, had been shot down over Damascus on October 21. The only thing they could tell us was that Itamar and his co-pilot had ejected their plane. Nobody knew if they were alive. Hefzi and I were extra worried because our daughter Tali was pregnant. *Will the baby grow up without its father*, I wondered.

Two weeks after the outbreak of the war, the symbol of the *Yom Kippur* war, Mount Hermon, also called "the Eye of the Nation" was finally back into Israeli hands. When our army was in 62 miles of Cairo and things were looking better, the UN security council assembled in great haste. Resolution 338 which called for a ceasefire had to prevent an even worse military defeat for Egypt. America put heavy pressure on Israel to start negotiations for a 'just and permanent' peace in the Middle East.

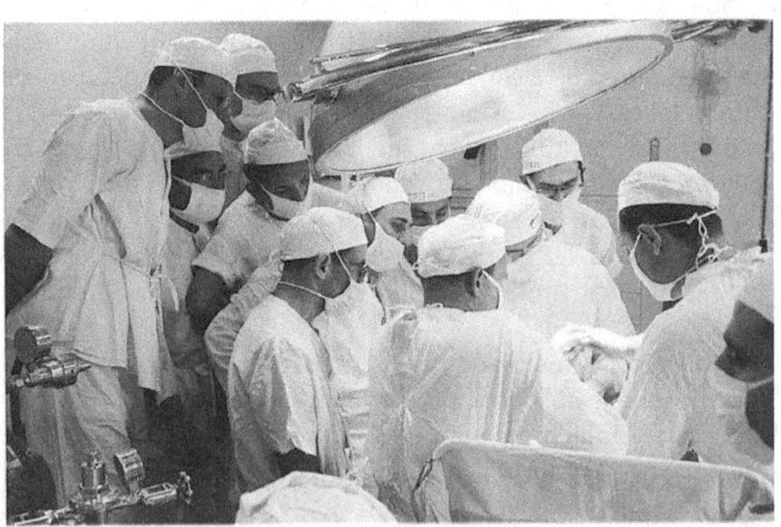

Despite the ceasefire with Egypt, border and air fights continued. Syria refused to participate in the peace talks that began on December 21, 1973. A week later, Syria renewed its attacks but their attempt to recapture Mt. Hermon in April 1974 failed. After a war of seven months and 25 days, Syria finally signed the ceasefire with Israel on May 31, 1974.

Against all expectations this religious war, an Islamic *Jihad* for Allah against the 'unbelievers' had ended with a miraculous victory for the God of Israel. Today, military schools always study the *Yom Kippur* war but because they are unable to explain the Arab defeat and Israel's victory, this war is classified as an 'impossible war'.

Besides the national crisis, I had big personal worries and wondered, *Is Itamar among the 314 Israeli POW's? Is he wounded? Is he still alive?* There were so many questions the Syrians refused to answer.
I joined the parent committee whose children were taken prisoner of war and together we demanded to know what was happening to our children. During a meeting with Henri Kissinger in the King David hotel in Jerusalem, I bluntly asked him,

"How is it possible that you force us, as 'confidence building measures', to make all kinds of promises, give away land, while the Syrians refuse to tell us if our captured children are still alive?"

"Eh, yes, well eh, you must not forget," Kissinger mumbled, "that with the Syrians, we are dealing with a different culture."

Even though we had won the war, there was no national joy as in 1967. Again, our small country had paid a high price for a war she had not sought: 2,688 Jewish soldiers had died and about 7,200 Jewish soldiers had been wounded or maimed during this traumatic war. There were no civilian casualties. Compared to the Arab losses (about 16,000), the Jewish losses didn't seem that high, but it was for our small country. People were angry and bitter at the government. David Ben Gurion had died of a brain hemorrhage on December 1, 1973. In 1974, Golda Meir and Moshe Dayan resigned. For many, the physical, emotional and psychological wounds of the *Yom Kippur* war would affect them for many years to come.

I knew there was no other option than to take things into our own hands. Freddy, my brother and I pulled out all the stops: even though our obvious pregnant daughter Tali pleaded to the American Congress, her mission failed. Freddy contacted a Lebanese man with Syrian contacts, also without results. After a tug of war that lasted several months, we finally learned via the Red Cross that Itamar was alive and being held in Damascus.

The prisoner exchange took place on June 1st, 1974. 68 Israelis, among them 23 officers, were exchanged for 480 Syrian, Iraqi and Moroccan prisoners of war. The Red Cross informed us that Itamar was wounded, but didn't specify how badly it was. At Ben Gurion airport, I stood with a medical team and anxiously waited for our freed POW's to land. Excited family members were kept behind a roped off area, but when the first soldiers began walking down the airplane steps, they ran towards them. Upon recognizing Itamar, my friend Olesh turned to look at me. I had become white as a sheet.

"You all right, Zvi? Lie down for a moment."
Thankfully, I recovered in time to greet my son-in-law who was struggling to breathe. Since none of the POW's had received a medical report, nobody knew what was wrong with him.

"Welcome home, my boy!" I said to Itamar. "You are the father of a two month's old girl – Lilach!" I sat next to him in the ambulance as we sped to Jerusalem with sirens blaring.

Israeli POW's in Syria

Wounded Israeli soldier - finally home!

It had been a big miracle that Itamar Barnea, one of the most severely wounded soldier, had survived his captivity. Even after he touched down with his parachute, the Syrians continued shooting. He had seven shot wounds in his legs and neck. The last shot in his chest was supposed to have been fatal but only injured his lung.

After Itamar was admitted to Hadassah hospital, we immediately took x-rays of his chest. I couldn't believe my eyes: where normally we see the lung, arteries and the trachea (windpipe), all we saw was a stump. The heart, usually on the left side of the chest, had moved to the center. The kinked trachea made it very difficult to breathe for Itamar. After a team of specialists began to care for the wounded pilot, we slowly began to understand his medical situation. The operation technique they used on Itamar, the so-called 'guillotine' was not known in the West. The Russian trained Syrian surgeon made a small cut in the chest, put his hand inside, pulled out the lung, cut it off and closed the stump with staples. Because I had done internship at the lung department, I knew that this kind of practices were unheard of in the civilized world. When a lung is removed, the mediastinum[2] must be balanced in such a way that the other organs will stay in their right place.

I consulted several Israeli lung specialists who gave their opinions and advised how we could help Itamar. After the first treatments, he was sent home for revalidation. As Israel then didn't have facilities to research and treat this kind of lung disease, we couldn't test the pathophysiology of his breathing problems.

Very seldom I took the elevator because I rather walked the stairs. However, on that particular day, I happened to be in the elevator with my friend Terry Davidson, an anesthetist. "Zvi," Terry said, "may I introduce you to doctor Karl Wasserman? He is a lung physiologist."
Of course, I told him about Itamar. This world-renowned lung specialist was willing to meet my son-in-law and study his medical problem. I knew that a few Israeli lung specialists had been in the States to study under Karl Wasserman and that he was highly regarded by them.

---

[2] Mediastinum is the cavity containing the lungs, heart, windpipe, esophagus, lymph glands, blood vessels and nerves.

Dr. Wasserman

"I've examined Itamar and would like to examine him further in Los Angeles," Wasserman told me a few days later. "I need more time to be able to understand what exactly is the problem."

Itamar wasn't improving, he could barely walk up the stairs and even didn't have the energy to lift his baby daughter. It was clear that something had to be done. The IDF was prepared to pay Itamar's trip to the USA but someone had to accompany him. Thus I joined my son-in-law on his trip to Torrance, Los Angeles and Palo Alto. After checking Itamar's lung functions by way of the most advanced tests, the specialists conferred to try and find a solution to his problem. All of them were convinced that the mediastinum had to be returned to its original position, but the big question was: how? Wasserman made an appointment with the Harvey Lash, head of the plastic surgery department of Stanford University. It would take three weeks to make an implant according to Dr. Wasserman's specifications. That was the first hurdle, but much more challenging was finding a surgeon willing to do this experimental intervention. After presenting Itamar to the Palo Alto private clinic of Stanford-University, one surgeon expressed his willingness to operate. Until then, Itamar and I were invited to stay with a family of the Hadassah organization. After the operation, which I didn't want to attend, Karl told me that they had decided not to implant because they feared infection of the lung stump. I was very disappointed, because there was no other solution. Unable to stay in the USA any longer, Tali flew to be with her husband and I returned to Israel.

Eventually, the team of specialists decided to fill the lung cavity with plasma. The Barnea family was finally able to fly home.

At first, everything seemed to go well, but a few weeks after his return I noticed that Itamar sounded hoarse. The x-ray showed that his body had absorbed the plasma and that the organs were on the move again. I immediately called Wasserman.

"Probably the best solution is that each time this is necessary, you inject the plasma into the lung cavity," the lung specialist suggested.
Even though I injected the plasma on a regular basis, I knew another solution had to be found.

"Why don't we do corrective surgery?" I suggested to Wasserman. Itamar was again operated on in the Stanford Clinic. The large amount of plasma he received over time had caused a lot of cicatrix, which made for a very bloody operation.

During that time, one of my friends did his radiology internship at Stanford. He offered to keep an eye on Itamar after the operation. When Itamar had an internal bleeding during the night, my friend immediately alarmed the medical staff, thereby saving Itamar's life. Dr. Wasserman had taken his Los Angeles research team to Stanford so they could treat his patient also after the operation.

Itamar stayed as a guest in the home of the Wasserman family until the wound was stabilized and he was allowed to fly home with his long implant.

Back in Jerusalem, I continued to treat him until one day, to my horror, I noticed the lung implant's plastic bag shining through the wound. A colleague plastic surgeon advised to operate immediately. He saved the lung implant by way of a rotating skin graft.

No longer able to fly, Itamar decided to study psychology. Today, he is head of the psychology department of NATAL, Israel's trauma center for victims of terror and war in Tel Aviv. Through his personal experiences, he tries to give others hope and help.

CHAPTER 28
Rova's Crown Jewel 1977

HaRova Hayehudi, or Rova in short, is one of the four traditional quarters of Jerusalem's Old City.

During the 1948 War of Independence, the Jordanians destroyed this Jewish Quarter. After the reunification in 1967, extensive archeological digs took place and only then the Quarter could be rebuild.

For centuries, Diaspora Jews longed to return to Zion and the liberation of Jerusalem was seen by many as a fulfillment of the hope of generations. The moment it became known that the Jewish Quarter was to be renovated, City Hall was swamped with requests. About 9,000 people wanted to live in the *Rova,* but there was only room for between six to seven hundred families and about 1,500 yeshiva students.

Hefzi and I also would like to live in the *Rova.* Family and friends thought we were crazy that we were willing to exchange our nice apartment at the Harlap for *Rova's* rubble heap.

The building at Misgav Ladach street, with a basement that was almost 400 years old, was sold by lottery. And we were the winners!

The building had been partially restored according to the design of Moshe Safdie, a well-known architect who was responsible for part of the rebuilding of the *Rova.* Because we didn't like certain structures, Hefzi and I decided to remodel part of it and built the rest of the house according to our wishes. Hefzi took a *Shabbaton* (sabbatical) to direct and oversee the building and restauration. Two floors were built on top of the old foundations. Large windows in the kitchen and living room looked down at the Kotel and towards the Mount of Olives. There was always something going on at the Plaza, the square in front of the Kotel. This could be an IDF swearing-in ceremony, a demonstration, Bar Mitzwa, a cultural gathering or just masses of people praying in front of the ancient stones.

Our home has often photographed because it was seen as the finest home in Rova. We turned the courtyard with niches and arches into an enclosed garden. The two-story high enclosure gives a spatial effect and is a small oasis in the middle of the bustling city.

Sitting at the dining room table, we enjoy the atrium and the view. We only gave the thick, age-old walls a layer of plaster and didn't touch it any further. Due to the ancient way of building, the temperature inside is constant and stable.

The living room has a cozy, European appeal and for visitors, it's hard to imagine to be inside

Dutch visitors in the living room

such an ancient Middle Eastern house. During our frequent travels abroad, often connected to our academic careers, Hefzi and I brought back many art objects. Throughout the years we also collected many painting, each telling its own story.

The small sitting room at the front looks down at the narrow street below. On the floor are colorful rugs and at the wall, under the window sill, a special stair rug. Because books are very important to me, they can be found everywhere in the house. To reach the newly built second floor, we built a separate entrance with stone steps. The bedrooms, bathrooms and my study are at the top floor.

A few stairs lead the visitor to a beautiful roof terrace with a great variation of trees and plants. I always bring visitors here so they can enjoy the beautiful views. This too has been photographed very often. Living in the Rova has its own challenges, the parking problem is one of them.

The Jewish Quarter has many interesting and beautiful houses, but this house is special.
To me, it is like a crown jewel, one that shows the development of the modern Israel in relation to her colorful past.

CHAPTER 29
Refuseniks and *Yad Vashem*

After my mother had become a widow for the second time, Freddy and I decided she should come and live with us in Israel. We found a suitable *Beit Avot,* parent's home in Kfar Saba, where she lived for many years. In 1979, Freddy was involved in the establishment of ELAH. This was the first Israeli organization offering psychosocial help to Dutch speaking Holocaust survivors. Also, their partners and second and third generation are able to receive help from professional workers who are assisted by volunteers.

Professor Menashe Har El figure whom I got to know during the yearly Palmach reunions. He assisted with the establishments of one of the first kibbutzim in Emek Beit Shean, and during a two-year period, amongst other things, smuggled Jewish children from Syria to then Palestine. Later, he became a professor of geography and with the Bible in his hand, walked through the length and breadth of the country. Hefzi and I participated in many interested trips with this outstanding teacher, both in Israel and abroad.

In the fall of 1986, Menashe led a group to China. I will never forget our *Yom Kippur* fast on a boat on the Yatzee River. Later, part of the group continued to follow the Silk Route, while we joined the rest on our return trip. During our stopover in Moscow we were informed that there was no further connection and that all the hotels were fully booked. (Only after we were safely home in Israel, did we hear about the Chernobyl disaster.) All the seats in the airport were occupied, forcing even the elderly people in our group to sit on the floor. It was one big *balagan* – chaos, so I decided it was time to take action.

"I'm going to complain to the management!" I told Hefzi and went in search of the person responsible. This man could, of course, not be found and nobody was willing to listen to me, let alone help. I contacted the Russian tour guide who was supposed to meet us, but she also didn't know what to do. Totally fed up, I decided to investigate myself. A door with a "Forbidden to enter" sign led to a corridor with many doors. I began knocking until finally one was opened and suddenly, I found myself in a room full of people sitting around a large table. They all wore uniforms decorated with many medals.

"Somebody here speak English?" I angrily asked.
When it seemed nobody understood what I was saying, I became even more agitated, talking even louder and more angry. Finally, they brought in someone who spoke English. In an effort to make myself look important, I said, "I'm secretary of the Israeli Surgical Association and personally know the Russian minister of health. I've have been guest at the Kremlin!" Of course, I didn't tell him that had been in 1967, during the international surgeon's congress. "I demand that the precarious situation I and my group presently are in will be solved immediately!"
When the translator explained my story to the important men around the table, everybody began talking at once and making phone calls. Of course, I had no clue what they were saying. Someone escorted me to the exit with the promise that tomorrow there would be a connecting flight to Israel. After solving this problem, we still faced another, urgent problem: where to find a place to spend the night?

"There are no hotels available," the translator told me. "You will have to spend the night at the airport."
This answer made me very angry, and suddenly there was a hotel available – the the Sputnik hotel, about 13 miles from Moscow. Even though travel agency *Aeroflot* insisted there was no bus available, one magically appeared out of nowhere. Relieved, we waited in line for the bus, only to face another challenge. "Unless you pay with Camel cigarettes I refuse to take you," the Russian bus driver threatened.
Thankfully, one of our group members had the foresight to take a carton of cigarettes, with which we 'paid' our driver. Quickly, we boarded the bus. "You know you can only depart when accompanied by a guide from *Intourist* (who were all KGB trained)," the driver reminded me.

"Unless you pay me with cigarettes as well, I refuse to bring you to your hotel," the Intourist guide threatened. Thankfully, there were enough cigarettes to appease her as well.
Everyone sighed with relief when we reached the hotel. I handed the hotel vouchers Menashe had given me to the desk clerk. "We don't accept those," the man told me. "You can only pay in rubles."

"Nobody in our group has rubles," I protested.

"Foreign currency can be changed at the exchange office," the clerk droned impassively.

"Where can I find that?"

It was in a nearby street, but opening hours were only between 3 and 4 p.m. Our exhausted group had to wait even longer before we finally could go to our hotel rooms. Anxiously, we wondered if there would be a connecting flight the next morning.

The Russians kept their word, there was a plane and that same day we safely landed on Israeli soil. Later, a seasoned Russia traveler told me that I should have tried to bribe those officials.

In the 1930's, Mijntje Asbeek-Brusse and her two daughters, Marianne and Willy (Esther) had moved from Chicago to Amsterdam. Mijntje lived in the Netherlands until 1979, when she returned to her family in New jersey, USA, I always stayed in touch with her. After Freddy requested Yad Vashem to declare Mijntje a "Righteous Gentile," she refused. Finally, after many years, Mijntje was willing to receive this special honor. The ceremony took place on January 7, 1987, in the small meeting hall of the Israeli consulate in New York. 93-year-old Mijntje was accompanied by her 71-year-old daughter Marianne, the grandchildren, great grandchildren and great-great-grandchildren.

Photo by Pim Van Heme
Wilhelmine Asbeek-Brusse gets hugged by her great-great-grandch dren, Jonathan Kobrinski, right, and his sister, Ronit, after she was ho ored at the Israeli Consulate in New York

Esther, Freddy's wife, had succumbed to cancer in 1983. In a mix of English and Dutch, Mijntje explained to the assembled people why she had used her small apartment as a hiding place for the Jews during WWII.

"I'm not religious; I believe that a person is a person."

"My mother is and was an amazing woman," Marianne said, "who did what had to be done. We never thought about the danger. We just did what we had to do."

A great-granddaughter added, "My great grandmother always said that what she had done wasn't special, but I knew that it was!"

"Non-Jews like Mrs. Asbeek-Brusse risked their lives and those of their families by helping Jews," Moshe Yegar, the consul general said. "At that moment, she didn't know when the war would end or if she would survive the war. Perhaps she and her children even would have to pay the highest price. This is a symbolic token, for in what way could we ever reward such action?"
Besides the medal, a tree was planted in honor of Mijntje in the 'Avenue of the Righteous amongst the Nations' in Yad Vashem in Jerusalem.

Finally, I had been able to honor one of the two women who had saved my life. However, despite all my searching and asking around, I could not remember any details about the woman in Assen. I personally wanted to thank her for the risk she had taken but how would I go about it?

In matters of determination and persistence, Freddy and I were very much like our father. Freddy didn't agree with Elah's policy to only give assistance to Dutch holocaust survivors. Amongst the Russian new immigrants were many traumatized survivors who also needed help. Freddy asked if I, together with Dr. Nathan Dust, was willing to establish a new organization that would be run from a small Jerusalem apartment: AMCHA[1].
After the war, "*Amcha*" - 'your people' was the code word to identify Jewish survivors. Today, this Israeli organization continues to actively support Holocaust survivors, their children and grandchildren. They give assistance through discussion groups, meetings, activities and conferences.

After the Six Day war, many Russian Jews began to request an exit visa. The Soviet government denied this document to most Jews and called them traitors. These so-called *Refuseniks* lost their jobs and became the focus of public hatred. In response to this treatment, an international campaign was launched: "Let my people go!" Those who did receive an exit visa were stripped of their Russian citizenship and had to pay high exit taxes. Even though emigration restrictions were removed under Gorbachov in 1989, academics still had to pay this exit tax.

[1] Mother later was greatly helped by talking to AMCHA professionals.

1982—Minister president Menachem Begin visits our surgical departments at the Hadassah hospital in Ein Kerem.

This so-called diploma-tax was often twenty times their yearly salary. This way, the Soviet Union tried to prevent a brain-drain when their top academics were beginning to leave the country.

In an effort to give Russian Jewish academics public support, the Israeli ministry of Foreign affairs asked us to bring this Soviet 'ransom' system under the attention of our international colleagues.[2] I travelled to the Netherlands to personally contact several academics. Often, I stayed with Koos and Net and of course, visited to see which new surgical techniques they were using.

Reception with Jerusalem mayor
Teddy Kollek

[2] The international actions were successful; in 1989 only 24,050 Russian Jews emigrated to Israel but in 1990, the doors opened wide: 199,516 arrived in Israel and in 1991, 176,100 Russian academics arrived.

CHAPTER 30
"Spoorloos" – Without a Trace

Ever since that day in September 1941, when Jews were no longer allowed to attend regular school, Guus Sluijter always wondered what had happened to Harry Klafter, his high school friend. When Guus retired from work, he decided to trace his friend Harry and began by asking at the civil register and the high school archive – nothing. Then he searched the telephone books, wrote to the RIOD and the Israeli Embassy in the Netherlands. Despite all his efforts, there were no results. Finally, in November 1989, Guus learned via the Red Cross that Harry Klafter now was called Zvi Eyal and lived in Jerusalem. He immediately wrote a letter to his school friend. An exchange of letters followed.

"Is there something I can do to help you?" Guus asked in one of the letters.

"You can," I wrote back. "Could you place an advertisement in the Assen newspaper? I very much want to thank the woman who saved my life but can't remember where she lived and what her name was."

Guus placed the ad, but when nobody responded, he decided to write to the TV program "Spoorloos" (Without a trace) and tell them about my request to find the woman.

Guus and I had not seen each other in forty-nine years but recognized one another immediately. We met in the home of Net and Koos in Kudelstaart in March 1990. Guus invited us to dinner to celebrate this meeting and also invited Johan Westdorp, another youth friend from Utrecht.

Guus Sluijter, myself, Mrs. and Johan Westdorp

In the morning hours of March 9, 1990, radio Drenthe broadcasted the following announcement,

> *"Tonight, the TV program "Spoorloos" will interview the 65-year-old Zvi Eyal from Jerusalem, who is searching for a family in Assen. In 1944, this family took in the then 18-year-old Harry and his 23-year-old brother Manfred Klafter after their escape from Westerbork. Information about the name of this family and their address can be given to Radio Drenthe or directly to the program Spoorloos."*

This announcement received quite a lot of reactions. That evening in the studio, I told interviewer Han van der Meer what had happened in the night from September 3 and 4 and how this woman had saved me and my brother.

"Why do you want to thank these people?" the interviewer asked.

"People like this woman are characteristic for a society," I told him. "Often, people think that the world's evil is dominant. These people are the mortar that keeps society together. They give us hope that there is something good in mankind. These people took moral decisions, not from behind a desk in an office, but did something concrete. They stuck out their neck. My brother and I survived because we encountered three such people during our flight. That woman in Assen was our first handgrip, the second was Jaap Borger in Heerenveen and the third one was Mijntje Asbeek-Brusse in Amsterdam. There should be monuments for those people!"

A writer of historical novels, who had done a lot of research on the city of Assen during the war, told us about a few possibilities that might help putting the jigsaw pieces together. After the broadcast, I received a list with telephone numbers and names of people that responded. The next day, I called all of the people on the list but the nameless woman living on the unknown address was not amongst them. As I had to return to Israel, Guus promised to keep searching.

The following letter (exerpt) is from my friend Johan Westdorp, dated June 2, 1990.

"Dear Harry, rereading the enclosed, promised letters from Westerbork[1] bear witness to the fact that you always were an adapt writer... Now to business: thanks for your last letter with pictures. Those you took in the restaurant in Middelburg are a poignant reminder of your memorable visit. Most impressive were the ones of your mother that you showed me. It is always difficult to say what goes on in your mind when you think back on 'things that pass'. Seeing your mother's picture brought back memories of the always good natured Mrs. Klafter in that special place on the Oude Gracht that always smelled of soap and perfumes. On Fridays, she sometimes baked those ultra-thin butter cookies and the table always looked festive. That same woman came back from the war lonely and bitter. No one returning from the camps could share his story with those who had just survived the hunger winter. I also wasn't ready to listen, for like you, I was too busy with my studies. Your picture resembled the mother I remembered from normal times: in a good mood, well dressed and interested in her surroundings. Am I correct to assume that you have a lot in common with her? Can you please tell her that I have a lot of respect for her art of living and admire her greatly? I hereby return the pictures of her teenage son that for many years lie forgotten, together with the school book, on my loft. Do I remember correctly that you gave me this picture to remember you before you had to depart for Westerbork?..."

I remember you telling me on the Oude Gracht about the century old anti-Semitism, referring to a formidable (2 volumes?) book in which everything was written down. You knew quite a lot about the subject... My best wishes for everyone that is dear to you. I worriedly follow the news about your country, especially because I know you live there. I hope to see you again – you are always welcome to stay with us, and if not, until the next letter. " Johan.

---

[1] The letters from Westerbork that were used for this book Johan had kept on his loft for many years. After he sent them to me, I put the envelop in my desk drawer and never looked at them. During the writing of this book, 23 years later, I finally opened the envelope and took the time to read them.

Visiting Johan Westdorp

The second letter was from Ben Verdonk, a high school friend. Dated August 30, 1990. An excerpt.

"Amice, how surprised I was to receive your phone call from Jerusalem. I tried to speak to you during the TV broadcast but they told me that was impossible. Unfortunately, I didn't see the program but recognized you immediately. That's why I contacted you. Yes, many years have passed, and how well I remember us studying at the HBS-B at the Catharijnesingelnr. 62, which now is a different school. I remember 'de boef' (rascal) and 'de Rochel" (phlegm) and especially our strict director, Mr. Spijkerboer. I had good contact with Mr. Westerbeek who taught us mathematics. At least two times I visited your home above perfumery Apollo, but only have vague recollections of it. I don't recall when you disappeared from school but knew you had to go into hiding. From the TV broadcast, I understood that you didn't find the people you were looking for. That is a pity. What did the people in Holland know about the terrible drama of the Jewish persecution? Nothing, absolutely nothing. Such a disgrace this could have happened. But it did and we didn't know about it. I dream often about it and while reliving those terrible things, I ask myself how this could have been possible. Thankfully, you survived, but I'm afraid many of your family members didn't and that is so terrible[2].

---

[2] I lost more than 100 family members in the Holocaust .

Later, we learned that the mysterious woman from Assen did watch the "Spoorloos" broadcast. Not wanting to be in the spotlight, she didn't react. However, one of her family members remembered something that happened during the war during the time he was imprisoned in the Wolvenplein prison in Utrecht.

"Remember those two brothers who were also imprisoned during that time? Wasn't their name Klafter? Wasn't the original name of that man, Zvi Eyal in that program also Klafter?"
After the woman reluctantly admitted that she had been the one helping those two youngsters, her family urged her to call the TV station.
In the summer of 1991, Guus and I drove to Epse, in the Gelderland province, where I my savior, Jannie Steinfort-van Aalst now lived. Finally, after all those long years, I could thank her personally.
During that emotional meeting, I also learned the name of that street in Assen: the Steendijk.

Steendijk in Assen

In November that same year, Hefzi, Jannie and I, drove to Assen. A journalist wrote an article about our visit to the house on the Steendijk in Assen that appeared in the local newspaper.

"... Yesterday, for the first time since that day on September 4, 1944, Harry Klafter (66) visited the house on the Steendijk... The woman who opened the door wants to stay anonymous. In the 1970's Zvi took his children to this neighborhood but couldn't remember the house. He kept driving in circles but didn't recognize the area.... Yesterday, for the first time in 47 years, the Eyals stood before the house where he and his brother asked for help.
"It is a pity that these heroes (Jannie Steinfort-van Aalst, Jaap Borger and Mijntje) are not used as true examples for our youth. Not Piet Hein, but these people are the heart of Dutch society. If there is some-

thing worthwhile in a human being, it is the instinctive way people like the woman from the Steendijk responded. Very often they want to stay anonymous. But they should be our examples."

In the years that followed, Jannie regularly visited us in Jerusalem.

Like Mijntje at first, neither Jannie Steinfort wanted to be honored by Yad Vashem as a "Righteous Gentile." Eventually, after a lot of persuasion, she agreed. On June 3, 1992, Yad Vashem officially acknowledged Jannie and a year later, she was honored in a special ceremony in a synagogue in Zwolle. Jannie regularly came to visit us in Jerusalem. It was a special moment when she unveiled her own name plaque in Yad Vashem. This courageous deed of Jannie Steinfort van Aalst is also mentioned in the "The Encyclopedia of the Righteous Among the Nations" – Rescuers of Jews during the Holocaust, the Netherlands. Part 2, page 712.

"Whoever saves a life, it is considered as if he saved an entire world."

Babylonian Talmud

CHAPTER 31
Academic Travels

While operating, I often used an instrument that had been invented by a Jewish Hadassah friend and was called the "surgical assistant." This arm was fastened to the operating table to keep the wound open during the surgery.

While attending an American medical congress, my friend arranged for me to give a speech to the personnel of the biggest army transportation base in St. Louis. I shared with the American soldiers who were present, how in times of war we turned our general hospitals into military hospitals by creating a center that could receive many casualties. Internal patients who could be discharged were sent home and all the hospital wards were turned into surgical ones. Using make shift installations certain terrains could be used to treat patients in tents.

Furthermore, I spoke of the mutual values of both our countries. America had a unique history, also because her constitution was based on Biblical truths.

As a token of their appreciation, I received the famous St. Louis gateway arch, which I still have on my desk.

Being a member of the American Surgical College, I often travelled to the USA. After a long trip to the Far East, I sometimes used a stopover to visit colleagues and friends.

Hefzi and I used each other's academic invitations and travelled throughout the

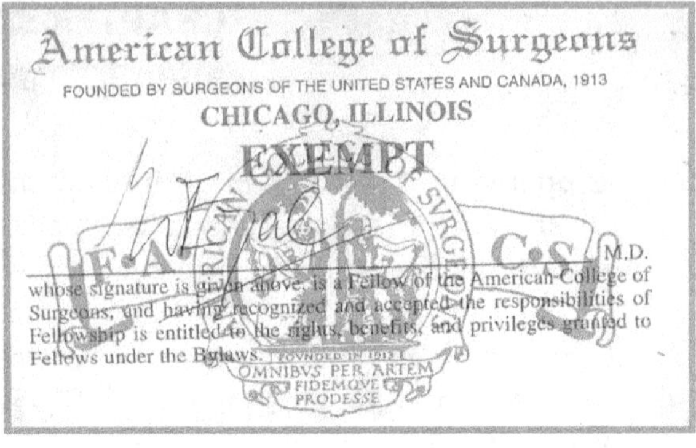

whole world: from Australia and New Zealand to Japan. One day, while Hefzi gave a lecture at a Congress in Tokyo, I visited a local hospital where my Japanese colleagues shared about their surgical methods. International travels are very expensive. Besides our regular salaries, we both received a special allowance that was used to cover the cost of our academic travels.

In my capacity as professor in surgery, I also had to teach the new generations of surgeons which was very rewarding.

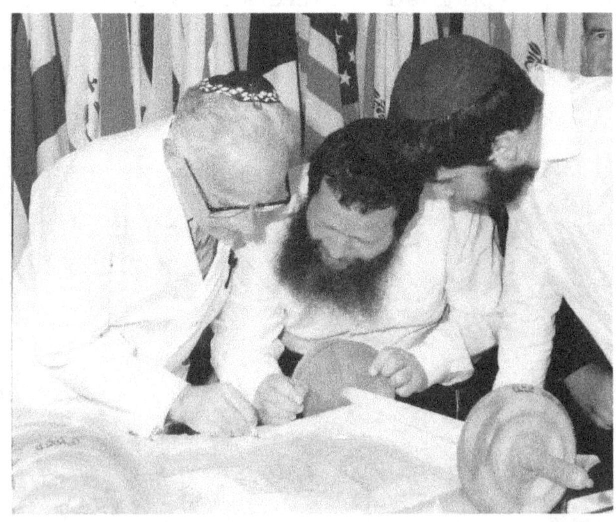

It is a great honor to write the last letter on a new,
handwritten, Torah Scroll.

CHAPTER 32
1995 -1997

In 1995, at the age of 70, I said goodbye to the Hadassah hospital in which I had worked so many years with so much satisfaction. Being retired didn't mean I was going to do nothing: I undertook the task to investigate malpractice suits. I advised, researched the medical procedures and treatments and many times traveled all over Israel to witness at court cases. Not used to mince my words, I wasn't popular in the medical world. For me, truth had to be central and if medical mistakes had been made, the patient had to be helped. While working as a surgeon, I never cut corners; I refused to do so now as well.

Hefzi and I were also active in the group "Professors for a political and economic strong Israel." It wasn't a political movement, neither right nor left but a group of academics that urged the people to face facts.

When Yasser Arafat was nominated for the Nobel Peace Prize, the group sent me as a delegate to protest in Oslo. The Israeli media refused to interview us.

"To bestow this honor to a known terrorist is the biggest intellectual crime ever committed in the Western World," I told the group.

Together with Meir Indor from Gush Etzion, who represented the terror victims, I travelled to Oslo. Meir and his six daughters were active in the Jewish Settlement movement.

Today, this group of professors continues to be active, but mainly through online publications. Every two-three weeks, Eli Pollak, a physicist at the Weizman institute, writes an article for the Jerusalem Post about the way the media often gives a misleading view on the situation. Ron Breiman also writes for the "Media Watch" column.

In September 1995, the Dutch Evangelical Broadcast Company aired a documentary called "At the end of the tunnel." Conny Mus interviewed both Hefzi and me in our home.

The documentary starts with an Arab patient in the Hadassah hospital, waiting for a heart transplant. The parents of a Jewish soldier, who had been murdered by an Arab, gave permission for this 'enemy' to receive the heart of their son. Not a single foreign newspaper mentioned this humanitarian deed.

Following is an excerpt of the interview.

"How can you be against peace negotiations?" Conny asked me.

"A surgeon is used to think in a certain way," I began. "A successful operation depends on determining the correct diagnose before you begin to operate. In politics this is different: prejudices are not being checked against the facts. A surgeon is forced to face the facts. For me, it is as if I'm in a dark tunnel and the light at the end of that tunnel is the oncoming train. The locomotive pulling that train is the Arab, Islamic world and the Palestinians. It is fueled by hatred. Yasser Arafat also mentioned 'the end of the tunnel.' By that, he means the destruction of the Jewish people. "

I told Connie about the parallels between then and now. The evening I urged my Westerbork friends to make a run for it, they laughed in my face.

They didn't understand that wearing the Yellow Star signed their death sentence. They were under the illusion that because they were strong and able to work hard, nothing would happen to them. The fact is, on arrival in Auschwitz they were immediately sent to the gas chamber.

"Standing on my roof terrace, I watch the "theater of the absurd': in the Temple Mount mosque they preach hatred against the Jews, while a few meters down below the Jews are praying for peace at the Kotel."

"Allah akbar, itbeeljehud!" screamed the Arabs during the 1948 Independence war. Today, Muslim women and children scream the same words, "God is great; (ritually) butcher the Jews!" They get the hatred against the Jews through their mother's milk."

I spoke about the similarities between now and the period before the Second World War and the danger of Islam today. Islam is an "über alles" religion. Non-Muslims are not tolerated in the Middle East.

"Year after year, we live with tension," I continued. *"In Israel, every hour we listen to the radio news broadcast, also at the university. People have children in the army and they worry about them. This fear is translated into different directions. Some people say, "Enough! I want to do everything for peace. Whatever it takes."*

"We think," Hefzi added, *"that we should do everything in our power to let the Arabs know that it is not worth it to attack us. Perhaps then we have a chance to live in peace a little longer."*

"Why are most intellectuals politically leftist?" Conny asked.

"The media is often led by left-oriented parties," I explained, *"who have disproportionate power, also economically. That also influences the academics. About 40% of them don't want to speak out because they are afraid to be seen as 'right.' Most of our group of 'Academics for a strong Israel' works in research institutes. Also, during big international conferences, we try to warn academics that the 'house is on fire.' When Arafat proclaims they will create a state with Jerusalem as its 'Judenreine' capital, and his charter says that they will liquidate the Jews, our academic group believes him."*

"A similar situation occurred during the time before WWII when people read "Mein Kamp" and reasoned, "What Hitler says is not important for inner consumption."

"Reading good books [see Appendix} is very important to understand the situation of the Jewish people and the problems, difficulties and challenges that cannot be defined by way of a solution formula."

"Nowadays, just to be re-elected, people use short-term policies and promise all kinds of things. They fix the water system and the sewers but they are not interested in what happens in ten or twenty years, or how they will look after and protect their own house.

"Israel's security situation is crucial. For us, Jews, it's 'to be or not to be.' Literally, the Arabs want "peace with Israel – piece by piece." The hatred propaganda and anti-Semitism, ingrained in the Islamic thinking, is a combination of the original anti-Semitism as it developed in the Christian world. After that came the communistic anti-Semitism, which has been perfected by the Islam."

"In Israel, we try to be 'mensch' as much as possible. Nothing is as hard to be human and struggle with guilt. A democracy (Israel is the only democratic country in the Middle East) is based on the Old Testament. The Ten Commandments are very difficult to keep."

"I lost three colleagues during the 1989 Intifada: Professor Melvitzki died when the Swiss airplane he travelled in was blown up by terrorists. Professor Katzir was shot dead in Lod and another colleague was killed by a knife in his back while he walked to the university."

"Through a miracle, Israel became a nation. It's a miracle Israel still exists. And we need a miracle to continue to exist."

By way of thanks for the interview, we received an antique vase from Shechem (Nablus) that we still have in our little courtyard.

CHAPTER 33
1997 till Present

My brother Freddy had been active on many levels since he moved to Israel in 1965.

It was such a shock for me when I heard that he lost his life through a fatal ski accident. My big brother passed away in 1997 at the age of 77.

American professor Nathan Saltz was seen as the founding father of modern surgery in Israel. He had been working in Hadassah hospital

since 1950 and I got to know him during my internal medicine internship in what now is the Anglican School in Jerusalem.

Saltz was an extraordinary physician. I greatly respected his empathy, and the thoroughness, quality and scope of his clinical knowledge. He introduced academic surgery to the Hadassah hospital and started a similar surgical training program in the USA. He believed that not only a surgeon was responsible for the care of the patient, but he should also share his knowledge and know-how with the students. During that time, it was common for the surgeon to be the omnipotent department head. The Hadassah hospital became the flagship of clinical surgery in Israel. Thanks to Saltz's personality and reputation, the best surgeons came to work with him. Many of the surgical department heads today once were students of Professor Saltz.

During the six-day war, Saltz's academic and surgical expertise (from WWII) played a key role in the treatment of hundreds of soldiers that were admitted to Hadassah hospital. During the Yom Kippur war, wounded soldiers who had received the first treatment from surgeons he once taught in the field hospital in Rephidim the Sinai received follow-up care in Hadassah hospital.

At the age of 65, my mentor transferred the responsibility of the surgical department to me because he was going to set up a new surgical ward in the Bikur Cholim hospital. He continued to work there as head of the department until he was 80 years old. He passed away in 2003 at the age of 91. At his funeral, I mentioned some of his quotes, one of whom was used on his tombstone.

I am so grateful for the time I could work under Saltz. Never during those years I ever complain that I had to work so hard, or that I had to be also present on Shabbat, or because there was no time to take a holiday. Saltz never told me how to tackle something or what I had to do. Not by preaching but by being an example I learned from him on how to become a competent surgeon.   That decision to become a surgeon was the best decision I ever made in my whole life.

Professor Nathan Saltz, my mentor, colleague and friend.

The 'quiet' years began when Hefzi's health began to fail. Her physical problems combined with the onset of Alzheimer made my world smaller but not less interesting. For sixty-eight years, Hefzi was my wife and soul mate. She passed away in January 2017, at the age of 91.

Today, I still try to attend conferences and talks about different subjects.
The growing anti-Semitism, spreading worldwide like a cancer growth, continues to be my biggest worry. It is so important that the youth of the western world learns from its history. They should be encouraged to ask questions, and their education should be based on: "Why did it happen? Why did we join them?"
For me, it is painful to realize that we cannot see the end of the tunnel and therefore it is of utmost importance to keep standing. We Jews have been doing so already for more than 4,000 years, but how I wish that my children and grandchildren realize what's happening, which danger threatens them. It is not for nothing that Israel's national anthem is called "*Hatikvah*" – the Hope!

Due to the long hours I worked in the hospital, I usually came home late. Hefzi ran the household and the only thing I had to do was make sure there was enough money in the bank to pay the bills. I didn't worry about how much she had spent. In the same way, I look at life now: enjoy what you have and don't think about what you don't have. This mentality also helped me to survive Westerbork. Isn't it a pity that a person only becomes wise by the time he's old? We should become wiser at a younger age.

The door of our house is always open for visitors – especial Dutch ones!
When they ask me for a piece of advice, I usually tell them:

**"*Continue to be curious*
Don't accept anything without thought
And keep asking questions!"

Zvi Eyal
Jerusalem, Israel
2017

A FEW OF ZVI'S QUOTES AND THOUGHTS

♦ Corrective surgery: you enter an area in which you don't know what to expect because there the anatomical changes. Sometimes you end up with a situation that you break out in cold sweat. The only think you could do then was take heart and continue.

♦ If you love your job, you don't perceive reading specialist literature as a 'chore'. My life as a surgeon was one big adventure; otherwise, I would not have been able to keep going. I'm so grateful for making that decision to become a surgeon. I was lucky to know myself, which gave me the courage to take a different direction.

♦ Before a surgeon operates on a patient, he first has to do extensive research and study the problem from different angles. The physician must be prepared for all kinds of surprises, so he will have alternatives during surgery. A surgery that is not well prepared by a surgeon is doomed to fail, that is why he can never compromise and must have a very high work ethic. That was my attitude to my occupation.

- How wonderful it was that I could become a surgeon and contribute to make people healthy.

- *Madah* = facts, information
  Yèdah = facts, knowledge of facts
  Deyah = what people think when confronted with facts.

- In order to prevent another war, it is necessary to keep history alive.

- The Islamic world is an enemy that will never disappear. We live in a world that is disoriented about what Islam is and implies. I see and always warn against the danger of prejudice, ignorance and the power of stupidity. People don't even bother to read a book or check if something is true or not. They don't put a question mark behind something and swallow everything that is being presented to them. Today, many people are lazy. The three monkey you can find everywhere in my home remind us of the danger of "see no evil, hear no evil, speak no evil"

- During the writing of this book, I was forced to go back in time, something I never managed to do before.

DECEPTION AND SELF-DECEPTION
Speech by Prof. Zvi Eyal, Netherlands, April 2016

My father's grave I cannot visit. Neither can his ashes be found, nor those of the more than hundred family members that were murdered by the Nazis. Each year as we remember the elimination of European Jewry on *Yom haShoa* (Holocaust Remembrance Day), we should ask ourselves how it was possible that the Jews didn't realize this approaching catastrophe. And why they didn't come to the right conclusion when there was still time.

Is this a question that is only asked after it happened? Does this mean that we cannot learn from history? Did the murderers conceal their plans? No, they openly announced it:

- In 1902, *The Protocols of the Elders of Zion* was published. This book, in which Jews are accused of world domination became the Bible of the anti-Semites.
- This was followed by modern additions, like Holocaust denial.
- In 1984, PLO head Abu Mazen's doctoral thesis was, "The dark background: the secret connection between the Nazis and the Zionist Movement." He accused us of collaborating with the Nazis to annihilate European Jewry.

The lie refuses to 'die' and until this very day, the book *The Protocols* is a bestseller in the Arab world and continues to be used for 'educational' purposes.

When Hitler wrote "*Mein Kampf*" in 1920, he used the *Protocols* to 'explain' the plans he had for the liquidation of the Jews....

In the 30s, Nazis marched through German streets while singing their infamous anthem: "*Wenn das Judenblutt vom Messer spritz wird uns gutt!*" (When Jewish blood runs from our knives, then everything is all right.)

Still, the people refused to listen.

During WWII, the Mufti of Jerusalem, the predecessor of the PLO, via Radio Berlin encouraged his followers to kill the Jews out of love for Allah. The same melody, although using different words, I heard in the beginning of 1947 when the British still occupied Palestine. During the Arab attack in Gush Etzion they screamed, "*Allah agrar! Itbach el yehud!*" – "Allah is great, butcher the Jews!"

Is there such a thing as 'theoretical, academic anti-Semitism'?
Did the Dutch Jews during the years before WWII ever wonder what happened to the Jews in Eastern Europe and Germany? If this might be relevant to them? Would they have believed that it could also happen to them?

Between July 15, 1942 and September 13, 1944, I have witnessed 93 trains depart from Westerbork, each carrying at least 1,000 people. Towards the abyss, under the leadership of the SS, helped by the Dutch bureaucracy and police, Dutch Jews were imprisoned and deported.
Step by step, organized by exact methods and deception. Psychologically, the victim deceived himself by denying the danger. "Wishful thinking' undermines acting in a sober-minded way.
How did Eichman sum up the result of his successful plan to destroy the Dutch Jews? "It was a delight to see how we could deport them without any problems, thanks to the help of the Dutch police and the bureaucracy."
And this was possible in a country that wasn't anti-Semitic!

I arrived in Westerbork in January 1942, at the age of 16. I grew up in a Zionist family and my father assisted German Jews who fled to the Netherlands before WWII. When the Germans invaded the Netherlands in May 1940, I didn't understand why some of those Jewish-German refugees committed suicide. My father understood very well and decided not to wait but to escape by ship to England. Eventually, we were caught in a Gestapo trap that had been organized by a Dutch traitor and my mother and I ended up in Westerbork. The German-Jewish couple who had tried to escape with us committed suicide. My brother managed to escape, but my father ended up in jail. After spending 2 ½ years in prison he was sent to Westerbork and from there deported to Theresienstadt and Auschwitz, where he was murdered.

In Westerbork, circumstances were fabricated in such a way that people deceived themselves by thinking that being sent east wasn't be so bad. Despite the terrible sight of those cattle trains in which hundreds of people were packed together. I even volunteered to join my friends for that first transport to Auschwitz. In the shadow of the catastrophe, in Westerbork people tried to live a normal life and stay human – a kind of moral victory.

Zionist- and religious youth movements took Chanukah candles to the barracks to encourage the people who were to be deported the next day. They wanted to show that the light of Israel would be forever.

Organized entertainment like concerts and revues was part of keeping up appearance in Westerbork. And like a play, the decors and scenarios were changed daily – one day revue, next day transport. From the imaginary to the realistic, from deception and self-deception to reality. Deceit went as far that only 'healthy' people deported. Sick people first had to be well or even operated on. After my grandmother had undergone a hernia operation, she was deported to Auschwitz. Prisoners held in the punishment barrack were always on the list of the next transport to Auschwitz. My brother was saved from that transport because a doctor injected something that caused a very high fever.
You will probably find it hard to imagine that during the evenings in Westerbork, I could finish my high school studies because of the help from professors and teachers who were 'in transit.' I find it hard to believe that I received permission to travel to Amsterdam for my exams at the Jewish Lyceum. On arrival, I was arrested during the biggest Razia that took place at that time but released when the Germans saw my *Ausweis.*' Trying to escape was no option because my mother was in Westerbork and otherwise she would have been put on the next deportation train to Auschwitz. After receiving my diploma, that same day I travelled back to Westerbork.

In 1994, my six-year older brother and I stole a radio from a storage shed. Now we could listen to the BBC at night. By then, we understood that Auschwitz meant a death sentence. When our names appeared on the transport list for Theresienstadt in September 1944, we escaped from Westerbork. In the pitch darkness, we ran over the moor, through the swamps and canals, while being chased by the Germans. It was a great miracle that 36 hours later, we managed to arrive safely in Amsterdam.

In 1945, I began my chemistry studies at the Utrecht University.
Assisted by the Jewish Brigade (part of the British army), in 1946 I joined a small group from the Zionist Federation to go to Palestine via the 'illegal' channels. Our 284-ton ship with 1,086 passengers was intercepted by the RAF and British fleet and escorted to Haifa.

Israel does not exist BECAUSE of the Holocaust,
but DESPITE the Holocaust.

We came to Israel to build the country and become a Jewish people. Since we have no other choice, we must learn from history. Each time and every year, like we do at Pesach, we have to ask ourselves the difficult question: what happened since the Shoah and the birth of Israel? We don't want to see the same symptoms of irrational hate culture appear and whitewash them. The deadly obsession of anti-Semites in Europe, the UN and the Islamic world is disguised by in all kinds of 'isms.' This is clearly visible, unless people fool themselves by all kinds of misleading explanations that are not based on facts.

The Arab/Muslim hate culture that surrounds us is characterized by lies and deception, murder and terror. They use the same pathological words which the Nazis used. Today's Islamic anti-Semitism is disguised by using and misusing concepts like, "freedom, democracy and sovereignty." These are rarely found in the Middle East. In the war against Israel, lies and deceit, murder and terror are justified while Israel is accused of racism, Nazism and genocide. Terrorists are called freedom fighters and seen as heroes – the world upside down.

Again, just like before WWII, the political correct and 'thoughtful' media and intellectuals try to influence the ignorant and prejudiced masses. As people no longer think critically, they do not recognize the fact that today's anti-Semitism is disguised in the cloak of anti-Israelism.

Words can be deadly weapons. The Western 'lie industry' is helped by the media and academics who spread the disguised poison. A deep gulf divides the arguments and facts they bring to defend their viewpoint.

How was is possible that a Nobel prize was given to one of the patriarchs of modern terrorism – Arafat? People deceived themselves by saying the argumentation was earnest. Unwillingness to face truth and facts prevents learning from the mistakes that were made; this makes it impossible to understand the present situation.

> *"Anti-Semitism is the symptom of a culturally sick society*
> *that cannot defend itself against the dangers that threaten*
> *her because she is unable to understand the pathology."*

Using concepts like 'double thinking' and 'political correct' are symptomatic for this disease. It is not limited to judging the Jewish people and Israel but also effects the ability to assess what is happening in Europe. The Islamic world's educational system and the media cultivate the hostility and hatred towards the West. Historical facts are non-existent while fantasies are presented as truths. This original sin of not admitting that you are being deceived and deceiving yourself triggers in me a déjà vu of what happened in Europe before the war. Again, the same pathology of not wanting to see and understand, the perverse misuse of concepts like 'democracy' and making peace with a 'culture' of which the fundamental idea *Jihad* (holy war), *shahid* (martyr) and infidel is.

"The most noble task is fighting deception with truth."
Albert Camus

BDS = Boycott, Disinvestment and Sanctions

This European and American boycott of Israeli products is being justified as legitimate criticism of Israeli politics. They deny it is a type of anti-Semitism. In fact, it is the ultimate expression of the 'modern' anti-Semitism in which not the individual Jew is attacked but the Jewish state. This happens with the help of the UN, EU, academics, media and is financed by your governments. Next to using double standards, they delegitimize, dehumanize, slander, scandalize and boycott. Historical facts are denied, history is rewritten and 'explain' truths that are taken out of context. Contemporary blood libels justify anti-Israel measures.

The snare of 'explaining' what happened, not based on facts and context is the disease of our present societies. It causes a normalization of evil and counterfeit, which makes it impossible to analyze, explain and fight against. The perpetrators become the accusers and those who criticize are accused of being anti-Islam. The tables are turned.

We live in a surreal phase of history. By suppressing our voices humanity is led like a flock to commit intellectual suicide. All this is accompanied by verbal rape and selective deafness.

"The anti-Semitic war against Israel is a laboratory
for the undoing and downfall of Western civilization."

As long as there are patches of light that illuminate the truth, it will be possible to see through the mist that is caused by double speech, lies and self-deception. Only then will we be able to stand up and survive the threatening gulf of global anti-Semitism and its bloodthirsty fantasies.

Like Emile Zola protested against Dreyfus' anti-Semitic process by writing *"J'accuse,"* I tell myself and the world:

> *"You are OBLIGATED to understand what is happening.*
> *Ignorance is criminal*
> *and by keeping quiet*
> *you share in the guilt of repeating the past."*

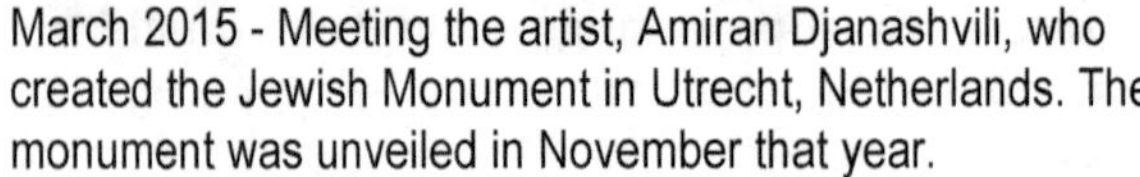

March 2015 - Meeting the artist, Amiran Djanashvili, who created the Jewish Monument in Utrecht, Netherlands. The monument was unveiled in November that year.

April 2016 - visiting the Jewish Monument Utrecht, Netherlands in front of the train station, with the names of my father, family members and friends who were murdered in Auschwitz.

Recommended Further Reading

1. Closing the American mind by Allan Bloom and Saul Bellow

2. The 101 most dangerous professors in the USA by David Horowitz

3. How imperial academia demolishes American culture by David Gelernter

4. Hitler's philosophers by Yvonne Sherratt

5. The intellectuals by Paul Johnson

6. The world upside down by Melanie Phillips

7. Londonistan by Melanie Phillips

8. Ins Westen nichts neues by Marke

9. The war of a million cuts by Manfred Gerstenfeld

10. The lethal obsession of anti- Semitism by Robert Wistrich

11. Les traisson des clerques by Julian Bender, 1927

12. The shackled warrior by Carolyn Glick

13. The Israeli solution by Carolyn Glick

Bibliography of English books
that were studied while writing this book:

A. Broken Silence by Betty Bausch-Polak en Elisheva Auerbach-Polak
B. Waiting for Hope. Jewish displaced persons in Post WWII Germany
    by Angelika Konigseder, Juliane Wetzel and John A. Broadwin
C. Underground to Palestina by I.F. Stone
D. Open the Gates—The Dramatic Personal Story of 'Illegal" Immigration to
    Israel by Ehud Avriel
E. Cast a Giant Shadow by Ted Berkman
F. Col. David (Mickey) Marcus by Zipporah Porath
G. A Prophetic Property by Kelvin Crobmie
H. It Takes a Dream - the Story of Hadassah by Marlin Levin
I. Siege in the hills of Hebron by Dov Knohl

My parents and I, at the beginning of WWII in Utrecht, Netherlands.
Notice the masked head light.

"If I am not for myself,

who will be for me?

But if I am only for myself,

who am I?

If not now, when?

Ethics of the Fathers 1:14 (Hillel)

IN MEMORIAM - Hefzi Eyal-Giladi
1925 - 2017

For 68 years, Hefzi was my wife.
She was part of me and I was part of her.
Together, we've been through so much.

On her tomb stone is written:

"חלמנו, נלחמנו והקשמנו!"

Chalamnu, nilchamnu veheeksjamnu!
We dreamed, we fought and reached our goal.
To be continued….

Most of my family -
Pesach 2017

Misgav Ladach street,
Rova,

Jewish Quarter

Old City of Jerusalem.

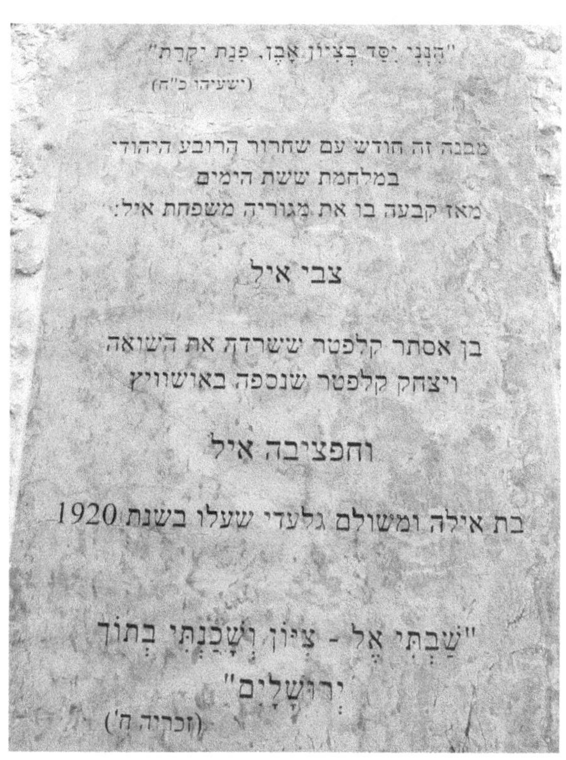

Translation of the commemorative tablet next to the entrance of Zvi's house

"Behold, I lay in Zion a stone for a foundation, A tried stone, a precious cornerstone, a sure foundation; Whoever believes will not act hastily." Isaiah 28:16

This building was renovated after the Six Day War liberation of the Jewish Quarter. From that time on the Eyal Family made this their dwelling.

Zvi Eyal
Son of Esther Klafter-Mok who survived the Holocaust
and Isaac Klafter who perished in Auschwitz

and **Hefzibah Eyal**
Daughter of Ayala and Mesholam Giladi
who made Aliyah in 1920.

'I will return to Zion, And dwell in the midst of Jerusalem." Zechariah 8:3

www.ingramcontent.com/pod-product-compliance
Lightning Source LLC
Chambersburg PA
CBHW061241120726
48001CB00001B/77